AT THE WORLD'S EDGE

Curt Lang's Vancouver, 1937–1998

AT THE WORLD'S EDGE

Curt Lang's Vancouver, 1937–1998

CLAUDIA CORNWALL

Foreword by David Beers

Mother Tongue Publishing Limited
Salt Spring Island, B.C.
Canada

Library and Archives Canada Cataloguing in Publication

Cornwall, Claudia Maria

　　At the world's edge : Curt Lang's Vancouver,
1937–1998 / Claudia Cornwall; foreword by David Beers
and introduction by Greg Lang.

Includes index.
ISBN 978–1–896949–17–8

　　　1. Lang, Curt, 1937–1998.　2. Intellectuals—British
　　　Columbia—Vancouver—Biography.　3. Vancouver (B.C.)—
　　　Intellectual life—20ᵗʰ century.　4. Vancouver (B.C.)—History—
　　　20ᵗʰ century.　5. Vancouver (B.C.)—Biography.
　　　I. Title.　II. Title: Curt Lang's Vancouver, 1937–1998.

FC3847.26.L35C67 2011　　　971.1'3304092　　　C2011–902531–0

Book design, layout and typesetting by Jan Westendorp
Cover photos by Curt Lang, 1972
Front cover photo illustration by Gordon Cornwall
First page: photo of Fred Douglas and Curt Lang: Foncie Pulice Photos, 1960
Last page: photo of Curt Lang and books by Don Slade, 1963
Dedication page: 7ᵗʰ Avenue and Heather, vpl 86646, photo by Curt Lang, 1972

Mother Tongue Publishing gratefully acknowledges the assistance of the Province of British Columbia through the B.C. Arts Council and the support of the Canada Council for the Arts, which last year invested $20.1 million in writing and publishing throughout Canada.

Nous remercions de son soutien le Conseil des Arts du Canada

Printed and bound in Canada by Friesens
Text printed on chlorine–free paper; inside pages are 10% pcw

FSC
www.fsc.org
MIX
Paper from
responsible sources
FSC® C016245

Published by:
Mother Tongue Publishing Limited
290 Fulford-Ganges Road
Salt Spring Island, B.C.　v8k 2k6
Canada
phone: 250–537–4155　　　fax: 250–537–4725

www.mothertonguepublishing.com

Represented in Canada by the Literary Press Group and distributed by LitDistCo in North America

To Gordon and Curt

View from Curt's place, in the 1100 block on Robson Street, 1972   PHOTOGRAPHER: CURT LANG

POEM

From the black pool, sky, bottomless dropped,
Fell away into the charred mirror of the brackish water.
The wood pool, clogged with twigs in the November dusk,
      Unnaturally still, pictured the evening's nakedness of trees.
      A gull passed in the sky.
With the same distant motion,
Another in the pool.
I saw then at the world's edge
That the sky's heaven had borne a daughter
And that the hawks and herons who draw the sky around them
Are too the dolphins of this other air.
There at my wish's window I leaned out,
      Complete but for wings and toppling at the brink of flight.

—CURT LANG, 1956

Contents

Foreword

THE WORLD THAT PRODUCED CURT LANG was East Vancouver in the 1940s and 1950s, a place capable of spawning a teenager who would cross the old Second Narrows bridge with a friend in search of Malcolm Lowry. It was a time when not only might an East Van boy care who Lowry was, but actually find and get drunk and argue with him as a form of worship. That Vancouver was capable of producing many young people who aspired to become what they believed the world badly needed and wanted—poets. How strange to read this. Was there really a moment when commercial culture was not so all encompassing, leaving room to imagine poets as brawling dynamos? So there was, Claudia Cornwall tells us, by telling us about Curt Lang.

This book is Claudia's journey to understand a man, and a moment she perceived as elemental. She knew Lang in his later years, and, she being a gifted reporter, decided to go back and gather his story in order to retrieve glimpses of a Vancouver that now is all but polished from view. Vancouver's current brand is World's Greenest City. Before that it wanted to be the future in a Jetsons sort of way, fashioning a metallic geodesic dome and whooshing SkyTrain to beckon the world to Expo '86. Those are the Board of Trade imaginations for Vancouver, of course, but the brands have stuck. Greenest? Cleanest? The Vancouver in this book was a muddy, mouldering, alcohol-and-drug-infused bohemia where crowds gathered to watch modernist painters debate, and blood flowed at literary journal launches.

This was a half century before Google maps. Had the satellite view of Vancouver been so readily handy then, perhaps Lang and his fellow bohemians would have felt deflated by the sight of their chosen home as last urban dot before the North Pole. They might have felt at once too far from everything and too globalized, the malaise that often grips me as a Vancouverite. Instead, they treated the rest of the world as if it could be conquered from any vantage given the proper words and brush strokes. And when Lang wanted to live in Paris, he just... went. Without money or even email. He made a virtue of poverty. The economy of the day, apparently, allowed a person to push off from Vancouver with a few dollars and coast until broke, counting on his ability to get more cash by gutting fish or herding floating logs.

The DNA of such presumptions is visible in Vancouver's remaining single-room occupancy (SRO) hotels, once the preserve of transient men living a version of Curt Lang's lifestyle, working some, coasting some, creating some, finding a roost for a week or a decade in the neighbourhood Lowry himself famously foraged for liquor. A friend of Lang describes their milieu as a stimulating mix of hoodlums and intellectuals. They were beatniks, who presaged the renegades of the sixties, and the mercurial Lang made me all the more curious about those bourgeois-hating Beats. Was it something heroic inside of them, or broken, that drove their reckless, yet deeply serious, pursuits? The person who just won't be ruled by money. Is he a better person? If so, what does it mean that Vancouver seems to have sealed off most decent ways to live on the cheap compared to the Vancouver Curt Lang inhabited?

Those who now strive to encase Vancouver in glass are profoundly uneasy with the SROS of the Downtown Eastside. The poverty inside those rooms is probably meaner, the drugs harder, than in the epoch Claudia chronicles, and nowadays a consensus seems to be forming around making the remaining SROS places of professional support for the addicted and psychologically damaged. This is not a medicalized caste to which Curt Lang would have seen himself belonging. He and his circle accepted squalor as a condition for creative life.

In the late 1950s, Lang and his friend Fred Douglas, having developed their own particular theory of art, inhabited a dilapidated, rat-infested studio and set about making paintings intended to bring local big shot Jack Shadbolt to his knees. I drove to the address, 1496 West Pender. There is no 1496 West Pender anymore. A drab concrete office building of 1980s vintage with a different number takes up the old spot and more. Having parked my car there, I watched one of Vancouver's current-prized industries hum along, tourists walking and rolling by in happy, sun-glinted clusters. All up and down Pender the shiny towers stacked their cubicled views of mountains and sea, views being another commodity expertly sold today in Vancouver. More bicyclists rode by. Their strained pedaling caused their candy-coloured graphite helmets to turn side to side, as if to confirm that, no, Curt Lang doesn't live here anymore.

David Beers, Vancouver, August 2011

Introduction

THERE WERE SIXTEEN YEARS between Curt and me. When I was a kid, Curt rarely appeared in my life but his visits always had great impact and always left me wanting more. He would just show up and do something astonishing: dance flamenco, play jazz on a flute, make bongos out of jars and leather and string, and then he would disappear again for months. It is difficult to convey how very odd these activities seemed circa 1959.

When I was in Grade 6, Curt walked into my school's office with a made-up story about a family emergency and yanked me out of class. "I thought I'd spring ya," he said, speaking in mock-gangster. We drove downtown and saw *Jack the Giant Killer*. This escapade did more than give me great pleasure at the time—it demonstrated the breakability of rules, and taught me the importance of every once in a while shooting a day right between the eyes.

When I was twelve-ish, I would sometimes be invited to Fred and Evelyn Douglas's place, where I was privileged to enjoy Evelyn's home-made beer and watch Curt and Fred write funny stuff. Their method involved drinking, shouting, interrupting each other, topping the other guy's lines and laughing their asses off while Ev wrote it all down and occasionally added her own wry lines. I vividly remember the writing of *Wabooba the Wandering Weirdo*, a radio play based (extremely loosely) on Jock Hearn's travels in Asia. That evening they performed the play for Al Neil, who literally rolled on the floor laughing until he gasped for breath. This alarmed me, and I wished they would stop the reading to give the poor guy a chance to recover. In the end it was all right—Al didn't die of laughter.

When I was fifteen, school and life at home weren't making much sense, so I moved out. Although I lived among friends my own age and stage, Curt was always in the background with a temporary job or an activity that might open a door for me. This often took the form of a "sorcerer's apprentice" type of position in a field in which Curt was adept and I was a helpless know-nothing. If Curt was welding a steel boat, I might be seen chipping slag and sweeping up. If Curt was log salvaging, I might be seen running along the shore setting rolling hitches on beached logs. If Curt was framing houses, I might be seen humping two-by-fours up the stairs. You get the idea: being a genius's less-brilliant little brother wasn't always easy.

During the boat-building episode, Curt and I shared a cold and grotty room above the welding shop. Concrete-block walls, drafty windows, chipped linoleum, mattresses and sleeping bags on the floor, electric space heater, little hope for advancement. We salvaged logs in the Fraser River to make money to complete the boat, while both the bank and the welding-shop landlord tried to take the partially built boat away. Curt fought desperately hard to make the boat happen, and he sacrificed his comfort (and mine, too) to keep the project going, but he was always under-capitalized and always going up too steep a hill. He did make a beautiful shallow-draft tugboat, though.

Curt was what a friend might call a "quick study" and a foe might call a "bluffer." He knew a surprising amount about a surprising number of subjects. He would intelligently discourse on history, optics, painting, economics, typefaces, architecture, photography, philosophy and more, sometimes all at once. He taught himself Spanish by translating Lorca. When he read a book, he seemed to just pour it straight into his head, where the book's contents instantly linked up with his mental model of everything.

Some of the doors that Curt opened for me stayed open. When I was twenty, I was able to use my log-salvaging experience to get jobs on the tugboats and coastal freighters. When I was thirty, Curt hired me to use a software tool that he and Jeff Chow had developed. That experience led to my twenty-five years as a technical writer.

In this book, Claudia interviews some of Curt's contemporaries and does a good job of describing his life and times in a Vancouver that has vanished—she even manages to evoke some of Curt's spirit. Of course, I believe it's impossible to convey fully my brother's depth, his brightness, his quick-wittedness, his sense of fun, his enterprise and his fuckoffishness. But then, I'm partial.

Greg Lang, Victoria

Curt Lang along the Sea Wall in James Bay, Victoria, British Columbia, 1976
gelatin silver print, toned, heightened with colour   PHOTOGRAPHER: NINA RAGINSKY,
COURTESY OF THE CANADIAN MUSEUM OF CONTEMPORARY PHOTOGRAPHY, OTTAWA

Will the real Curt Lang please stand up?

CURT WAS A BEATNIK, POET, painter, photographer, beachcomber, boat builder, fisherman and software entrepreneur. He was born in Vancouver in 1937 and died in 1998. He and Freddy Douglas, an artist and photographer, were known as the two hippest guys in Vancouver during the late fifties and sixties. This book is my portrayal of Curt and the wild and crazy scene that swirled around him.

I remember hiking in a forest with my husband, Gordon Cornwall, hearing him tell our two then much-younger children about a Druid wizard named Clang, who bore some resemblance to Curt. We were climbing higher and higher through the Douglas firs. A low fog hung round the trees. The story revolved around a major construction project the wizard was mounting. There were obstacles, delays, frustration. And then Gordon was overcome by sadness. He couldn't continue. "It's too close to the bone," he said.

In an earlier and less sophisticated time, people might very well have regarded Curt as a wizard. A shape-shifter he was. Not only did he transform himself several times during his lifetime, but the people around Curt saw him in radically different—wildly different—ways.

"Not much of a lady-killer," said Don MacLeod, a former bookseller who had known Curt in the sixties. Whereas his cousin, Denise Goodkey, who grew up with Curt, said, "He was quite a Lothario, you know." Bob Sutherland, an artist, recalled, "Curt did not have a great amount of respect for women at all." Yet Gill Collins, a girlfriend of Curt's in the early sixties, said, "He was affectionate and tender." Nina Raginsky, a Vancouver photographer, also used the word "tender." She said, "Underneath that scruffiness, he was tender." Perhaps this was why Curt's brother, Greg Lang, said, "Curt could be catnip for the girls."

Curt's best friend, Fred Douglas, told me, "He was like his name—'courteous,'" Greg warned me, "The hardest thing for you to capture will be the malice. That is going to require an act of imagination." Gordon reflected, "There's a phrase at the end of Ginsberg's 'Footnote to Howl' that reminds me of Curt—'The extra brilliant intelligent kindness of the soul.'" Bob James, a programmer who had worked with Gordon and Curt, had a different impression: "Curt was always disrupting things." Jim Polson had been a friend of

Curt's in high school. They had travelled to Europe together and afterwards had drifted apart. "I got fed up with the role playing," he said. Tod Greenaway, a photographer and artist, had known Curt since the seventies. He assessed him like this: "He was such a mixture of extreme perception and extreme thickness. Lurched from one to the other on a bad day."

And what do I remember? A lot of details. Curt was a man who liked blackberry pie, apple pie, pumpkin pie, any kind of pie except nut pie. He hated turnips, background music and weak tea. He liked the English short story writer, Pritchett, admired Virginia Woolf and Nigerian writer Amos Tutuola. He was amused by Spike Milligan and the schlock science fiction movies directed by Ed Wood. Curt read Thucydides. He was learning ancient Greek and he built himself a pedal canoe that could go like the wind. He liked baths. And he toyed with the idea of making over-sized armchairs out of foam rubber. He wanted them to look like the furniture in an old comic strip that featured a lazy, fast-talking character known as Major Hoople. Once he tried to make a helium suit that would allow him to leap into the air as effortlessly as the astronauts did when they strode about the moon. Curt didn't like Christmas. He referred to children as "short people" and he winced when they fought. He used to talk about the berserkers—wild Norse warriors who fought with a frenzied fury known as the berserker rage. He said they would gnaw on their shields and weep while waiting for the battle to begin. Curt was interested in the different ways in which the Greek god Hermes was depicted—especially the different hats he wore. A couple of months before he died, he gave his friends garlic peelers as a parting gift. He could talk to anybody. He was tidy. He kept his rooms cold. He liked bentwood-cane chairs. He neglected his van. He had published poetry and his name was on two patents. He loved parties but hardly ever took a holiday. He co-authored a book about the Internet and published a dictionary of Chinook jargon. He met Robert Graves and Malcolm Lowry. He gave a presentation at the General Motors Research Institute. He had small hands and blue eyes. He was five feet, ten inches tall. He was married twice. He liked blue-and-white Chinese bowls with fish painted on the bottom and chewy white bread.

Michael de Courcy, an artist who has created paintings, photographs, installations and videos, contributes to *Ruins in Process: Vancouver Art in the Sixties*, a website and digital archive. When I asked him if he knew Curt, he said he didn't, although he had come across him in his research. He said, "He was some kind of saint." I laughed and said, "I don't think so." Then Michael said, "Well a legend, then."

Curt sometimes reminded me of the legendary character Odysseus. Not a saint, not perfect, but human in his striving, his hunger. Consider this scene in *The Odyssey.* The sorceress Kirke, who lives on the island of Aiaia, warns Odysseus about the perils that lie ahead. She tells him that square in his ship's path are sirens who sing so beautifully they will lure any innocent men who hear them to their death. If Odysseus is to escape, she says, he must plug his oarsmen's ears with beeswax. "But if you wish to listen, let the men tie you in the lugger, hand and foot, back to the mast." Odysseus must instruct his men not to untie him, no matter how much he begs, not until the voices of the sirens have safely faded. Armed with this knowledge, Odysseus explains to his men what Kirke has reported. He says, "Seirenes weaving a haunting song over the sea we are to shun, she said, and their green shore all sweet with clover; yet she urged that I alone should listen to their song. Therefore, you are to tie me up, tight as a splint."

You notice how Odysseus subtly spins Kirke's message. She does not urge him to listen to the sirens' song at all! She merely tells him what to do if he wishes to hear it. Of course, he wishes to hear it—and strengthens his case by slightly altering her message. I can see Curt doing this. He, too, would hunger to hear that beautiful singing.

Curt was self-reliant and adaptable. In the seventies, when he wanted to take advantage of the soaring demand for fish, he built a boat and sailed north. In the early eighties, as high-tech dawned red and rosy on the horizon, he quickly understood its potential and taught himself how to use computers. More than anyone I ever met, he was alive to new possibilities. He understood that things are always changing and was willing to explore and learn. Innovative and visionary, Curt was at home in Vancouver, a city that dwells more on the future than on the past. He liked to start things—the edgier the better. He didn't like to tidy up loose ends. Usually he didn't reap the financial benefit from projects he began, though others often did. Curt's legacy was not great fame or fortune, but a reaching, inquisitive spirit, hard to capture.

Claudia Cornwall, North Vancouver

1. Wild and memorable poets

A JELLYFISH SWAM BY, TRANSLUCENT, pulsating. Curt Lang, who lay on a wooden dock in the sun, reached down with his gin glass and scooped up the gelatinous, slithery creature. Then he passed it around for the assembled company to admire—Malcolm Lowry, the celebrated novelist; his wife, Margerie, an actress and writer; the not-yet-famous Al Purdy; and Downie Kirk, a teacher. The cocktail proved such a hit, that Curt presented everyone with a gyrating jellyfish. He was only sixteen, decades younger than his drinking companions, but very much their equal. He could talk as well as they could and read with as much understanding. The only thing he couldn't do was hold his liquor the way they did. When it was time to go home, Curt was so drunk he couldn't negotiate the long steep path up from Malcolm's North Vancouver beach cottage to the road. Al Purdy carried him to his car.

Curt was a tall, restless teenager. Because of his looks—blond and blue-eyed—and his name, "Curt," people sometimes thought he was of German ancestry. But that was not the case. "Curt" was short for "Curtis" and his background was Scottish and English. Curt lived with his parents, Hope and Earle, and his much younger brother, Greg, in a small house on Dieppe Drive in Vancouver.

Curt attended Gladstone Secondary, a high school on Vancouver's east side that had just opened its doors in 1950. He sometimes applied himself to his studies, but never for very long, and he often got D's. Curt's sensibilities were engaged far more by what he was experiencing outside school than in it. During the summer of 1952, he worked on the

Princess Elaine in the Canadian Pacific Railway coastal fleet. For six weeks, he washed dishes from Vancouver to the Gulf Islands one day, and from Vancouver to Powell River the next. I found Curt's recollection of that time in a sheaf of loose papers:

> After my days off I would go down to Pier B.C. at midnite on Sunday. Granville Street almost silent but soft & rich with neon lights. The boat below me (I stood on the elevated ramp where the taxis come) still & lighted. The tenor whirring noise of a train, a far off crash of boxcars being coupled. The June night soft around my bare arms. The water rattling in the pilings and rhythming with reflections of all the lights on the dock. I went down the iron catwalk stairs, down to the sheds & through the wooden gate. Walked over ropes and hoses & up the gangway. The car deck, white and yellow & black, all its light on, humming generators. Nobody there at all.

Curt Lang from Seamen's Log Book
1955 PHOTOGRAPHER UNKNOWN

At Gladstone, Curt became good friends with Jim Polson, whom he'd known since his days at Renfrew Elementary School. Jim recalled that Curt hung out with a pretty rough crowd. "He wore drapes and a ducktail haircut," he said, when I visited Jim at his home in Coquitlam to talk and drink tea. "I think he got beaten up a few times. It didn't really suit him. He wasn't as stupid as they were." (Drapes were like zoot-suit pants—high-waisted, wide at the knee and narrow at the cuff. The fashion didn't last much longer. Soon tight jeans à la Marlon Brando in *The Wild One* took over.)

Jim, who became a teacher and librarian, was quiet and bookish. Though Curt liked books, he was anything but quiet. He used to embarrass Jim when they walked home late at night by turning a whole street percussive. As Curt wrote:

> If you grab a lamp standard firmly with both hands, dig in your shoe soles and then tug-push, tug-push strongly the top begins to whip back and forth in the air (the whole thing is pliant), at first in little sweeps, and then as you continue to tug and push in the rhythm of the pole, it goes wilder and wilder until you can give just little pats to it and it goes so fast, it almost breaks in two. The wires hang down inside the pole and they make a pleasant ringing. It is a noble sight to stand, drunk, at the end of a suburban street and look back along it to see all the poles for blocks swaying crazy and swirling the shadows.

Jim didn't think it noble at all. He worried about the people in their working class neighbourhood needing to sleep. "I thought it was pretty bad," Jim said, "but Curt seemed to think they deserved it for being bourgeois."

Curt and Jim were both science fiction fans who read and collected pulp magazines like *Fantastic, Amazing* and *Galaxy*. When Jim spotted an ad in the paper inviting people to join a science fiction society, he asked Curt if he wanted to come along. Curt did, and then got into quite an argument with the group's founder, Norman Browne, over the relative merits of certain comic books. Of greater moment was his meeting another club member, a rangy man with a rough-hewn voice and no-nonsense manner—Al Purdy.

After Al died on April 21, 2000, the news splashed across the front pages of the *Globe and Mail*. The story said: "He was acclaimed yesterday as the greatest English-language Canadian poet of the twentieth century." But when Curt and Jim got to know Al in 1952, he was working in a mattress factory. He was six foot, three inches, with strong capable hands, ideal for the hard work of stapling mattresses. Jim told me he found it surprising that Al became a poet. "He was crude. I didn't think he was very sensitive. But Purdy had the drive to write poetry. He just kept writing and eventually got better." Al had self-published a book of poems in 1944, *The Enchanted Echo*, and spent his weekends and evenings teaching himself to write. He was one of a breed that has almost vanished today—the proletarian poet.

Al and Curt became friends, despite the age gap of nearly twenty years between them. Doug Kaye, a friend of Al's from the mattress factory, remembered Al could be fiercely protective of Curt. Doug said that he, Al and Curt once made wine in his cellar. "My wife said she didn't want Curt Lang around the house any more. I told Al this and he said, 'If he's not welcome, then neither am I!' Al came and took all his bottles of wine that we had put down. He shoved the corks down in the bottles, drove off with them and put them under his bed. The wine was still fermenting and so that night, the corks started popping out and the wine was spilling out all over."

Doug Kaye, unidentified friend, Al Purdy, Curt Lang, Toni Kaye, 1954,
Kitsilano Beach   PHOTOGRAPHER: EURITHE PURDY

At times, though, Al treated Curt as an annoying kid. Jim recalled, "Al was cruel to Curt. Once Curt was standing on the running board of Al's car. They were arguing about something and Purdy just pushed him off. Curt banged up his legs." On other occasions, Al and Curt were co-conspirators who turned on Jim. He recalled, "I was helping Purdy move on Fourth Avenue somewhere. I was on the running boards, holding a table on the roof. They started to take my pants off." Then, said Jim, "Curt and Al paid me an unexpected visit after we had been out drinking. I was sleeping in the attic of my parents' house. It was about one o'clock and there was a knock on the door. My mother opened it. Curt and Al pushed past her and came upstairs. They shoved a bottle in my mouth and began to ransack my books. They took all my science-fiction books. Later Purdy packed them all up and sent them to England. Science fiction books were prized in England and not much valued here. Purdy had a deal with a bookseller in England. He would go to used bookstores, buy up the science fiction, mail it off to England. With the money he made, he bought poetry."

In his final years of high school, Curt didn't have a clear idea of what he should do. He was writing because he enjoyed it. He was not sure he wanted to make it his career, although, at sixteen, he had already achieved some success. In the winter of 1953–54, *Canadian Poetry Magazine* published one of his poems—a eulogy/rant for Dylan Thomas who had just died.

ON THE DEATH OF DYLAN THOMAS

Could I find words
I'd revile you
Till your hair fell down
And the sparks leaped.

Could I level my tongue
I'd curse and blacken
Your withered souls
Till they curled and dropped

From the wearing place
For a poet is dead!
And not one of you little donkeys
Has wings to fly
Or tears to cry with.

The strange thing about this poem is that Curt always *could* find the words. He could talk himself into and out of most situations. And he could converse knowledgeably—or at least sound knowledgeable—about most subjects. Much later his friend, the poet Jamie Reid told me, "People used to say, 'Curt, you talk too much, you don't do too much.' Curt said, 'I'd rather talk than do anything else.' Talking and drinking were the two things he liked to do best. So talking and drinking were what you did when you were with him. Curt was a wit. He could make you laugh. If you were drinking, you would be laughing with him most of the time. Sometimes gut-wrenching laughing."

* * *

At Gladstone, Curt had one teacher whom he liked and who encouraged him—Downie Kirk, his German instructor. Jim Polson described him as a "small enthusiastic man. He would almost foam at the mouth he was so enthusiastic." Downie summered at a cottage on the beach at Dollarton, across Burrard Inlet from Burnaby. From the beach, you could see an oil refinery on the Burnaby side. You can still see its cylindrical tanks and bright lights sprawling along the south shore of the inlet. To the north, on the Dollarton side, sea life abounded—crabs, mussels, seabirds and seals. Even the odd whale swam by. Behind the beach, a great green rainforest filtered long shafts of golden light. Downie's cabin was part of a collection of about ninety shacks that sprang up on Roche Point in the 1930s. The squatters had no legal right to be there; they hadn't bought their land and paid no taxes. They lived free and unfettered. Many of the cottagers built their places on stilts, so close to the sea that the high tide flowed right under them. British Columbia had a long history of tolerating beach squatting, allowing people to throw together a cabin out of driftwood or scrap lumber, and leaving them alone. The Dollarton community was one of the largest of such settlements in the province.

Most of the beach dwellers only came during the summer. But a few residents—among them, the author Malcolm Lowry and his wife, Margerie—stayed year-round. Downie befriended the couple who moved to the beach in 1940. When Lowry's novel *Under the Volcano* was published to great acclaim in 1947, he began to receive a considerable amount of foreign correspondence. Downie, who spoke French as well as German, helped Lowry translate it.

A dark novel set in Mexico on the Day of the Dead, *Under the Volcano* tells the story of an alcoholic at the end of his run. Considered one of the best books of the twentieth century, it was eventually translated into many languages and filmed by John Huston. By the early fifties, the initial flurry of interest in it died. The royalties dwindled to a trickle, and Lowry was living in relative obscurity. Nevertheless, when Curt discovered Downie knew the renowned writer, he immediately had the idea of going to see him. He convinced Al Purdy this would be a worthwhile thing to do and persuaded Downie to arrange a visit. In "Lowry: A Memoir," Al wrote: "Curt Lang, a 16-year-old who could talk the round collar off a theologian, assured me the guy was good." Al described the event further in his autobiography, *Reaching for the Beaufort Sea:*

> We turned right after crossing the Second Narrows Bridge, there was a lot of water on our right; we passed an Indian graveyard; there were a lot of trees, too. Maybe fifteen miles of trees and water, then we parked my little English Prefect at a wide spot on the road. Downie Kirk located a path that led straight down into the middle of thick woods, and seemed to know the way. We walked about a mile, caught the gleam of water again, and a sort of driftwood house appeared out of the greenery. It was built atop log pilings on the beach, and looked almost like a houseboat.
>
> The man who emerged from the driftwood house looked short because he was so heavily built. Sporting several days' beard, pants held up with a piece of rope, bloodshot blue eyes, face nearly beet-red, he seemed a drunken bum. And I wondered: how can this guy be a great writer?

Even though Al had misgivings, the first visit was a success. They talked and drank, and then talked and drank some more. Curt showed Malcolm a few of his poems "suitably impressing him," as Al wrote in "Lowry: A Memoir." They consumed the two bottles of Bols gin Al had brought, and headed back to Vancouver where they bought more supplies at the liquor store near Main and Hastings. Before returning to Dollarton, Al showed Malcolm his own poems. "He read them like a famous man and said little."

When Curt was much older, Sheryl Salloum interviewed him for her book *Malcolm Lowry: Vancouver Days*. He told her, "We would read our poetry to each other, enjoy it, show off and argue about it." Malcolm sometimes sang, not well, but with enthusiasm, and played the ukulele, also not well. They spent hours talking in the sun. Curt said:

> I remember once when we were all cheerfully stoned, Malcolm appeared among us in his shorts and thundered off the end of the jetty into the chuck. The water's cold here, but he was strong and energetic. He'd swim around and yell, then he'd come blowing and puffing and struggling against the current and climb up the ladder back onto the jetty. When the feeling of satisfaction would die down somebody else would jump in and do the same thing all over again.

By April 1954, Curt could no longer wait to leave school. Like Al, who had dropped out after completing Grade 10, he quit—two months shy of graduating. When I visited Gladstone, I was allowed into the library to look at the high-school yearbooks. The one profiling the class of 1954 mentions Jim Polson: "One of a knot of intellectuals; a first ranker who says he's had an overdose of formal education. Will probably wind up as a pseudo scientist of some kind. Likes to make impromptu speeches." But there is no reference to Curt. I suppose because he didn't graduate, he didn't merit one. It is as if he slipped through the walls without leaving a trace.

The summer of 1954 was Malcolm's last on the beach. For several years, the District of North Vancouver had been planning to turn Roche Point into a park. The shacks had to go. Malcolm and his wife left in August. In the fall, Al and Curt returned for one last nostalgic pilgrimage. Al wrote in "A Memoir of Malcolm Lowry":

> I returned to the beach shack with my friend and a beautiful girl. We brought along a bottle of wine and drank it on the road, regaling the girl with tales of Lowry, about the savage mountain lions in that dark forest, striving to impress on her what a genius each one of us was. At the end of

Lowry's dock we poured what remained of the wine into the sea, accompanied by a suitable oration. All were impressed with the literary solemnity of the moment. But I think that Lowry himself never made such gestures. He was always himself, whoever that strange person may have been.

Malcolm would never feel as well anywhere else. In 1955, a psychiatrist he was consulting in England forbade him to work on his new novel *October Ferry to Gabriola*, it upset him so much to think about his old home. Curt and Al did not see Malcolm again. But the connection among the three men had an afterlife. In April 1957, Malcolm wrote to Ralph Gustafson, a poet and professor at Bishop's University in Quebec, who was editing the *Penguin Book of Canadian Verse*. He suggested that Ralph include some poems by Al and Curt;

> Two wild western poets came to see my wife and I in the bush on Burrard Inlet one stormy night some years ago, and I enclose you some of the recent work of one, which seems to me—the typed one—damned good. This fellow Curt Lang was scarcely out of his teens and he impressed me mightily as being a type I thought extinct, namely all poet, whose function is to write poetry. His address is Curt Lang, 517 Pine, West Montreal, Quebec. I think the written poem would be better without the *on retina* in the first line, and the final couplet is weak; but the other two have a kind of fury, and the architectural one at the end, a really terrifying quality, that seems to be very rare and original in a poet, whatever the merits of his typography or indeed however he means it to be printed; I do think he is worthy of inclusion, even if you have to kick me out, for he is a young bloke who could use and deserves that kind of encouragement in my opinion. (Not that I couldn't or don't, but I'm older.) The work of his friend on that occasion, whose name I've unfortunately mislaid is also worth looking into; his name is Al something or other, but Curt Lang would put you onto his work which again impressed me by its originality, intimacy and power. He is an older poet who has published a chapbook or so, but both are well worth watching and he, too, is worth considering in my opinion but

maybe you've already made your selection. I've met a lot of writers but I have rarely been impressed by such dedication on the part of anybody as these two, and as for Lang he might well have genius.

I have a fat sheaf of poems that Curt wrote. Many never saw the light of publication—typed on onion skin, scrawled on the back of envelopes, pencilled on graph paper, one on the back of a hospital x-ray report. The ones that Lowry so admired are there too—and also, as I discovered, amongst Lowry's correspondence, in Special Collections at the University of British Columbia. Lowry was close to death when he wrote that letter to Gustafson. And he'd got it wrong about the two friends, the western poets, visiting on a stormy night. They came on sunny afternoons and if there were storms, they were only in someone's mind. Still in the letter, Lowry *sounded* all right.

Is "Poem, Architectural" that perfect fierce poem—as he thought? Here it is; I'll let you decide:

POEM, ARCHITECTURAL

The murderers build towers
for the insane, for lovers.
Grey stone on stone
leaved with
ivy,   ivory,
flutings of marble

Pavements meet pediments,
climb into collonades,
curl to Corinthian capitols,
(scrolls over roof)
burgeon into pigeons, pigeon coloured stone
rises on wings.

Below caryatids groan.
(Dark caryatids, murderers' mothers.)
From the highest windows the madmen leap.
(demented by portico angels)
The utmost cupolas sway in ignorant sleep
backed by a blue
(it is such a blue!)
Far away rain prepares a green lie.
The jungle jumps in its tangled net.
At the city's gate
the furious convolvulus tears at the wall.
and grass, a green trouble,
barks at the stones.

In May, Ralph Gustafson wrote back to Malcolm Lowry. He tried to contact Curt but the letter was returned "addressee unknown." By June, Malcolm was dead—too much gin and too many barbiturates. When his *Selected Letters* was published after he died, Al was asked to review the book for *Canadian Forum*. Testily, he signed the piece "Al Something-or-Other."

Today the mudflat shacks, including Malcolm Lowry's, are gone, bulldozed in the late fifties. North Vancouver created Cates Park where they once stood. In 1980, it named a walk in Lowry's honour. More recently, it erected a stone plaque to indicate where he lived. It does not mention that he was evicted from the place he loved more than any other.

Al did not forget those days with Curt. In his later years, he divided his time between a cottage in Ameliasburgh, Ontario and a home in North Saanich, British Columbia. He saw his old friend very infrequently but Curt's infatuation with Al's sister-in-law, Norma, remained vivid in his mind. Later Curt had many other girlfriends and married twice, but his young hopeless love stayed with Al. When Curt died, Al wrote a poem about him that appears in his collection *Beyond Remembering*:

FOR CURT LANG

O Lydia, Lydia, why are you sound asleep
while all night long I suffer in the alley?
—HORACE

How awful to spend the night in an alley
trapped in a little English Prefect
wide-awake and dreaming sexual dreams
at age 17 in 1952
beer-drunk and comically romantic
forbidden to love delicious Norma
afflicted with a permanent erection
condemned to this dreadful fate
by your hard-boiled friend Purdy
thus allowing Norma a good night's sleep
Ah yes the parallel to Lydia's boyfriend
is obvious—but skip from Rome to Canada
Curt died of cancer in Vancouver
two months back and I am now 80
unfit for all but literary endeavours

Well I remember going out to the Prefect
again to see if Curt had killed himself
for love or lust or both
and thinking "migawd the poor guy"
his pale face at the car window
imploring the night piteously
"Oh Norma, Norma, why are you sound asleep?"
And will you hate me forever Curt?
—but now it's 1999 and he's dead

Talking to Norma on my return
to the house—she quite agitated
and possibly aroused
but wanting her beauty sleep
and that is the way it was?

But Norma has forgotten the incident
as she grows old and me older
the new millennium around the corner
which makes such things trivial
but think how lucky I've been:
this lifetime of writing excitement
and itching torment *to get it right*
a double reward for being alive
like a rolling Niagara of what I am
thus reversing the flow of time's river
stand confronting that Greek mountain
(yah Parnassus)
admiring but without envy
of all the great masters
reversing time to meet myself there

—AL PURDY

Like a fly in amber, teenaged Curt is locked forever in Al's car, locked forever in Al's poem, locked forever yearning for Norma forever. When I told Curt I wanted to write a book about him, he said rather sharply, "I'm not dead yet!" But now he is dead yet. And I am doing it, and I worry about locking him in to these pages.

2. That beautifully unworldly, reasonless rampaging of my old self

CURT, AL AND JIM CONVERGED ON MONTREAL in October 1955. Curt, who hitchhiked, arrived first. He showed up on Irving Layton's doorstep, introduced himself as a poet from British Columbia and wangled a place to stay. "I would never have had the nerve," said Jim. Then Al came, having spent a few days visiting his mother in Ontario, and Jim, who rode the bus (through the United States since the Trans-Canada Highway was not yet built).

Their grand tour of Europe was about to start. The three men had saved for a year to afford the trip. Al had tried to persuade Doug Kaye to join them, saying, "Doug, we're not getting any younger, you know." Doug, now eighty-four, chuckled as he told me that. "I didn't want to go," he said.

After a short visit in Montreal, the friends crossed from Montreal to Le Havre on the creaky *Ascania*, a Cunard liner. The *Ascania* was truly at the end of its life; it was scrapped after this voyage. The passage was rough. At night, the rolling vessel bashed them into the walls of their cabin, and their arms, still aching from recent inoculations against diphtheria and small pox, throbbed with pain. In other respects, the week at sea was boring. According to Jim, "It was a British ship and old ladies organized sing-songs on the deck—'Knees up Mother Brown.'"

Curt, Al and Jim had made no prior arrangements about where to stay in Paris, but they found a hostel near Place Pigalle. This was the heart of Paris's red-light district—made famous by nightclubs like the venerable Le Moulin Rouge, which opened in 1889, the year the Eiffel Tower was completed. In the past, many artists had lived in the area—Henri de Toulouse-Lautrec, whose prints immortalized it, but also Pablo Picasso, Pierre-Auguste Renoir (who waited on tables here in his youth), Edgar Degas, Maurice Utrillo. Curt's impressions inspired his poem "Paris 55."

```
Paris 55

The place was full of phony artists when I was there,
(But the  stones had beauty)
The fleas in every hotel chanted poems
While sucking the blood from American tourists.
The girls waited in dark doorways
The way they were supposed to; and even
Bronze  statues in fountains watched themselves
Avidly when no one else was looking.
I kept wondering what was the plural of 'pimp'
Everytime I escaped from one.
Disenchanted? No, the iron pissoires
After the traffic stopped made a lovely sound.
And on the boat train to Dieppe
I kept thinking of the sweet-faced girl
I saw on the Rue de la Ancienne Comedie
Who discovered a run in her stocking,
Stamped her feet three times, and said:
"Merde! Merde! Merrde!"
```

After some time in Paris, the trio went south to visit Gary Ness, a painter they knew from Vancouver. He was living in a ruined church in Chémery. When Ness decided to return to Paris, Al went along, to help carry Gary's paintings. Curt and Jim did not see Al in Europe again. Though they had been planning the trip with great anticipation, their relations had turned rancorous. In January, when he was back in Canada, Al wrote to Curt to explain:

> There were also several reasons why I decided to go on to London with Gary, not least among them being that I was somewhat disenchanted with Polson. You may recall a few words I had with him that were not finished by any means, I should say resolved. This is trivial except for the effect it had on the whole trip. You and I (please don't laugh) were sometimes able to understand each other, and among the expectations, or perhaps the only one, I had for this trip was that that feeling should improve, the communication be clearer and more explicit. If you misinterpret the above then you do not have my feeling for it, which as I confessed is difficult to say. I won't elaborate the Polson part, I merely say the thing is, and seemed to me an underlying hostility and antagonism on his part.

This was nothing new. As Jim said, "I was friends with Curt, and Curt with Al Purdy. Al and I were never close. I think he felt the lack of his own education and, in social situations, he would turn on the weakest person there, which would often be me. He would tease me, try to embarrass me."

Curt and Jim sailed on to Majorca, one of the islands off the east coast of Spain. Robert Graves was there and Curt was hoping to meet him. As Jim recalled:

> We went fourth class, sleeping on deck. We arrived in the morning. I remember the wonderful smells of almond, lemon and orange trees. And they burn a lot of charcoal which has a pleasant smell as well. Majorca was wonderful—seventy degrees. It was so cheap. A bottle of wine cost three cents. The bottle would cost more than the wine.
>
> We bought masks, snorkels and a spear. I was not a very good swimmer. Curt wasn't bad. I remember the clear, pale-blue water and then the dark water beyond—the deep water where there was a sharp drop-off. Seeing it, made me feel apprehensive.
>
> We went down steep steps to the beach. They were marble steps, natural marble, polished from use. Once we were swimming and suddenly

there was a great splashing and shouting. I could see the spear thrashing up and down. It was Curt having a battle with something he had dragged up from the deep, a ray. Then Curt subdued it and brought it to shore. Fishermen had already caught it once, cut off its tail. It was near dead, anyway. But when Curt stabbed it, it had jerked in reaction and Curt thought he was being attacked.

We did meet Robert Graves. Curt buttonholed him on the street. Told him that he was a Canadian poet. I was squirming with embarrassment. But nothing embarrassed Curt. They chatted for a few minutes, but Graves did not invite us or anything.

After Curt and Jim toured the rest of Spain (visiting many gypsy nightclubs along the way), they returned to France. Curt's brother, Greg Lang lent me a diary which Curt started on this trip. A brown and battered, water-stained volume stamped, "Richardson and Co., 176 Charing Cross Road," it smelled musty. The first entry is from Saturday, March 23, 1956, when Curt was back in Paris. It was raining slightly that day, a bit sombre. Curt wrote: "The past is always so alive. It encroaches like a green tide on every hour and day, breeding a sadness in everything. A summer sun reminds me of lost summer suns, the rain of misspent days." Two days later: "All the usual discontents and doubts banging around inside." But not everything was lost—at least not yet: "I went into the street wearing sandals and very proud to see them covertly admired."

By early April, Curt and Jim were in England. Then Jim returned to the continent while Curt stayed on in London. Curt met a woman—Adrienne, a waitress in a restaurant called the Stock Pot. When he first saw her, she was wearing an attractive black dress and had her hair wound in a thick plait. Curt wrote: "It is not that fable of love one hears of, but I like her, am a little content with her, her face fascinates me endlessly, she is passionate and entirely womanly, and needs my help. Why not her?" In a letter to Curt, Al commented: "Your Adrienne sounds attractive. I mean a person that dreams such dreams…" Jim told me that she was very nice—blonde and plump. She was also pregnant—although Curt was not the father of the baby.

On April 26, Curt wrote: "Still no money, porridge and poverty." The prospects of escaping grinding destitution seemed better in Canada. Britain was slowly emerging from its post-war economic slump; rationing only came to an end in 1954. By contrast, Canada was riding a megaproject-fuelled boom, constructing the Trans Canada Highway, the St. Lawrence Seaway and the TransCanada Pipeline from the East to the Leduc oil-fields in Alberta.

Curt said good-bye to Adrienne at Euston Station on June 13. As he left her there, he was struck by the expression on her face. "She does care for me, and I for her," he later wrote in his diary. He boarded a steamer for Montreal. Three days out from London, walking on deck, he saw that the mist and rain erased the horizon completely. Curt was reminded of something he had been thinking a few weeks before:

> I discovered on a beautiful day in London, when I awoke to look at our jungle, that all the trees in the back were sopping wet. The air smelled delicious and the greens fairly walked in circles they were so bright. That day I discovered that I actually like dirty weather. Now I think back on Vancouver days spent in the park in Al's car drinking old Dublin. We sat with the water hanging in the air dressed as mist, oozing out of trees, drip-ping off leaves. It was so present and ubiquitous that it entered our talk and our brains and our limbs, and, I see now, my heart. Those days at the time seemed an epitome of wastage—sad, bitter ale in the mouth, dreamy talk, and the incessant, glum-faced weather. However, the trees grew finely green in all the rain.

As the ship ploughed west, Curt contemplated what attracted him to Canada, espe-cially the North Pacific Ocean. He wrote about the coast so alluring to him, his language almost trance-like:

> The Queen Charlotte Islands, cedared, rich, breathing a perfumed wind in long audible sighs. The sea becomes green, the islands are named after Indians as the others are named after Spaniards. The tiny bays have brown clay banks with forest starting up immediately, and birds—crows, gulls, runners, fish hawks—endlessly patrol and crowd the shores. Then farther north to Kamano [Kemano]. A glacier pours into the sea, making it an opaque milky green. The islands are rock-granite, and have no trees. Only

a sheathing of ice that glitters all summer long. And finally Prince Rupert where it rains and rains and rains.

But he was also bothered by the idea that he was taking the easy way out, and wrote: "And I? I am becoming safe. No more burning itch of discontent, no more seeing the wall fall down and the weather come in. Where is that beautifully unworldly, reasonless rampaging of my old self?" He needn't have worried. He was hardly becoming safe.

* * *

On June 23, the day after arriving in Montreal, Curt was working in a hospital emergency ward. Curt found a room on Lorne Avenue near McGill University and his thoughts turned to Adrienne. "Received a letter from A. today. She is worrying and very unhappy. My motives are, I suppose, mixed, but all I want is to have her with me, and try to help make things right for her. Oh, balls! I can't help worrying about her."

At the beginning of July, Curt landed a job as an orderly at the Allan Memorial Institute of Psychiatry. The notorious Dr. Donald Ewen Cameron was director at the time. He had a theory about curing mental illness which involved erasing existing memories and rebuilding the psyche completely. To "wipe the slate clean," he used electroconvulsive therapy and sometimes put his patients into drug-induced comas for months on end. Intrigued with the possibilities this might hold for mind control, the American Central Intelligence Agency began funding some of his experiments in 1957. The program wasted hundreds of lives. I remember Curt telling us, that when Dr. Cameron entered a room full of patients, their fear was palpable. He said he never met anyone whose presence had such a chilling effect.

Curt borrowed $200 from a friend, Doug Kaye, to pay for Adrienne's passage to Montreal. She wired him that she would be sailing on July 13. "I pray that she can teach me to love. To teach a blind man how to see," Curt wrote in his journal. Curt promised to pay Doug back, as soon as he could. But other priorities took precedence. Years later, when Doug bumped into Curt in a restaurant in Vancouver he shouted, "You son of a bitch, where is my money?" Shamefaced, Curt pulled out his wallet and gave Doug twenty dollars. When I spoke to Doug on the phone recently, he laughed and said, "He still owes me $180. I don't suppose I'll ever collect it now."

After Adrienne arrived, the couple moved into a rooming house on Pine Avenue (now Avenue des Pins), not far away from Curt's first place. Curt was pursuing various writing projects—an adaptation of Haida myths, children's stories, a film script for the National Film Board. But none of these seemed to pay anything. "Working some for the CBC. High hopes for remuneration." Then in a letter to Al: "Money is running goddamn short." He was making $33 a week at the Institute—starvation wages. He was hoping to get a better job—either with Trans-Canada Air Lines or the Distant Early Warning Line up north (which paid $425 a month). And, in case that didn't work out, he had applied for a second job at the general hospital. "You can imagine what that would mean. No time whatever to live," he told Al.

In late August, Al and his wife, Eurithe, moved from Vancouver to Montreal. Al intended to live on the unemployment benefits he had accumulated while working in Vancouver—and write. Al and Curt hatched a plan to collaborate, but the joint effort was stillborn. In October, Curt wrote to Jim who was in Vancouver by then, attending the University of British Columbia. "Al displays his usual charm. We are supposed to be writing a play together. An alleged comedy. But I am so pissed off with it that I can't work on it more. I shall leave it to his heavy genius."

At the end of October, Adrienne had her baby. I didn't learn this from the diary but from a letter which Curt sent to Jim Polson: "Adrienne has dropped her calf." Was Curt really as callous as he sounded, I wondered, as I read that? Or was this a way he had of writing to his friends? A posture? His tone was different in his diary—"to teach a blind man how to see." Adrienne's baby was soon adopted; a friend knew a couple anxious for a child.

Somehow, in Vancouver, Curt's mother, Hope, heard the news and wrote to enquire about it. Curt wondered who could have told her. As he related to Jim: "Your name was mentioned but we all knew you wouldn't have said anything. When I heard what actually happened I was really most surprised; however, everything is all right. I told mama the child was stillborn and she is satisfied and we have all resolved to say no more about it. I hope you didn't scold your mother too severely." Apparently, Jim's mom was the source of the leak.

Curt continued to struggle with writing. He complained in his journal that it had degenerated to pointlessness. And then on December 18, this:

Sitting today with Al and Irving in a pub. The conversation was mainly on the merits and demerits of Orwell, Irving being pontifically against him. Nothing much said. Talk progressed to our own work. He edicted (if there is such a word) that my work was nothing and that I had no idea of poetry. All this said so cocksurely that he seemed to expect me to agree!! He really began to bother me when he said, with complete conviction, that he was great and would be read and loved a thousand years from now.

In January, Curt was still working as an orderly, then at the general hospital:

An Eskimo from the territories had somehow gotten his foot wet and it had been frozen in the 70 below zero weather. The foot was quite black and looked like the man they found in a bog in Denmark. It smelled like the mummy room in the British Museum and appeared utterly lifeless, almost as if it had been transformed into a carved foot. When they began to amputate and made the first few incisions a vile stench of gangrene filled the room and beneath the black leather the dead flesh was an intense red and somewhat gelatinous. The thin bones of the foot were cut with an abrasive wire. The young man was 19, named Winingluk, very pleasant faced, spoke no English.

By February 6, Curt was out of work. In his diary: "Thinking of dashing back to Vancouver although I dislike leaving my friends here."

Nine days later, after a long bus ride, he was at the coast. He did not ask Adrienne to join him and they were never together again. "What peculiar deadness pervades my relationship with people? At first, with Adrienne, I built an hypnotic image and became bored with it later, gradually falling into our estrangement."

"You silent sonuvabitch!" Al roared across the continent at Curt in a letter when he found out that he had left town. "I don't think you should have left Moriel [Montreal] for a construction camp in British Columbia. I'm in a helluva state without you. Adrienne, according to Leslie, hates my guts and thinks me responsible for you not marrying her (the silly bitch!). I have no one to talk to but myself and spring is damn near here for your absent edification."

3. If one casts completely free

CURT ARRIVED IN VANCOUVER on February 15, 1957, to find a city hinting at spring. Nevertheless, he was not much happier. In his journal: "Many thoughts on self and writing. Between depressions I can get along. The whole business of living and perceiving is like walking along a thunderous beach. All around waves rise up and tumble/fall. In the spun foam are meanings." If the meanings were in the spun foam, if they were thrown up by a lithe and dangerous sea, what happened when the waters were calm? Did they disappear like the foam?

Al sent a companionable, friendly letter. He gave Curt the news about his Montreal acquaintances and told him about his attempts to get paid for writing:

> I've read several more National Film Board scripts and am rather disgusted. They're not infantile, they're far worse. The people are so goddamn normal, they're monstrosities. I don't think I can do that sort of stuff at all. I miss you here, doesn't seem quite the same. Perhaps we see through each other more clearly than most, even the heart pumping in its red gelatin, the synapses and relays of the brain clicking spasmodically… perhaps motivation most of all. I dunno… It is quite frightening to observe how your judgment of people changes with regard to how they treat you. You'd think everyone was desperately searching for a mirror of some kind, as I've said before. An identification bracelet to jingle pleasingly at times… Sometimes I think most of my own identity is in other people's opinions which I must conform to.

I'm supported in mid-air by cables of glutinous thought, anchored by opinions… and there seems to be no clear consistency of thought or action… all is governed by belly hunger, woman hunger, thought hunger, loneliness, growing older… Write, Al.

Curt did not go to a construction camp as Al thought he might. In April, he was labouring on the docks as a stevedore:

Today loaded flour sacks for eight hours. At fifty pounds each, it was very wearing. Terribly dry. Flour dust impregnates my clothing and forms a second skin on my arms and face. Am weary of this sort of thing. Towards five o'clock, as we pushed one of the last loads out of the freight car into the shed, a drop of water fell from the roof. The colours of the label printed on the sack were red and blue, a faded, powdered, flour-charged red and blue. Then this drop struck the letter "a" in "trade," turning it into a half inch arrow of bright, blood red. Why that tiny drop could so refresh me I don't know, yet one half drop of soft cool rain water cleared me and made me cheer up when I could have drunk a gallon of beer.

In May, Curt had a job aboard a salmon troller *Spray No. 1*, in Queen Charlotte Sound. His skipper was Leo Carter, a thirty-one-year-old from Prince Rupert who had begun fishing for halibut when he was fifteen. He'd acquired his own boat when he was twenty-four and that season was vying for the position of highline boat—as Curt wrote: "the man who made the most lovely money of the season." Later, Curt described his experience trolling—a bittersweet memory:

The calm night, all black and soft and the sea gently rolling and splashing on the hull after a red sunset. The universe-size tiredness after the work… then the radio on into the silence so rich after the motor roar and the twenty hours of static on the fisherman's band and from Frisco a woman's voice singing "Dark Moon." All in the quiet velvet of silence and fatigue after terrible labour.

And the grey dawns when the raw clock-bell tears sleep down its soft centre. And the skipper tumbled out with a curse for me and a curse for work. He started the motor—oh agony of the day's noise. And climbed to the forepeak, thumping the deck over my head, clanking the nigger-head and grinding the anchor winch.

I, hating to move, zombieing into my salt clothes and oilskins, tumbling into sea boots. With numb, vague fingers, hands sore with work, I stumbled up on deck into the biting morning with a bit of breeze picking spray off the grey waves and flinging it at me. To the stern, and creaking into the cockpit like an arthritic, so loathe to start the toil again. Grabbing the cold-stuck covers off the gear buckets. Grasping the wires and putting a lead ball overboard, but it always cut my hands, and thumping the gurdy into action and running out the lines. Flinging hooks and clipping. All of my body a shuddering wish to die.

No coffee, no half hour to summon up heart, but dive right into the fray with the cold green coho lashing up the water (yet black from the earliness) and thumping their thin skulls with the gaffs and gill-hooking them in to the suddenly-running-with-blood checkers. How I hated these early fish—their same selves no matter the hour—lashing their element as I ripped them from it and desperately killed. A hundred by seven o'clock. A hundred six-pound coho to gut before I could eat a tin of acid oranges and swig a cup of poisonous, strong instant coffee. Then when the sodden work had straightened me up and it was morning full blast I was as ravenous and stomach-fierce as the salmon that bit my steel in their frenzy. But I had to clean them so a hundred packets of salmon guts into the wake for the gulls and gunnies and a hundred times my razor knife slashed their soft bellies from arse to throat and chopped out around my thumb their red-fringed gills. Then to ice them, and down that dismal hold onto my knees in the snow ice, and lay the difficult buggers just so with a sachet of ice for a hot water bottle. Then to cook a meal, and so on, through a lengthy day till dark rest.

I know what it's like very bloody well. The drunk and the herring stink of Namu and all, but I look back on it as if it were paradise, so sharp an edge has nostalgia.

Curt and Leo did well that summer, especially around the Goose Island Grounds—a group of islands called the Duck, the Goose and the Goslings. In one month, Curt earned $800—a sum he hoped would last him a year. He came back to Vancouver in September, but was hungry for new experiences, and headed east to Alberta. He did not go in the style you might expect of a man newly flush with salmon money. He set off with $5 in his pocket. On the way, he was shanghaied to fight fire in a world made ghoulish by flames:

> I wandered through a landscape of trees made of artists' charcoal that drew black pictures on my white shirt. The ground was, too, as black as Satan's breech, except where a tree had fallen and consumed itself to fine white ash. Then the twisted pits a foot or two deep where roots had been eaten away—all the tortuous paths of the roots exposed and empty but for a bit of ash. From these pits came coils of blue smoke and, if you broke the bone dry shell of earth over the root tunnels at their ends, red coals grinned out of their graves.

And then he arrived in Banff, penniless. This horrified the "fair" Pamela whom he had come to visit. He wrote that her true colours showed:

> Alas, a true blue bourjaw indeed. Left to the humanitarian task of support-ing her fine bohemian lover boy, she displayed little grace. Had she given with humour, or god's eye, refused with some sign of life—all would have been well. But why does any transaction of money call for such damna-ble seriousness? Christ, she could do anything if she would stop being so damn hyper serious-pompous-ponderous-hypocritical-niggardly of im-pulse whatever the bloody impulse. So who flipping well cares? About money. Do what you will with it but treat it with the contempt it deserves.

I must admit, in reading this, I have sympathy for Pamela. An awkward situation, when friends ask for money. She probably worried that if she said, "Yes," Curt might ask again, and then what? And if she said, "No," he might be annoyed. No wonder she pulled a serious face. But Curt was testing the boundaries, pushing hard at the social niceties, carving out an identity for himself. In his world, money wasn't supposed to matter. If you had it, you spent it, if you didn't have it, you coped. You weren't supposed to *worry* about it. That was giving it too much respect.

In Raymond, "deep in Hutterite and Mormon country," Curt laboured mightily for a few farmers, "sweating in the super sweet aphrodisiac smell of alfalfa." He drank in the immense sky and then hitchhiked home, over the Kicking Horse Pass, the Blood Reserve, through the Kootenays, Nelson, Trail, Greenwood, down to Creston and Bridesville, over Anarchist Mountain in the Monashees, through sage-scented Osoyoos and along the Fraser Valley to Vancouver. Once there, he camped out for a few days in the studio of a friend, Jock Hearn. He wrote: "I slept in the dust, among the tartan spiders and nearly died of the smell of my sleeping bag." Jock was a bluff Scotsman, a psychiatric nurse and a painter, whom Curt met at a Stanley Park exhibition that the Federation of Canadian Artists organized. He called him a "rousing horrific painter and a sterling fellow." The two not only had art in common, they both had been seamen— Jock in the merchant marine during the war, and Curt, of course, on the CPR fleet and, latterly, on a fishboat.

* * *

Then Curt moved to a house at 3408 West 39th Avenue near UBC. He had intended to use his summer earnings to buy some time for writing, but found himself in a dry spell— and often dissatisfied with what he did write. He took long walks. He visited Jock, with whom he liked to argue about painting. He observed: "Jock very definitely works from a method. His sketchbooks are seeded with little maxims and rules." Curt called on David Marshall, a sculptor, whom he first met at Jock's place. And he also learned to play the guitar. In his diary: "Very exciting to make music for the first time. It isn't so hard either since music seems to follow rules. My fingertips feel scorched, though."

In late October or early November, Al asked Curt to join a book venture—printing a volume of both their poems. "Why not call it *Two* in large letters and print the Italian Roman, French and all language translations of "two" on the cover in smaller letters? Let me know on that. I think it a novelty, if not exactly a brain wave. I beg you on my house-maid's knee to include both 'Beachcomber' and 'History Lesson.'" Curt replied: "About the book. First off, haven't got the money. Second thing I don't like my old stuff very bloody much anyway. Will certainly have the money next summer and wouldn't mind getting it printed but to get any extra cash now would entail far too much effort and would probably be impossible. The usual winter unemployment has assumed astronomical proportions this year. Have written a few new things which is very heartening. For a time I had given up all claims to being a poet but the last efforts aren't too bad I hope."

Why didn't Curt take Al up on his offer? Was it really the money? Or his highly critical, self-censoring attitude? Or something else, his forceful desire to move on? One of the poems Al liked, "The Beachcomber's Lying Song," presages the future. Ten years later, Curt would *be* a beachcomber, "standing among the rocks and kelp whips," wrestling with errant logs. And like the beachcomber in this song, not content—certain that "the whole story lies beyond."

THE BEACHCOMBER'S LYING SONG

Here where the clouds lie, the great sea does not remember us.
That sea that swallowed lovers, land, mapmaker's sight,
A ship loaded with oranges, the holds stacked with suns,
And went down far from port, with it went Portuguese sailors,
A dog, a trunk of books, a yellow-haired girl and five green cockatoos.
      To this no point, but that we know it.

Now here we stand watching the gulls carry our wishes to sea.
They, tough, winged brethren, fly with the ships—
A lying shifting constellation, not to be steered by.
And we stand, desperate as locked gates;
Cursing their wings and jealous of their flight.
      Out go the lighted ships, at dawn, at noon, at any hour,
And we are there to watch;
      Standing among the rocks and kelp whips,
Or high, high on the shore, among the pines and cedars,
Watching till the ship dissolves in the sky-sea-dissolving white
Or till the last clear, winking port light is swallowed
By the kraken-sliding night.

It is true we have our relics and our secrets.
The two stony vertebrae of some prehistorically beached whale
Dug from an inland hill.
The Indian masks, the bundles of dried kelp,
The great sized skeleton of a strange crab.
Our beachwood, twisted, pungent when burning,
Our knowledge of the winds.
Our wondrous sea meals and our watchings
Of the insidious, still, green-windowed bay.

But they are lies, all lies contrived for our amusement.
Proof and credentials, foolish things—
Only the tides tell half the truth,
The whole story lies beyond.

Strange how the sea does make us think ourselves immortal,
Consider ourselves as fit for such a trip—
Think on the legend of my forebears;
Two in prison, one is dead, the other lost at sea.

—CURT LANG
3308 Dieppe Drive

And then a long-distance quarrel. Al had sent Curt a play of his to read but when Curt commented on it, he complained:

I didn't think I'd be placed in this position again, that of defending the way I write and interpreting my own words to you so that you'll understand what I mean. So here it is: this is NOT a dull play. But let's not kid ourselves: in a moment of extreme intensity I might write what some would consider great poetry, but never a great play. I'm just not capable of it at this time. But everything I write makes me more capable, everything I read ditto. Nowadays, my mind hardly ever stops working; in fact,

I observe myself with a kind of wonder. That sort of thinking is bound to make for cold-bloodedness. (Observe my reaction to my mother's death when she died night before last; or would you call that honesty?). You may or may not have got the idea that I'm money grubbing for the CBC; if so, you should know better. But somehow out of a clear blue sky I am not going to write a masterpiece of simplicity and experience and wisdom and knife sharp poignance. An apprenticeship is necessary, and I'm not sure if it ever ends.

"You seem appalled to be 'in the position of defending the way I write and interpreting...'?" Curt replied. "Not so bad really is it? Had I wrapped you round like a warm cozening fungus you'd have said nothing of interest and perhaps wriggled a bit (from pleasure or horror). ...Perhaps I was venting spleen of my own that rises from my own feelings about the art, for when all is said, here, I am working little. Needless to say, I envy your productive state no matter what I think of its result. I vacillate so widely that at moments I am dizzy from it all. I even consider a life so far from the arts that I would not hear a murmur of them."

Curt would eventually do that, but not just yet. Towards the end of the year, he worked as an extra in a National Film Board production about Matthew Baillie Begbie, a judge in the colony of British Columbia from 1858 until his death in 1894. A colourful character, Begbie became known as the "hanging judge," although the *Encyclopedia of British Columbia* says that this reputation was undeserved. Curt was an extra with a bushy beard, who nodded thoughtfully when the Begbie character, played by Vancouver actor and sculptor Robert Clothier, extolled the virtues of British justice. He didn't *say* anything.

By January 28, 1958, Curt had decided to pull out of town yet again. He wrote to Al: "Shall arrive in London absolutely flat. Have a multitude of foolish reasons for this madness." But he didn't really seem to have much of a plan or an agenda. What followed was eighteen months of an incredible ride. Curt turned his hand to many things in many different countries—a situation made possible by his own adaptability and a time which was much less bureaucratic than our own. Rules? There didn't seem to be many.

* * *

Curt caught a bus to New York and in mid-February sailed across the Atlantic on the *Saxonia*. By the beginning of March, he had a place to live in Chelsea off The Kings Road and found work. He wrote to Al: "Have a job in a lousy joint for two nights a week. It's called 'Hades' and is got up all black with dripping candelabra and quite good drawings of devils and devilleses (?) with infernal epigrams written on the tables."

On May 20, after a winter of what he told Al were poorly paid "survival jobs," he left London for Belgium. He landed at Ostend with a sixpence in his pocket which he threw into a ditch. "I have often said that if one casts completely free, good luck is bound to turn up. One cannot land on one's feet if one hangs onto little things. Mind, I had some moments of fear before I left lovely Dover, but once on the boat where there was no possibility of turning back, I felt alright. I know it is bad to be hungry, but I have experienced it before. If I can keep my cheer all will go well." And it did, thanks to a generous woman with whom he hitched a ride to Ghent, a town in the Flemish part of Belgium. In his diary, she was a "Walloon acquaintance." But to Al he wrote: "met a fairly well-off Dutch broad in a big American car. The inevitable happened." She gave him 200 francs so he was able to stay in a cheap hotel and eat in a restaurant when he had expected to sleep in a field. All his life, Curt skirted closer to the edge than anyone I knew.

Jamie Reid told me a story about Curt that may, in fact, be apocryphal, but is certainly illustrative of an attitude—a cool confidence that prevails in the tightest of spots:

> When he was in Europe, he got on a boat in the Mediterranean. For some reason, somehow, he fell overboard. He said the water was warm. He was floating in the Mediterranean, nobody around. The boat that he fell off was gone. It was calm. He said, "I wasn't worried at all. I felt completely relaxed." He just stayed there, treading water in the sunlight. He said, "I knew because I was on a shipping route that boats were travelling all the time, that sooner or later, if I tread water long enough, for a day, two days, that a boat would come past me." And, of course, it did. He may be one of the few people who have fallen overboard under any circumstances who felt completely relaxed about it in the open ocean.

After hitting rock bottom on a road near Ghent, Curt earned some money on a television show in the American pavilion at the Brussels World's Fair—the first after the Second World War. This was enough to get him to Germany: "And in Köln [Cologne] the gallery has very good 15th century paintings. Fearful monsters and headless saints. Saint Nocosias stands with the top of his head neatly whacked off and holds it in his hand in his mitre (like a cranial ice-cream cone). He has a neat fringe of blood on his forehead." Curt wrote to Al, that with an acquaintance he made in a Frankfurt hostel, "a sunburnt, rather ragged type," he travelled to Nice on the French Riviera. "Quite skint as usual." I was both amused and chagrined to read about what he did there. His letter goes on:

> With a few hints from my friend, I soon had the method down pat. You walk into a youth hostel and pick out the prettiest or kindest looking or whatever dolly that is there. Now I have an old coat with large side pockets, one of which I rip open. I approach very ragged and sad looking and request the loan of a needle and thread, give a shrug of the shoulders as I display the torn pocket, and a forlorn smile. Well such is the nature of young, pretty women that in a trice you are sipping coffee and telling the tale while they sew up said pocket. Thus, I ate and fucked for almost two months.

* * *

I was telling my husband, Gordon, and my son, Tom, these stories while we were walking along the Lynn River in North Vancouver one cold Sunday afternoon, a fine spray rising from its bubbling green waters and swirling through the tops of the trees.

"I don't know what attitude to take towards this," I said. "On the one hand, Curt was so sensitive." I related an anecdote Curt's brother, Greg, had told me. Curt had been out at sea for two weeks in a grey boat, on a grey sea under a grey sky. The fish were grey and there was grey ice in the hold of the boat. When the boat arrived at Gibson's, Curt saw a purple Edsel on the dock—the first colour he'd seen in a long time. It made him weep with joy to see such a cheerful colour."

"He was *aesthetically* sensitive," said Gordon.

"Yet the way he treated women was..." I trailed off, not knowing or perhaps, more truthfully, not wishing to end the sentence. Then I spoke about how he had described Adrienne's baby. Gordon winced.

"Was he actually unfeeling? Or was it a manner, a style he had adopted—especially when he was with men?" I asked.

"Just tell it," said Gordon. "Curt was a mixture. We're all a mixture. And Curt was more of a mixture than most."

"Besides," said Tom, "who wants to read about some nice person who never does anything wrong?"

I was seeing the underside of casting free and I wasn't sure I liked it.

Sometime in the summer of 1958, Curt returned to England. He boasted to Al: "One stroke of amazing good luck after another has been carrying me for the past while and I am still riding the crest." He was living in a hotel, The Regency, in Ramsgate, an old seaside town in Kent. This turn of the wheel had begun spinning in Monaco, as he explained to Al:

> Well then so the next is an English girl—no mere wandering student—
> who pulls up at the hostel in a Sunbeam Talbot sports car looking for
> someone to go back to England with her. She had been at Monte Carlo
> with her brother, who runs a flourishing hotel cum school in England. He
> picks up the paper and discovers he is being sued for 13,000 pounds by
> his mad partner and so the dolly is left alone. Naturally, although I don't
> want to leave the south of France, I figure it would be a lark to roll up on
> my friends in London in such fine style so off I go, figuring on going back
> to Nice after about a week in England. When I get there her brother offers
> me a job teaching English and whisks me off to Ramsgate and when I see
> all the stunning French cunt I stay.

"Oh, Curt," I thought. But then, as Greg had reminded me, I wasn't meant to see this letter. I could hardly complain about its language. He continued:

> Went for a midnight swim with a little red-headed bitch a week ago and
> dived off a jetty about fifteen feet high into four feet of water and a pile
> of sharp rocks. Arrived back at the hotel (it is on the beach) dressed in

a wet bathing suit and a very decorative coat of blood from arse to tip. However, four stitches in the scalp and the liberal application of Dettol to the scratches cured that.

* * *

By the end of August, Curt was no longer teaching. He was off to Spain to buy a hotel for someone he called "his employer." Was this the man who owned the hotel cum school in Ramsgate? Curt reflected in his diary: "I have decided—as much as I can decide anything in my life, bearing in mind that fate rules all—to make my living at sea. It fulfills the qualities stipulated by my character as I know it: stimulation to educate me and a hard life to balance my inclination towards easy living. Also, at this late date, even a touch of romance."

In September, he was a seaman aboard a yacht captained by a Norwegian called Jens Nilsen. Curt sailed from Palma, in Majorca, by way of Ibiza, to Gibraltar and there got a job looking after a boat named the *Margaret Louise.* On December 3, he received two months' worth of mail and from his mother, learned about Jim's marriage to Lindsay. He wrote to Jim: "I wish you the best this poor world offers." He also recounted:

> I have been broke and stranded in half the ports of the Mediterranean and in the other half drinking like a duke and spending silver money. I have had ephemeral affairs in Paris, London and Marseille with women good and bad, but though dangerously close, haven't had the fortune to find someone who gave me a feeling that did not disappear when my ship pulled out. At the moment I am first mate of a yacht in Gibraltar but that will last till a better thing comes along. Gibraltar is one of the last of the last of the old-fashioned ports. Stinking with life. Spaniards, Greeks, Hindus, thousands of English soldiers and sailors, whores all over the place. Like I imagine old Shanghai.

Then on December 20, while the *Margaret Louise* was safely moored, hurricane-force winds swept in from the southwest gusting to eighty miles an hour. Curt kept watch all night and the top deck was only slightly damaged. But, on Christmas Eve, he received news that Jens Nilsen drowned during the same storm, when his boat foundered off Cape Palo, on the coast of Albania:

> I talked to Ken Wardley after the wreck of the Fidoothea. Apparently a ventilator was carried away by a breaking sea and they began to take water fast. Nilsen, so said Wardley, refused to bail, saying it was hopeless, and drank a lot of liquor before going overboard. I find this hard to take, knowing Nilsen for a tenacious and sober man. Wardley put on two life jackets and oilskins and leapt into the sea, when he came ashore in the heavy surf he was stripped naked and, when he spoke, coughed sand into his hand.

Curt sailed on the Dutch *De Goede Verwachting* to Casablanca and spent New Year's there. In January, back in Spain, he joined another ship in Algeciras, the *Warrior Geraint*, which he was expecting would sail to Barbados. While waiting to depart, he

Curt's ports of call, from log book, 1958–1959

took flamenco lessons from a man called Antonio. He rode a scooter out of the city and gazed over its green hills. The trip to Barbados didn't come off and in February, Curt headed back to London. "I am living with a French girl called Bernadette, who in the buff looks like one of the pinups from la Vie Parisienne of about 1920," his diary reads. They had a room near Russell Square with an immense bed and a large and complicated decorated fireplace painted white. The morning sun streamed in the window, but Curt was discontented. He was working as a porter at Lyons and he hated it. "Bernadette said I was 'trop négligée sur la question d'argent'" (too careless about the question of money). He observed: "That is quite true, I must return to a state of solvency."

In May, he was in Paris, busking with a man called Ivan. It started to rain and Ivan got sick. Curt's luck finally ran out. Curt did something I didn't know you could do. He sold his passport to the Canadian Embassy for repatriation. In June, he sailed home on the Cunard liner *Ivernia*. The voyage was uneventful, save for his meeting the painter, William Kurelek, in the bar. They shared a few drinks and discussed painting; their acquaintance was commemorated by a photo of Curt with Kurelek, which I spotted in a book by Patricia Morley, *Kurelek: A Biography*.

On his way across Canada, Curt stopped in to see Al who was living in Ameliasburgh. The visit fell flat. As Al, evidently skeptical of much that Curt had to say, wrote to Earle Birney:

> Curt Lang passed through here on his way to B.C. He had a guitar and a fund of Rabelaisian stories. Once we were simpatico, or so I seem to remember. But gone now, I'm afraid. How the hell does it happen? But I mourn the past. He was sent back at the expense of the government because of some contretemps or other. Smuggling on a boat in the Med, ball bearings and so on, he said. Also skin-diving for an archaeological expedition and coming up with amphorae of wine from an old Roman ship. How did a Roman ship have Greek containers of wine, the name I mean—or do we call all such containers amphorae?

I wondered about Al's lack of sympathy. I, too, felt something like that, reading Curt's letters from Europe. Curt then was quite different from the man I knew. Was the hard shell he seemed to have a kind of affectation?

* * *

On August 14, Curt was in Vancouver and wrote that he was going to a coffee house near UBC "to be interviewed as a beat." This was the first time Curt referred to the notion, although he was certainly living the life.

May 19, 1959 Paris
Have sold my passport to the Canadian Embassy for repatriation. Have been singing in the streets with Ivan & making out at it till we got rained out & Ivan got ill. Better put myself into the hands of the government than undergo unnecessary misery.

I dreamt I saw Joe Hill last night, Alive as you or me.
But Joe, I said, You're ten years dead, I never died said he.

In Salt Lake Joe, I said to him, Him standing by my bed,
They framed you on a murder charge, said Joe, But I ain't dead.

The copper bosses shot you Joe, they killed you Joe said I,
Takes more than guns to kill a man, Said Joe, I didn't die.

Joe Hill ain't dead, he said to me, Joe Hill ain't never died,
Where working men are out on strike, Joe Hill is by their side.

Joe Hill's alive he said to me, And smiling with his eyes
Where working men are out on strike, Joe's there to organize.

From Copper Mountain out to Trail, In every mine & mill
Where workers strive to organize, It's there you'll find Joe Hill.

August 14, Vancouver.
Tonight I made the scene at the Black spot to be interviewed as a beat for a broad called Laury had said I should go. It was very sad even though at first I was angry; at the reporter who came on nothing & when we told him he was just going to amuse the public with a few cliches agreed that yes it was a big joke but lets play the game & give them some shit but he could have been real & said no, give me some opinions; at the cats around the table who came on pompous like it was all a big put down. But sad. No one could communicate.

Curt's diary from 1959

36

By 1959, the idea of living beat was very much in the public eye. Allen Ginsberg had expressed it searingly in *Howl* (although the word "beat" only appeared once in the poem). Ginsberg first read *Howl* in 1955 to a stunned audience in the Six Gallery in San Francisco. After Lawrence Ferlinghetti published it in 1956, it provoked an obscenity trial because of its frank sexual language—"who let themselves be fucked in the ass by saintly motorcyclists, and screamed with joy." Ferlinghetti won the widely publicized case because the judge decided the poem was of "redeeming social importance."

In 1957, Jack Kerouac's *On the Road* was published. The sprawling, largely auto-biographical novel tells the story of Kerouac's experiences hitchhiking across America and his encounters with influential beats—Allen Ginsberg, William Burroughs, John Clellon Holmes, Neal Cassady and many others. The book made Jack Kerouac into a celebrity, the subject of many articles in the popular press.

What gave rise to the new zeitgeist is not easy to say. This generation grew up in the shadow of the Second World War. Some of the older beats, Kerouac, for example, served in the military. (His tour was brief: he had eight days of active service, and was honourably discharged on psychiatric grounds.) Younger beats, like Curt, had fathers who enlisted. For many of the men who survived the war, marrying, buying a house in the suburbs and enjoying their families looked pretty good. But the beats eschewed all that, feeling alienated from a society occupied with materialistic pleasures. Perhaps they considered them evanescent. You cannot discount the fear of nuclear devastation. In 1952, the United States detonated its first hydrogen bomb at Eniwetok Atoll in the Marshall Islands; in 1953, in Nevada, it tested its first tactical nuclear weapons; in 1954, it conducted another hydrogen bomb test on Bikini Atoll; and in 1956, it practically obliterated the tiny island during a second test. In 1957, Nevil Shute's powerful novel *On the Beach* was published, describing the world after a nuclear war in which every-one dies, victims of either the initial blasts or the subsequent deadly fallout. Was this a generation in mourning? Maybe. The beat fondness for black (often satirized) would suggest it.

Curt's interview was at the Black Spot. The name was a joke, a spin off the White Spot, a chain of drive-in restaurants which featured a white-and-green colour scheme and a hamburger menu. The Black Spot, located at Dunbar and West 28th Avenue, was decked out with black walls and had an all-black dress code. It offered coffee, poetry and jazz. A place for young musicians who were just getting started and wanted to try out new ideas, its patrons were mostly students from U B C and from nearby Lord Byng High School.

The conversation at the Black Spot did not go well. When Curt said the reporter was just amusing the public with a few clichés, the journalist agreed and said it was a big joke, "but let's play the game and give them some shit." However, "the cats around the table" were no better. They "came on pompous." It was sad, Curt thought, "No one could communicate."

Curt, back from Europe, August 1959
PHOTOGRAPHER UNKNOWN

4. Naked in the VAG

FRED DOUGLAS AND CURT were such close friends that people often thought of them in tandem. Jock Hearn coined complementary epithets for them: "Cloudspin" for Curt and "Wordweb" for Fred. To this day, they are still bracketed together. Gregg Simpson, a Bowen Island artist and jazz aficionado, called them "the young firebrands, Curt Lang and Fred Douglas," in a 2008 post on the Vancouver Jazz Forum. When Paul Wolf, a former gallery owner and a painter, wrote about being introduced to the art scene in Vancouver, he related that first, he met "a mad-looking gentleman who painted, by the name of Fred Douglas" and that "he had a buddy… a poet called Kurt Lang. He said, 'I'm not really a poet. I'm a psychopath and I don't like working.'" In early 2011, bill bissett, a famously unconventional poet and visual artist, told me, "They were a duo." He was speaking on his cellphone from Toronto, on a bitterly cold afternoon, while walking to a showing of his work at the Secret Handshake Gallery. He went on, "There was some kind of parallel with the Hermann Hesse book *Narcissus and Goldmund*. The book made a big impression on me at the time. Freddy was the more introspective, domestic one [Narcissus]; and Curt was the more socially adventurous one [Goldmund]."

In 1999, just eight months after Curt died of cancer, Fred felt a terrible pain gnawing at his gut. A sinister coincidence, I thought. In the emergency ward at Victoria's Royal Jubilee Hospital, a physician found the cause—a tumour the size of a grapefruit. A few days later, a surgeon excised it—at midnight, the only time he could book the operating

39

theatre. Fred's condition was serious, but his prognosis was much better than Curt's had ever been. The doctors diagnosed the problem quickly and were able to operate—something that was never possible with Curt. After recovering from his surgery, Fred started a six-month program of chemotherapy involving one week a month getting injections and the other three weeks off, recuperating. In February 2000, I phoned to ask if we could talk about Curt, and he told me to come on an off-week when he would have more energy.

I had known Fred almost as long as I had known Curt. Named Alfred, but always called Fred or Freddy, he was born in 1935, the eldest of seven children. Like Curt, he grew up on Vancouver's east side. "As a teenager, he was a bit of a hoodlum," Lisa de Bourcier, his daughter, told me. Then she corrected herself, "Not *a bit of*; he *was* a hoodlum." When he was eleven or twelve, he stole bikes, later cars. He attended Templeton Secondary School and "did everything he could to get banned from school," Lisa said. In Grade 7, he was suspended for drawing nudes—pin-up-girls—on the back of his friends' jeans jackets. Like Curt, he never graduated. He quit school in Grade 10, and worked for Mel Perry, a commercial photographer.

When I first met Fred over dinner at Curt's place in 1987, he was an assistant professor of photography and drawing at the University of Victoria, a position he'd held since 1979. An energetic conversationalist, he spoke quickly and eagerly and loved to tell stories. He was also a dandy. One New Year's Eve, he showed up at Curt's in high retro, wearing a hot fashion item from the late fifties—a new pair of strides. The trousers were custom-made at Modernize Tailors, a Chinatown establishment which, belying its name, hung on to all the old patterns. Goon Wong started the business in 1913 and his sons, Bill and Jack, still carried on. Fred gave me the exact numbers that allowed you to calibrate a wearer's cool. A modest drape was twenty-six inches at the knee to fifteen at the cuff. Standard was twenty-eight inches to fourteen inches. Only the very daring would venture a ratio of thirty-two to twelve. Fred told me that when he was a teenager, it was not unusual for fifteen-year-olds to order tailor-made pants. He and his friends knew a lot about cloth then and understood the differences between worsted, gabardine, serge. On Wo and Modernize were the two tailors who could satisfy this fussy clientele.

On the spring afternoon I drove to Fred's house in Lynn Valley, he was noticeably tired—grey. His eyebrows, which used to dominate his face, seemed less prominent, and his beard, wispier. As he beckoned me in, a large orange cat wound itself affectionately around Fred's foot, and he kicked it roughly, sending it scurrying away. I curbed my inclination to pet it. We talked for a while about chemotherapy, about the strange and unexpected things it does. Then we sat down beside a window looking onto a couple of tall cedar trees and I set up my tape recorder. When Fred started speaking he was uncharacteristically subdued, but soon warmed to the topic of the old exploits.

Fred met Curt in 1957, while going to the Vancouver School of Art (now the Emily Carr University of Art and Design). Curt wasn't a student—he was modelling at the school to make money for another trip to Europe. But the two had much in common; music was their passion. Curt had an acoustic guitar and Fred, a trumpet. "I'd get up at five in the morning and practice," Fred said. "It was an enchanting thing to do and in those days, I didn't have a thought for anybody else." Once when Curt was sitting on the porch in front of Fred's bungalow on Pacific Avenue, a little girl came along.

"Hi," she said.

"Hi," said Curt.

"Are you the guy who plays the trumpet?" the girl asked.

"No," Curt said. "That would be my friend."

"Well," she said, "you can tell him to take that trumpet and stuff it up his ass."

Fred laughed at the recollection. "I guess that was something her mom and dad were saying."

Soon Fred came to the conclusion that art school couldn't teach him what he wanted to learn. While Curt headed off to an adventure in England, Fred dropped out, rented a cheap studio and painted. When Curt returned to British Columbia in 1959, he worked for a while counting fish on the Cluxewe River at the northern end of Vancouver Island. As soon as the salmon run was over, he came back to Vancouver, but had nowhere to stay. He reconnected with Fred, who invited him to live at his new place on Richards Street near Hastings. "I wanted to learn about poetry," Fred said. "He wanted to learn to paint. So I showed him how to paint. He showed me something about writing poetry. It was a very good time. We were totally anarchist or communist or whatever you want to call it. We had so little. It was easy to share."

Fred's studio was in a rundown building that once housed offices, but "it was no longer good enough for that. We got it really cheap. They were just holding the property, in hopes that something else would happen, so they'd rent it off at less than cost. That came to an end, though. We got evicted because John Ralph, another guy who was living in his studio there, went out naked into the washroom and these old women, who had a language school there, walked in. A bunch of us got kicked out. Then we moved to, you know, where Georgia and Pender meet."

Fred Douglas, circa 1961   PHOTOGRAPHER UNKNOWN

Even though Fred and Curt weren't studying at the School of Art, they took a keen, mostly disapproving interest, in what was being taught. Fred explained:

> The accepted mode of avant-garde work around here at that time was a kind of compromised abstract expressionism that was often called abstract impressionism. People would do what they called "'inscapes" which were landscapes painted in moody colours. Jack Shadbolt, [John] Koerner, [Gordon] Smith, [Bruno] Bobak, Tak Tanabe—these people were doing what we saw as a polite version of abstract expressionism that was self-consciously trying to be West Coast. We didn't have any respect for those people. We favoured a kind of linear abstraction that was popular in Paris and Europe at the time. Nobody around here knew much about it, or anything about it mostly. Deyrolle, Vasarely, Manessier, Singier, Pillet were some of the people involved. The historians around here have heard of Vasarely because that became op art, but they still don't know about the others.

To air their differences, Curt and Fred challenged the man they called "Jack the Shad"—Jack Shadbolt—the most prominent of the abstract expressionists, to a formal debate. Jack, who was born in England, established himself as an artist in Vancouver in the 1930s. A tall, powerfully built man with broad shoulders, he was ruthlessly competitive. His influence on the local art scene was legendary. If he didn't like you, you were finished in Vancouver. Jack was the head of drawing and painting at the Vancouver School of Art, where he had started working in 1938. Curt and Fred were confronting an authority on his own turf.

Jack, of course, didn't have to take on these young bucks, but he didn't brush them off or delegate the discussion to a younger colleague. He was confident and articulate; he probably thought he could mop the floor with them. When I called Jock Hearn, who was then living in California, to hear his impressions of the event, he told me that the school was worried about it. "They were so horrified at the idea, they had numbers to call the police. None of us had any intention of starting a riot though," Jock said, laughing. Although this was 1960, the *sixties* weren't really under way. Diefenbaker was the prime minister of Canada, Eisenhower was still president of the United States. The term "counterculture" hadn't been invented.

In a room permeated by the smell of oil paint and turpentine, the two sides staked out their positions. Fred said, "Jack wasn't humiliated." But neither were he and Curt. One afternoon, while I was having tea with David Marshall and his wife, Carel, at his house in Vancouver, he told me how he remembered the affair. By then he was a man in his early seventies, with slicked-back, white hair. Before we shook hands, he brushed the stone dust off them onto his worn patched khakis. He had retired from teaching, but still sculpted, and large abstract marbles occupied the spaces between the fruit trees in his backyard. He recounted how, during the debate with Jack Shadbolt, Curt and Fred disparaged Jackson Pollock, who maintained his painting was like a tangled hedge in which you might find a golden crown. "They said, 'We have removed the hedge.' That sort of dramatization was quite effective. It struck me as an illustration of how they were getting right down to the goal, the spectral roots of art instead of all this romantic hodgepodge."

David was right about Curt and Fred wanting to excise the sentimental—maybe even the emotional—from art. As Fred said, "We had taken the notion that a painting was a peculiar arrangement of coloured shapes on a flat surface, and were trying to relate it to logical positivism, to the ideas of A.J. Ayer." Logical positivism was a theory advanced by a group of Viennese philosophers in the 1930s. Anti-metaphysical and scientifically minded, they influenced the British philosopher A.J. Ayer, who argued that for a statement to be meaningful, it had to be verifiable. Fred added, "I suppose it was a last gasp of modernism, of optimism that we were going to go into a bright future, although we never really understood it that way." Fred's ideas about art changed over the years. He admitted, "There's way more to language and painting than we realized at the time. We were full of bullshit. But we could talk fairly well, especially Curt."

"Did you make any converts?" I asked. "Oh, no," Fred replied. "It wasn't our ambition to create converts. We wouldn't want them. We had contempt for everyone. We were aggressive. We felt like doing it. That's mostly why we did it." Fred told me that Curt gave another talk at the Arts Club, then a private restaurant for artists, musicians and actors. "I wish I'd recorded the talk because it was full of devilish witticisms," Fred said. "Curt was saying that a lot of painting done in town didn't have any kind of structure to it. It was slapped on. He went further and said that there were a couple of artists in the audience who did that kind of work, like Bobak. People were appalled. They couldn't believe anybody could do that. We were both pretty fucking harsh."

* * *

Bob Sutherland, a friend of Curt's from the late fifties, left home at thirteen to escape a "difficult situation." Art turned out to be a lifeline for him. He said, "It was either art or crime. I figured art was a much better way to go." In 1978, Andrew Scott, writing in the *Vancouver Sun*, called Bob a "painter's painter." Bob remembered Curt this way:

> Curt was extremely sarcastic and caustic. Not just a little. A young lady on the scene would come up and he would say, "What are you supposed to be? Who do you think you are?" Absolutely try and destroy her. And then I'd feel sorry for the girl and say, "Forget what he said. You know Curt, he's just like that." Fred would do the same thing. Meanwhile Curt would be standing there with this really sarcastic look on his mouth. He had a mouth that registered his sarcasm physically. I saw him years later when he was working on the boats. It was in the Safeway. I just had a successful show in New York. He started with me again. He said, "What are you doing, just hanging around? Not doing anything? I'm working on boats. Do you have a job?" I said, "Curt, f-off! I haven't seen you for twenty years. I'm glad to see you. Do you have to talk to me that way?" He smiled and said, "I am glad to see you." You had to do that. A lot of people couldn't do that because they weren't used to fighting for what they had. He was one miserable son of a gun. But he was my friend.

According to David Marshall, Curt perfected the insult to a high art. Sometimes he was so original, David was taken aback. "I'd think, wow, that's a really creative thing." Once, David told Curt about an annoying acquaintance. Whenever this man wanted something from him, he would try to manipulate David by saying that one of his relatives had just died—his brother, his uncle, a cousin. Curt thought about the situation for a second and then suggested, "Here's what you say: 'A painful death, I trust.'"

Fred thought the brash kick-ass attitude, for which both he and Curt were famous, was a result of growing up on Vancouver's east side:

We had the moves down. I don't think anybody had it down any better than us.

In the forties and fifties, there were gangs of hoodlums in Vancouver. They were all over—the Broadway and Main gang, the gang on Oak Street. The Grandview Park gang was one of the most notable of them all. Everyone was wearing strides and long hair. The beats were related to hoodlums as much as to intellectuals. Curt and I came from the east end and we had that going. The working class districts could do it better. We felt totally confident. We brought that to whatever intellectual pursuits that we had. I don't think that other people at art school or university could get that attitude as strong as we had it.

They also honed their self-confidence. They argued exuberantly; their discussions included a lot of yelling and shouting and "Fuck you, Douglas." They sharpened their wit by playing tricks on each other. Greg Lang, Curt's younger brother, wrote in an email: "Fred suffered from terrible bouts of depression. Curt walked into their shared studio and found Fred staring off into space, deep in an existential fug. After not speaking for a long time, Fred put on his best spaniel eyes and asked, 'Curt do you *believe* in me?' Encouragingly, Curt said, 'Sure, Fred, I believe in you.' And Fred sprang his trap, shouting, 'Aha! So you're admit you're a *Douglasite!*'" They devised inventive games— running gags that involved improvisation as well as repetition. In the same email, Greg recalled: "To be an asshole was one thing, but to be a 'professional asshole' was another thing entirely. When discussing professional assholes, they would contrive to work the words into nearly every sentence, pronouncing them with enjoyment. (I suspect that this would have been around the time people in their world started passing around business cards.)"

Fred and Curt were maestros of verbal pyrotechnics, but they also had their own brand of unspoken humour—such as the middle-finger stealth attack. They'd be engaged in conversation. One of the two would sense the other had let his guard down. The victim, suspecting nothing, would be looking straight at the perpetrator—whose middle finger would slowly rise from behind the cover of a newspaper or book he was holding. They kept sparring all their lives—even when Curt was dying. I remember the two having tea together. Curt dipped the spoon in his cup, let it become nice and hot, and then, while Fred wasn't watching, laid it carefully on his arm.

Constantly dishing it out and taking it, they didn't worry about hurting each other's feelings. Their swagger gave them an edge. They'd try almost anything—and the stories about them took on a life of their own, which just added to the edge. Don MacLeod, the bookseller, told me that once Curt took offence at something a woman at a dinner party said, and dumped a plate of spaghetti into her bosom. "Did that really happen?" I asked Fred.

Fred's eyes gleamed. "It might have been so. He might have done that." I thought to myself that, if Fred didn't know about it, it probably *didn't* happen. But then he related a second story which perhaps, after telling and retelling, was what gave rise to the first. He said, "I do remember one night that I was sitting with him in a nightclub and there was this wife of a musician who had huge breasts, enormous breasts and this low neckline. Curt kept on looking at them like this—"

Fred looked intensely at the air beside him. I imagined a woman with a blonde beehive and wearing a tight shift sitting there on one of Fred's empty kitchen chairs.

"—and all of a sudden went 'Wraghhhhhhhhh!'"

Fred plunged his head into the imaginary woman's décolletage and shook it vigorously from side to side. By now most of his usual energy had returned. Fred relished anecdotes like this, but he didn't want me to make too much of the incident. He began reminding me of other aspects of Curt's character:

> Curt always was different than the others, you know. He wasn't as hip. He was like his name, "courteous." It might be interesting to look up the word "courteous" to find the root of that because it goes back to the days of chivalry. It figured highly in those days. To be courteous is to acknowledge somebody's difference and welcome them. It's one of the most basic of human skills or sensibilities—that ability to take a foreigner, or somebody other than yourself, and open yourself to them. Curt was more like that. He could see people's feelings. I couldn't.

Despite Fred's caveats, Curt's reputation for wild high jinks remained formidable.

Greg, Curt's brother, gave me a vivid sense of it when he talked about how it was for him coming along fifteen or sixteen years after Curt:

> I'd be drinking with my pals down in the Anchor Hotel in the mid-seventies. We'd go to the Alcazar or we'd go to the Cecil, which wasn't yet a strip bar. It was where the bohemians drank. The remains of the beatniks would be in the Cecil. And I'd join a table around midnight and there'd be a bunch of people I didn't know sitting there. And someone would say, "Oh, this is Curt Lang's younger brother." Everybody would go quiet and look at me like I was now supposed to do a backflip or something. I'm now supposed to do something shocking or astonishing. In many ways, it was a pretty fucking hard act to follow. To get this, "What's going to happen next?" from these old beatniks was a bit of a shock.

* * *

The studio Curt and Fred found at 1496 West Pender Street was a mouldering, dilapidated building to the southeast of Stanley Park. Roy Kiyooka had a place a few doors away at 1422 and many other artists, writers and musicians lived or worked in the neighbourhood—Claude Breeze, John Newlove, Dale Hillary, Al Neil. Jamie Reid rented above Takao Tanabe's "dust-filled" studio, and he remembers the area as "fabulous":

> All of the houses were slated for destruction. Ours was in bad decay because the landlord wasn't there, he was in Edmonton. We overlooked the waterfront, Stanley Park, the Lions. We paid $60 a month rent. If you live there today, you'll be paying $200 a day. Friday nights were party nights. People from the bars would come and we would have a party there twice a month. I would be able to afford my breakfast on the basis of the beer bottles that were left behind. I would go and buy breakfast and cigarettes for me and my girlfriend. I couldn't pay the rent but I could do that. When I couldn't pay the rent, I just went to the real estate company and told them "we don't have it" and they would say, "Well, pay it when you've got it." Nobody would come around and demand it. I think if we'd stayed there

for six months and not paid, they wouldn't have done anything. The guy knew that the property was going to be valuable in the future. It was only a matter of waiting twenty years. He had enough money, it didn't matter. He was holding on to the land.

Later Jamie added in an email:

The good old days. We had cardboard walls in the back rooms, burlap walls covering plaster and lath in the front room overlooking the harbour. The place was a firetrap. When we ran the bathwater, red-coloured water would come out until the pipes came clear, and sometimes they wouldn't. We had pigeons in the attic, dozens of them. When their cooing and scrabbling on the beams got too much for me, I'd pound on the ceiling with a broom, and a cloud of pigeons would burst out of the attic over the tracks and out over the harbour.

Among the local amenities was the Pilot House, in the basement of the nearby Parkway Inn at 1997 West Georgia Street, a kind of coffee house cum party space cum speakeasy, run by Joe Pilot, a notorious character of the era. This was where Jamie had his first serious conversation with Curt—on the night of a poetry reading. Jamie recalled that Curt "remarked on the intensity of my poems and critically added that I was trying to bring it out of an awfully fucking tight keyhole, as he put it, and he wondered if I had a Roman Catholic upbringing on that account. The combination of confidentiality and provocation in his approach appealed to me, and I thought he had given voice to a real insight."

Curt and Fred lived on almost no money. Fred said, "Lots of times we'd just have rice with butter on it. Curt would insist—you know those blue fish bowls that he liked—he'd say, 'We'll have it on those.' It would be a ritual. It would be something. It would be like supper. It would be made into something." Even though they often didn't have enough to eat, they kept painting—painting anything they could get their hands on, paper, cardboard, bedsheets—canvas if they were lucky. Large geometrical, abstract paintings, very brightly coloured.

Their place was a storefront, a marine engine shop that they cleaned up and converted into a studio. "It was still a hell of a place," said Fred. "It was completely rat infested." Every night he and Curt would put out traps. And every morning, there'd be a couple of dead rats. But it didn't seem to make any difference. There were always more rats. As soon as they went to bed and turned the lights off, the rats came out, running all over the floor, making sharp, scratching noises with their claws. Fred said, "It was horrible. You'd feel one of the rats come over you. They became brazen. They'd stop on you. You'd feel their weight and then you'd feel the warmth of their bodies. You'd shake the cover; sometimes you'd have to shake it a couple of times before the things would move."

Fred recalled, once he was painting and he had to take a leak. He was really interested in his work, so he walked backwards, towards the bathroom, keeping his eyes on the painting the whole time. He unzipped, stepped into the bathroom and looked down. "There was a fucking huge rat sitting on the edge of the toilet. He was shocked, too. I went, 'Ahhhhhhhhh!' My cock hanging out, I felt exposed." Fred knocked the rat into the toilet and slammed the lid shut. "I flushed it. I must have flushed it six times. Then I opened it up. He was drowned, but he didn't go down."

A few years after Fred and Curt left the old marine engine shop, it was demolished. The night it was torn down, a friend of Fred's was driving home to West Vancouver. Fred recalled him saying, "I saw this kind of black shadow moving on the road ahead of me. As I drove closer, it was just a sea of rats coming out of that building. They were taking off for the waterfront. There were thousands."

* * *

Finding a regular job was not a top priority with either Fred or Curt. Nevertheless, they managed to land work as janitors in the Vancouver Art Gallery (VAG). "What a fiasco," Fred recalled. "We never did very much work. I'd say, 'Look there's not very much work to do, why don't we just do the work and then fool around?'" But they never did follow Fred's suggestion. "We'd just think of doing things."

Paul Wolf, who spoke to me on the phone from his home in The Pas, Manitoba, remembered races at two in the morning, "They had carts that you would move heavy stuff around on. They were flat, just about three inches off the floor. They had casters on them that went in any direction. You lay on your belly and pulled them along with your hands."

Fred told me, "We'd have races through all the galleries like sports car races. We got really good at it. We learned that to go around a corner you could grab one wheel and stop it and spin. Of course, you'd leave black marks on the floor. We'd do it night after night. There were black marks all over the place. They'd leave us notes begging us to please clean-up. Fred and Curt left notes, too; they'd criticize the exhibitions, calling their reviews, "The Janitors' Report."

One night after a costume party in the gallery, some monk's habits were left behind. Fred and Curt immediately donned the robes and began chanting, entertaining each other in this way for hours. Things got wilder. A guitarist dropped by and Fred remembered that Curt got ceramic pots out of the gallery store. He set them up as drums so he could accompany the musician. "Boom, boom, boom—all night," Fred said.

The zenith—or nadir point, depending on how you looked at it—of their careers as janitors, began as an act of charity:

> Jesus, I remember one night in the winter, we'd let people in to sleep on the couches—people who didn't have any place to sleep. We let them in night after night. I'd wake up at seven in the morning and get them out of there. The staff started to come in by nine and I just didn't want to get caught. One night, I had a girlfriend sleeping with me. We were naked on this couch. The fucking alarm didn't go off. When I woke up, I saw this guy, and he saw two naked people lying on the couch. He was funny because he didn't want to lose his cool. But of course he did. Who wouldn't? Instead of leaving right away, he looked at a painting for the longest time, then spun around and ran out. I had to go and collect everybody. They wouldn't get up and I had to argue with them.

When the ragtag visitors were finally on their feet, they couldn't go out the back door because it was locked. Fred had to walk through the lobby with his woebegone troupe following. "I was so embarrassed that I looked down at the floor. I didn't know who was in the lobby. I could see people's feet but I didn't have enough nerve to look up and see whose faces were there." Fred and Curt were not immediately sacked. They kept their jobs for a little longer before they were finally let go. Looking back, Fred was astonished, particularly by Doris Shadbolt's forbearance. "Even though we'd done everything wrong, she was still nice," he said. That's probably because Doris, Jack Shadbolt's wife and the director of education at the VAG in the early sixties, had no idea about what was going on. Years later, Paul Wolf met her at a cocktail party in Ottawa. He told her what had been happening behind the scenes. "She was absolutely horrified. At first, she said, 'Fred wouldn't do that.'"

Curt's paintings had never been displayed anywhere except on the decaying walls of his own studio. He was just a janitor, not a graduate of any art school. Still he thought there might be a chance to get a show in the VAG. With his friend, art student Walter Langdon, he went to see William Dale, the director of the gallery. As they talked, Curt clenched and unclenched his fists, in what he intended to be a suggestive manner. Robert Reid, an eminent typographer and book designer who taught at the Vancouver School of Art in the early sixties, recalled in an email: "Curt took great delight in telling me this story because he wanted to illustrate for me how violence, or the threat of violence, could intimidate people. Most people in Canada are not confrontational, and can be bullied very easily." In March 1960, Curt got his show, *Exhibition of Geometric Abstract Painting and Sculpture*, the gallery's 20th group show. I am not sure that Curt's gesture was really necessary to pull off this coup. William Dale was something of an iconoclast himself. When he took over as director in 1959 he announced, "There are only two or three works of art worth the name in the gallery's permanent collection." Curt's radical ideas might have appealed to him. In any case, for three weeks, Fred, Curt and their friends— the painters, Jock Hearn, Evelyn Gilbert and Shirley Buss, and the sculptors, Peter Paul Ochs, David Marshall, Robert Clothier and Frank Perry—had forty-two works on display. The program read: "This serious group of young artists are searching for an expressive style free from the accidents of visual impressionism, the painters relying almost entirely on colour and line, the sculptors on contour and mass. In keeping with their unity of aim, the artists' names will not be attached to the painting and sculptures."

Despite this self-effacing attitude, the "neo-constructivists," as they called themselves, did get some media attention. On March 10, an anonymous critic in the *Vancouver*

Province wrote: "The experience with which they are concerned is the purely artistic experience, from which all romantic, sentimental, literary and 'soulful' elements are banished for what they are—claptrap."

As Curt explained in an undated diary entry: "We are breaking new ground. In our work we have chosen to disregard all associative elements—to think of painting as construction in two dimensions. The idea was to strive for precision of line and flatness of surface and ignore the random effects of calligraphy and draughtsmanship, impasto and brush stroke, fading tone transitions, and indefinite edges, not because there is anything wrong with them as techniques but because they would only be impedimenta in our present researches."

More recognition followed in April. The same artists got an exhibit in the New Design Gallery on Pender Street. The event was important enough for Ian McNairn, a professor in the UBC Department of Fine Arts and the curator of the Fine Arts Gallery on campus, to host the opening night reception. Since Abraham Rogatnik and Alvin Balkind founded The New Design Gallery in 1955, they had showcased the latest, most provocative, most imaginative paintings and sculpture in the city. It was official: Fred and Curt were leading edge.

However, none of this success produced any income. Fred and Curt were still eking out an existence in a rat-infested hole. Fred said:

> We never sold anything. Now and then we tried to. Later when Curt was doing those landscapes of Vancouver at night, he tried to sell some of those. Nobody would buy them, I don't know why. I guess if the work isn't contextualized in some way, if it doesn't belong to a group, that's what happens. The Bau-Xi would handle a certain kind of artist and another gallery another kind. [The Bau-Xi Gallery opened in 1965 in Vancouver to showcase emerging and established Canadian artists.] I guess it's still like that. The work would have to seem to be coming from somewhere. It wouldn't matter if it was great work. We never realized that. I thought that years later.

In another undated diary entry, Curt wrote: "We must travel light." For the time being, he saw no other option.

5. Smoking Gideon

ENGLISH BAY. A broad sweep of beach flanked by high-rises. Palm trees at the midpoint—Vancouver's boast. You *see* how warm it is here, just like California!

This was where Curt's mother, Hope, liked to spend time in 1929 or 1930. She had left her parents' home in Fort MacLeod, Alberta, to join her sister in Vancouver. Instead of looking for work as she was supposed to, she came here and picked a comfortable spot on the sand. "It wouldn't necessarily be sunny weather. She'd be sitting there in her skirt and her stockings and shoes on the beach. And have her eyes at half mast. Looking at the... looking at the guys. Trying to look mysterious." That's what her sister, Clara Hague, said anyway.

This was also where Curt had a job when he was a teenager, working in the old aquarium (now the English Bay Bathhouse). He sold tickets to the visitors and used a clever sleight of hand to shortchange them. When he boasted about this to Jim Polson, his friend did not approve. He still doesn't.

The October day that I'm describing was cold and bright. The sea was that dark blue colour it always is when the wind whips the water into cresting waves under a sunny sky. I had arranged to meet John Newlove in the historic Sylvia Hotel. Now an award-winning poet, this friend of Curt's from the early sixties had lived very near the rat palace Curt and Fred had on Pender Street. Since then, he had moved to Ontario. But when I learned he would be visiting Vancouver to give some readings, I asked whether we could talk. I told him I wanted to hear about Curt and the milieu in which he lived at that time.

John Newlove said to come around noon. We had never met, only emailed back and forth and talked briefly on the phone. He would be with someone, he said. I didn't know whether "the someone" would be male or female, but I looked for a couple. I saw two men sitting by the window. I walked over to them. "John?" I asked. The tall, heavy-set one nodded. I smiled and told him that I was Claudia. We shook hands.

He introduced me to his friend, a bearded man with dark hair. "George," he gestured. I shook his hand, too.

George picked up a jacket that was draped over the back of a chair and I sat down. John explained that he was drinking lime and soda. I was surprised since on the phone he'd mentioned he intended to drink wine, but I told him, "Maybe I'll have that." He said, "It's passable." I started talking about the traffic. Crossing the bridge had been slow. And the parking. It was always hard to find a spot in the West End. I'd had to circle around. John was sympathetic. Then I asked how long he would be staying in Vancouver. He looked startled. "There must be some mistake."

I said, "You're not John Newlove?"

"No, I know him though. Haven't seen him in years."

I asked, "What does he look like?"

"He was tall, slim."

I got up, nodded to the two men, walked away from their table and began looking again, now mistrusting my intuition. A tall, slim man approached me. He had intensely blue eyes and that white hair it is easy to imagine as blond. He smiled.

"Are you John *Newlove*?" I was not going to make another mistake.

"I saw the whole thing. I was curious to see how long you'd go on. You were both such polite people, I thought you might talk all afternoon. Maybe he would have been a better interview."

I was both amused and disconcerted. This man was much more of an *observer* than I was. I'd have leapt up, wanting to clarify the misunderstanding immediately. (But I'd have missed something that way.)

John Newlove died in 2003, three years after this interview. The day I met him, he walked stiffly—with a cane. But he spoke with animation and I didn't notice any signs of illness.

John came to Vancouver from Saskatchewan in 1960 and then lived here off and on until 1967. Then he moved to California and later to Toronto to take a job as an editor with the publisher McClelland & Stewart. One of John's poetry books *Lies* won the Governor General's Award in 1972. The *Canadian Encyclopedia* is complimentary: "His poetry of drifters in contemporary space and historical time had gained him a reputation as a major chronicler of loss and alienation." John was also a notorious bad boy, according to Peter Auxier, another friend of Curt's. Peter was one of the founding members of the *Georgia Straight*, the outrageously titillating voice of sex, drugs and rock 'n' roll. In an interview at his house in Kitsilano, Peter said, "I remember once we were in a topless restaurant. John ordered a hot dog. The waitress came up, leaned over him, and he couldn't resist. He bit her breasts. I don't think he drew blood. But of course, he was thrown out of the place. We tried to impress on him that he should mind his manners, even in a place like that. There was a lot of unpredictable behaviour in those days."

Those days were a world away. Sitting across from one another in the low-ceilinged, dim part of the pub, we spoke in low, modulated voices. "I knew a guy in Saskatchewan who painted. He knew a guy in B.C. who painted. I got lucky through these accidents," John began, as he sipped his red wine. "I met all these people—painters and the downtown guys, Freddy and Curt, and the TISH guys whom we regarded with contempt, which was unnecessary. We were ambitious in different ways." (UBC students founded TISH, the poetry newsletter that ran from 1961 to 1969. They were influenced by Warren Tallman, an English professor at UBC, who was much taken with American Black Mountain poets such as Robert Creeley and Charles Olson. Many of the writers who contributed to TISH went on to start other publications. Dan McLeod, for example, helped found the *Georgia Straight* which he came to own.)

George Bowering, a prolific novelist, poet and historian with eighty books to his credit, told me in a recent email that there was some mingling of the university and downtown poets. "For example, Maxine Gadd and Judith Copithorne were to be seen on the UBC campus. I think that we started to merge when Warren Tallman asked John Newlove to a party or two."

On one mingling occasion, a number of people were stapling TISH together in Peter Auxier's living room. Peter told me Curt had the idea of imitating Cossacks who drank vodka laced with cayenne pepper. After everyone tossed back a few, Curt said, "Now you know why those Cossacks could get on horses and ride for a hundred miles." Curt got drunk and fell asleep while the work continued. The stapler broke down and the TISH folks began using a hammer to staple the newsletter together. Then they threw the stapled newsletters on top of the sleeping form of Curt. So there he was, in the living room, covered with magazines. After a while, he rose, shook off the magazines and announced to the world, "I had nothing to do with this," and went back to sleep.

Curt Lang, Judith Copithorne, Fred Douglas at UBC *reading,* 1963   PHOTOGRAPHER: DON SLADE

The rivalry between poets came to a noisy head at least once, on Saturday, November 30, 1963. Fred, Curt and Judith Copithorne were invited to read their poems at an international fall fair on the UBC campus. A picture of the three of them, taken ahead of the event to advertise it, shows Judith sitting in a comfortable armchair, beside a bookshelf, and Curt and Fred standing behind her. The three look surprisingly collegiate, Judith in a neat skirt and simple top, Curt and Fred, clean shaven with short-clipped hair, wearing dress shirts. These rebels evidently feel no need to look the part. They seem calm; obviously, they have no idea what's in store. The reading took place upstairs in Brock Hall, a mock Tudor building at the north end of campus. Groups representing about twenty countries sang, danced and sold ethnic foods in different rooms. The atmosphere was chaotic; visitors came and went.

This was not a particularly literary setting, but when the university poets got wind of the fact that downtown poets had been asked to read at UBC while they were not, they got huffy. They showed up anyway and demanded equal time. Voices were raised. There was pushing and shoving. Some of the spectators, who had not signed up for a melee, tried to leave; others, who were very interested in such a contretemps, pressed forward in order to see better. Despite the confusion, Curt remembered something. He went downstairs and spoke to two gentlemen outside who nodded their heads and then followed him. Curt strode back into the room with two bagpipers in full Scottish regalia, marching behind him, amidst skirls of piping. Curt didn't say anything, but the martial music, at close quarters, did the trick. The audience quickly dispersed.

TISH engendered much controversy. Robin Mathews, the Canadian poet, professor, and political activist, railed against the American influence on the newsletter. He urged Canadian writers to break away from both U.S. and British literary models. This aspect of TISH's history has been explored at length and with much fireworks elsewhere. Curt, however, disapproved of TISH not so much on nationalistic grounds, but because of its university affiliation. To him, that smacked of careerism, safety, of *not* burning your bridges. Curt and many in his circle of friends were definitely not safe. As John said, "I don't know how to say this without sounding like a cheap comic book. But I was also a bum on welfare. I used to fight too much."

Over the years, I heard many stories about the fighting which I attributed to a vein of machismo that ran through hipster-beat culture. John would drink and get belligerent—punch people, even women. George Bowering recalled in a recent email:

> Once, when we were all living on Yew Street below 4th in the 60s, John Newlove came down his stairs and out the street door with a hammer in his hand, heading toward Freddy Douglas's French car, a Citroen, I think. John was telling Fred in his Newlove voice we all loved, the voice that came between tight teeth, that if Freddy did not get Curt out of Newlove's apartment, Newlove would destroy his nice car with that hammer.

It wasn't just John, though. Once Peter Auxier and Curt got mad at John and smashed the hood and fender of his car. Another time, a man called Gerry Geisler fought with Curt and broke his ribs because he suspected Curt of playing around with his wife. So Fred decided to beat Geisler up in retaliation—went up to his house and was going to land one on him as he opened the door. When his wife answered, Fred almost punched her instead.

The man across the table from me spoke quietly. I had to listen intently to catch what he said over the bar's relentless background pop music. It was hard to visualize this measured and thoughtful person lashing out—angered and quick. We all hide a lot. John said:

> I'm surprised that I like Curt so much, but when you get old you start remembering the people who were kind to you. And the people who made you think. When you're about the same age, you can't stand the idea that somebody is... I think the current word is 'mentoring.' I don't like the word and I'm quite sure that Curt Lang didn't think that it was one of his missions in life to develop this little brute with a fast right hand from Kamsack, Saskatchewan, into a poet.
>
> I think he found me interesting. He hadn't run into that particular kind of fish before. When I think about it, I don't understand, because he treated me as if I were an intelligent human being. And I was. But it sure as hell didn't show. It took Curt Lang to figure it out. 'He's got a brain. Let's turn the on switch.' It sounds like bragging. It isn't.
>
> I had written a couple of verses to see if I could do it. I don't think he

made me write poetry. I think *I* made me write poetry. He made me think about it. The basic question is "Why did I start writing poetry?" to which the answer is "Who knows?" But it's important that you meet someone who's serious, so that you don't start writing Hallmark cards. But I don't think he made me write poetry. There was something inside me that did. But he made me read, without making me read. Curt Lang never in his life said, "You should read this book." Never. He was always lending books. But he never said you have to read it.

No, but you always did, I found. Even after Curt died, I was still reading books he'd lent me. I'd have the impulse to call him and ask what he thought about them and then realize with a start that he wasn't there and I couldn't. John went on, "The primary influence was the conversation, the constant flow of ideas. Good or bad? It didn't matter too much. It was the energy. Once Freddy Douglas said, 'This is more about language than ideas.' Fred's an epigrammatist. I've got this thing in my book. Philosophy—it's from Fred Douglas. It's on dealing with difficulties. Fred says, 'If Immanuel Kant, Genghis Khan.' He said that years ago."

It took me a minute to get it: "If Immanuel can't, Genghis can." I laughed. John went on:

Brilliant. These guys were so brilliant. Most of the time they didn't get around to writing it down. It wasn't important to them. Curt did write poems. He did paint, but it was not the point. He had so much energy. If he felt like writing a poem, he wrote it. But it was all speculation about life and ideas.

The only poem I can remember is a big piece called "Hair Bomb." I didn't like it because I was an aggressive young bastard who wanted to get published. But I remember Freddy saying that the good thing about it is that you can start anywhere. You don't have to start at the beginning, you don't have to go to the end. I've always remembered that. I'm very much into technique and control. The whole idea offended me at the time. But it seems to me now to make some sense in terms of thinking about Curt.

And I saw some of his paintings and I thought they were good, but I didn't know. I didn't think any of that was his primary purpose. He was very much a Renaissance type.

The only thing I have against Curt is that he was too busy to make a record. But then you can't ask—I'm not saying he's a saint—but I can only think of the analogy. You can't ask a saint to get off his cross and write his diary at six o'clock every night. That's not what it's about.

What was it about then? Something was nagging at me. Another conversation I'd had—with Jim Polson. He had said:

I got fed up with the role playing. Curt liked to play the poet. He used to do this with young women. We used to laugh at it afterwards. Then he started doing it with me. He would look at me to see if I was impressed. I resented that. I have a very low tolerance for bullshit. Curt immersed himself in poetry. But what bothered me was the way he would be looking at you sideways to see how you were reacting. There are some people who pursue an activity in a solitary way. They would do it on a mountain, by themselves, for the love of it. I had the feeling Curt needed an audience. I had the impression that he liked to play the role of poet, of hearty fisherman, of bluff entrepreneur.

I told John what Jim had said and asked him what he thought:

I can see where somebody would say that. But I don't think it's true at all. I think it was all genuine. But yes, he could be the Renaissance saint, the gentle Indian, Rousseau… He didn't try to impress anybody any more than he was trying to get fucked by those women. It happened. But I can see why somebody would think that. Because one day Curt was this, and one day he was that. And you were never quite sure how much he believed in it. But I think in every instance he believed in it. He was trying it out to see if it fitted or not. I can see where somebody would say "poseur." But I think he knew that, too. And he tried out the postures. But he wasn't a fake. Ever.

So who was right? John or Jim? What can I tell you? At least that Curt was endowed with more chutzpah than anyone else I knew. That time at the General Motors Research Centre in Detroit—where people were paid to invent the future. Curt standing up to speak, thinking, "Yeah, right Curt, here you are talking to a roomful of research engineers."

How did this dropout, poet, painter, fisherman, boat builder and inventor end up at the research campus of the world's largest car company—its university? He wasn't *posing*, although he certainly wasn't the kind of person you'd expect to find there. But I am getting ahead of myself. This was all long past Curt's poet days. Back to John:

> We're in Freddy Douglas's house and there's this wonderful conversation about painting and reading and poetry. But all I could think of was that Freddy has a big loaf, the equivalent of wonder bread. And he was poor, too. But I'm always thorough. I was more poor. "Freddy, could I have some bread?" He said, "I don't have any bread man." I thought, "I can't deal with this. I can see the damn thing." And then my mind snapped... You remember the language of the time... Freddy would be sitting at the kitchen table. And Roy would be wandering about. And I'd be staring at the bread. And Curt would probably be waiting for this irrelevant shit to get over so that he could finish the sentence.

"You like him a lot, don't you?" he said.

"I do," I said, relishing the present tense and thinking that when someone dies, our relationship with them doesn't die. But I wonder if it eventually crumbles, like a house that no one lives in that falls into disrepair.

John began speaking about Curt's kindness. He had already written a little about this to me. He had explained that the painter Roy Kiyooka let him move into his basement where another painter, Claude Breeze, was already staying. One day, Curt who lived nearby with Fred Douglas asked him to lunch. John wrote: "It was only a few years later that I realized he had known how poor I was (absolutely poor) and how little I knew my way around; he had, I am convinced, arranged the meal and put up with my nonsense simply because he wanted to feed me."

62

As we were talking, John returned to this idea. "The key thing to me was that lunch. I couldn't ask Roy Kiyooka or Claude Breeze for food. They would have given it to me. But I just couldn't. And he laid on this—not, 'Here have a sandwich'—a real damned lunch with wine and everything. Just let me babble on. Didn't sneer at me."

John was so strapped that sometimes he couldn't even afford to buy tobacco. Paul Wolf told me that he used to collect all the cigarette butts from the public library. "People smoked in libraries then," he said. "He'd bring them home, break them open and make a can of butt tobacco." Even when he could pay for tobacco, he economized. John recalled: "I'd used my welfare to buy a tin of tobacco. And I didn't have five cents for the papers. So I went into a hotel like this one, walked into a room and zipped one of the Gideon Bibles because it's really nice paper. Kiyooka saw me rolling a cigarette with Bible papers. And Curt said, "It's a harmless pretension." Does that sound like him? It was meant kindly. He was wrong actually. It was not a pretension. But it was like him to see that it could be and it didn't matter."

Curt did not have a reputation for kindness at the time. On the contrary, his brother, Greg, had warned me. "The hardest thing for you to capture will be the malice. That is going to require an act of imagination." I asked John about this, too. He recalled:

> If he thought someone was full of bullshit, it was like having your throat slit by an epigram... When my first real book came out, there was a party at Freddy's, not for the book, just a party. Somebody showed Curt the book and he looked through it, and he really cut me. He said, "That's not the way you do it." Now I think he was horribly wrong. The way you do it is the way you do it. But he was just so intelligent. It really hurt, it really hurt badly. And when I tell you that, it sounds like he was being evil or jealous. But he wasn't. It wasn't the way he would do it. He couldn't see the utility of it. There was too much structure. Too old fashioned, I would think. But he was born with understanding. Other people like me and Al Purdy had to make everything up from the beginning. He didn't get that. There are different kinds of intelligence and his was so quick that I don't think he could quite understand the slow people.
>
> The more I say I understand about him, the less I understand. That's

perhaps the problem you're going to have.

John and I spent a couple of hours together. But I was not the only one who wanted to mine his recollections. A young filmmaker who was working on a documentary about him came by to see when he might be free. He was already planning his shots. The filmmaker put his fingers to his mouth and sucked on air, cautioning, "Don't smoke too much now, I want to get it later!" And John amiably agreed. To me, he said:

> There's this man, he's highly intelligent, but he just doesn't understand anything. One of the things that I think happened in the early sixties in Vancouver was that you didn't think of yourself as a poet. It was just a damn thing you did because it was interesting and you wanted to figure out how to do it. And I'm trying to make a connection. They're doing the film because I'm a poet. But they don't understand. I'm John Newlove, comma, who writes poems. I bet Curt would have said he was an intellectual. I think he would have liked that. I don't think he would have said, "I'm Curt Lang, comma, the poet, or, comma, the painter." I don't think Freddy would, to this day. Freddy is one of the great spirits. When you look at Freddy you have to remember that it's okay for elves to have heavy beards.

I turned off my tape recorder and put it into my bag. John said, "You've brought back to me a period that I thought of as full of strife but that was because I didn't have any money or a place to stay. It was when I became me."

John beckoned to the filmmaker and I went outside, blinking in the bright fall light.

6. Just arson around

THAT SHIMMERING JUNE AFTERNOON, sunshine flooded Hope Pedrini's small room. Curt's mother was living in Haro Park Lodge, about half a mile away from the Sylvia Hotel where I talked to John Newlove. Hope sat on the bed in front of an oil painting of sunflowers. Eighty-six years old, she looked younger. White curly hair framed a round face and her eyes were a startling blue.

I met Hope for the first time when Curt was dying and she came to the hospital to see him. We didn't talk much then; I left so Curt could have some time alone with her. He rarely talked about his family. The only thing I can remember him saying about his mother was that he longed for her delicious pork roast when he was tramping around Europe on hardly any money. I wanted to know more.

I sat beside Hope on the bed and Sandra Foss, Curt's cousin who had arranged the visit, sat on one of the two chairs in the room.

"How much do you love your mommy?" asked Hope, looking at a photograph of herself, much younger, with dark hair, an unlined face and a wide smile. Curt was in the picture, around three years old. His cheek was pressed against hers, his arm was flung around her neck and he was laughing. "This is how much I love you, Mommy!" Hope said. "If Curt were here to hear me tell this story about him calling me 'Mommy,' he would say, 'Oh, Mother!'"

Hope was born in 1913, in Vegreville, Alberta, a town much favoured by Ukrainian immigrants. She was the fifth of eight children. Virginia, John, Neil and Clara were older;

Alice, Kate and Pearl were younger. Hope's father, Stephen Dillingham, was an editor, publisher and journalist, a brilliant mercurial man. In 1898, at the age of twenty-six, he started his first newspaper, the *Brandon Independent* and married Clara Bayne from Ontario. In 1900, Stephen sold the *Independent* and worked for a while in the United States, where the first three children were born. The family returned to Canada, to Saskatchewan, where Stephen edited the *Langham Times*, established a paper in Aberdeen and later founded the *Biggar World*. He sold that and, in May 1909, moved to Fort Saskatchewan in north-central Alberta, a town that boasted forty-nine businesses and an $8,000 opera house. There Stephen edited the *Fort Saskatchewan Herald*. Even though he triumphed over his rival, the *Weekly Chronicle*, which ceased publishing in June 1911, his two-year stay in the town came to an inglorious end.

It seemed money wasn't his forte any more than it was Curt's. In September 1911, four of Stephen's employees despaired of getting the $400 in wages he owed them, and they sued. Stephen did not produce the money. On October 27, Joe Newman, who was acting as town bailiff, came to seize the printing press, to sell it and turn the proceeds over to the employees. Stephen reacted impetuously. He captured Newman and detained him. Then he declared the bailiff was "a prisoner of war" and nailed the front door shut. Inside, along with the bailiff, were Stephen, his wife, Clara, and their four children, the youngest just eighteen months old. When the police chief, Thomas Stacey, arrived to rescue his bailiff, Stephen was ready for him. He had stockpiled three buckets of lye as ammunition. Stephen broke a window and threw one of the pails of lye at Stacey. In retaliation, the police chief fired two shots, one of which whistled over the youngest child's head and missed Stephen by six inches. Stacey, seriously burned by the lye, narrowly escaped losing his sight. In the trial, Judge Taylor said to Stephen, "You did a dastardly deed; there is no doubt about that." He reminded him, "The maximum sentence, as you perhaps know, is life imprisonment." But he was moved to mercy by considering the fate of Stephen's wife and children. He sentenced him to six months in Lethbridge jail and said, "I trust and hope and pray that my clemency will not be misplaced in your case." Stacey was also charged—for "shooting with the intent to kill." He was acquitted, but resigned as chief of police. (In 2009, the Sheeptown players in Fort Saskatchewan restaged Stephen's trial as part of a local history project and I am indebted to them for their script which closely follows the original court case.)

Upon his release, Stephen carried on as if nothing had happened. He moved to Vegreville, about sixty miles east of Fort Saskatchewan and then to Stettler. In 1918, he headed south to Fort MacLeod, his large brood in tow. He began working for the *MacLeod Times* and in 1920, took over the publication. I expected that a newspaper in a farming centre would deal mainly with agricultural issues, but Stephen's editorials ranged over many topics—hell, spoonerisms (ridiculous blunders in speech), the social revolution in Turkey, freedom ("keeping your spirit unconfined is worth seeking"), Mother's Day, Herbert Hoover's fulminations against the British rubber monopoly (in Stephen's words, "sublimated buncombe"), prisons... Surprisingly enough, considering his own experience, he took a hard line: "The only way to control the criminal is by abject fear. The only cure from crime is quick, sure and severe punishment."

Stephen loved language. His daughter, Hope, told me, "He was self-taught. He read poetry and memorized long poems, like Longfellow's "The Wreck of the Hesperus." That's how he would entertain his kids, reciting these long poems." Sometimes his passion for words took a quirky turn. Stephen got it into his head that he wanted daughters named Hope, Faith and Charity. Everyone else in the family thought this was a bad idea, so when a baby was born in 1913, he said to them, "You tell me what name you want. We'll put all the names in a hat. We'll pick one and that's what we'll call her." Everybody told him what they wanted and he wrote their choices on pieces of paper which he put into a hat. He got his daughter, Clara, to pull one out. It was "Hope." So the baby was named Hope. Only many years later did Stephen divulge that he had written "Hope" on every piece of paper. And he did get his Faith and Charity, but only as second names. Hope's younger sisters were Kate Faith and Pearl Charity.

Stephen was also an alcoholic. He went on long binges, sometimes disappearing for days. Hope said, "Once after a very long toot, he came back, put out the paper after a three to four week break. There was an editorial or news story about how he had suffered a Rip Van Winkle experience and had gone to sleep. Curt loved that story." Hope's mother, Clara, held the family together through the frequent moves, the tight money and Stephen's drinking sprees. In Fort MacLeod, she was the publisher of her husband's newspaper, handling the printing, distribution, and other practical details. After successfully running a concession stand at Fort MacLeod's Golden Jubilee celebrations in 1924, Clara started another business, Dilly's Café. She was an excellent cook and the restaurant soon became popular. Hope waited on tables in a uniform that her mother, also an expert seamstress, sewed for her. Sandra told me, "The uniform made the most of her beautiful bosom." At that, Hope flashed a broad smile and exclaimed, "I still have it!" She said, "I flirted, when anyone was flirtable enough. I was a born flirt, what can you do?"

Fort MacLeod thrived in the early part of the twentieth century. Because people were convinced the town would become the primary population centre in southern Alberta, real estate prices skyrocketed, and numerous handsome stone houses were built. Then, in 1912, the CPR moved its divisional point (repair shops and other services) to Lethbridge. Two hundred jobs were lost and the community went into a tailspin from which it did not recover until the 1970s. In 1924, the town itself declared bankruptcy and the local economy began suffering a couple of years before the Great Depression took hold across Canada. Many businesses, including the Dillinghams', were hit hard. Curt's grandmother, Clara, took matters into her own resourceful hands. What she did was a secret for years. Finally in 1963, Virginia, the eldest sibling in the family, died and the Dillinghams got together at the funeral. Afterwards, while they were sitting in a car, chatting companionably, Hope finally spoke openly about what happened. As she explained to me:

> I just burned the house down. It was arson. I was arsin' around. It was
> the only money they had. I never confessed. My mom asked me to do it.
> She was desperate. I lit a basket filled with waste paper, moved it close to
> some curtains. She thought if anyone investigated, she could say it was
> an accident, a foolish girl had set fire to the house by accident. But if she
> did it—an adult—there could be no such explanation. I worried that the
> police would come and get me and put me in jail. I was worried that they
> would look at me and *know*—that they would catch me unawares.

In those days of coal and wood stoves, house fires were common. (I noticed an ad in a March 1926 issue of the *MacLeod Times* which said, "Fire? Many recent local fires have accentuated the necessity of insurance against loss by fire. Reliable companies get our rates.") Forensic investigation was then in its infancy, making it more difficult than it is today to distinguish between an accidental fire and arson. In any case, the police did not investigate. The crime was not discovered. The insurance money staved off financial disaster, but Hope worried and brooded. She said, "I felt pretty guilty—that I shouldn't have done it."

When Hope was about sixteen or seventeen, she made her first visit to Vancouver. Her sister, Clara, was already there, working for the telephone company. Hope moved in with her and was supposed to look for a job, too. But she did no such thing. She went to English Bay and sat on the beach, looking as alluring as possible. Denise Goodkey, another of Curt's cousins, said:

> I don't know how long she'd been there without finding work when the landlady, or somebody, squealed on her. She was going down to English Bay and hanging out with the guys. She may even have been bringing some of these guys back to the suite. Must have been, otherwise how would the landlady know that she was fooling around with boys and wasn't seriously looking for work. They put a stop to that.

Hope returned to Fort MacLeod in disgrace, but in 1931 was back in Vancouver. Again, she lived with her sister, Clara, on Nelson Street and, in 1935, met Earle Lang. "I met him walking down the street. I made eyes at him," she said. Earle seemed sophisticated to her—worldly. He smoked a pipe and was playing in a jazz band, semi-professionally at least. He was the youngest child in a family of girls, apparently much doted upon by his mother and sisters. When Denise asked Hope why she married him, she responded with characteristic frankness. "By then, I had slept with so many men, I thought I should marry one of them."

Soon after the wedding, Curtis Earle Lang was born—on January 20, 1937. That year, in April, Franco's troops attacked the Basque town of Guernica, inspiring Picasso to paint the masterpiece of the same name. In November, the concentration camp Buchenwald became operational in Germany and, in December, the Japanese occupied the Chinese city of Nanking, killing about two hundred thousand of its inhabitants. Though Vancouver seemed far away from these troubling events, in reality, it was not. Britain and France declared war on Germany on September 3, 1939; Canada joined a week later. Along with a million other Canadians, Curt's father, Earle, enlisted. He was sent to England, where he served as quartermaster but never saw combat. Hope said, that while he was overseas, he didn't write to her. He wrote to his mother instead, and asked her to send him money—and nylons.

Hope did not pine away at home. She got a job at Spencer's department store on Hastings Street and enrolled Curt in Athlone School for Boys, a private boarding school at Arbutus and West 49th Avenue in Vancouver. Hope said, "I put him there so that I could flirt around, so I could be free, although that wasn't what I told my mother!" Hope borrowed money from her mother to pay for the uniform and the school fees. Curt hated the school, hated the uniform, hated the shorts that came with it, hated the way wearing them made his legs go blue in the winter and hated the discipline. He didn't get on with the other kids whom he thought were "stuck-up." And he was terrified of the headmistress, one Mrs. V.A. Dryvynsyde. Hope said, "I picked Curt up on the weekends, when he got loose." On Sunday nights, he'd beg her not to take him back—but on Monday mornings, he'd be there regardless.

When Earle was finally demobilized and returned home, the family moved into the old Vancouver Hotel at the corner of Georgia and Granville. After the war, the building, which had been used as an army recruiting centre, was empty. A small company of thirty-five vets, angry about the acute shortage of places to live in Vancouver, seized it on January 26, 1946. Under the leadership of Bob McEwen, a big man weighing two hundred pounds and standing over six feet tall, not easily intimidated, they marched to the hotel and told the lone soldier on duty that they were taking over. Then they hung a fifteen-foot-by-three-foot banner outside, reading, "Action at last veterans! Rooms for you. Come and get them." By evening, the hotel's Spanish Grill and Ballroom was thumping. The vets had organized a dance and that night more than a hundred of them bunked down in the place. The next day, seven hundred vets had "registered" in the hotel. The following week, the federal government and the City of Vancouver hastily put together a plan and found money to operate a hostel.

When I wrote about this for the online magazine *The Tyee* several years ago, I discovered that many vets who'd stayed in the old hotel had fond memories of it. It was cheap; rooms were about $20 a month, with clean linen supplied. Even better, perhaps, the residents were in their twenties or thirties and a party atmosphere prevailed. Hope remembered that, too, saying, "It was lots of fun. People were always dropping in." Few families stayed in the hotel, so Curt wouldn't have had many friends his own age. But he got his first bike while living there and explored the streets and alleyways nearby, acquiring an intimate familiarity with downtown Vancouver. "Scared the hell out of me. Didn't scare him," said Hope.

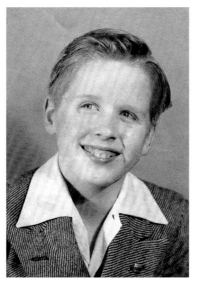

Curt about age eight, circa 1945
PHOTOGRAPHER UNKNOWN

Eventually, in 1947, the city council and the federal Department of Reconstruction and Supply agreed to provide permanent rental housing for the vets. The Langs moved to 3308 Dieppe Drive in Renfrew Heights, an east Vancouver subdivision of six hundred units created by that agreement. All its streets and places were named after First and Second World War battles—Vimy Crescent, Falaise Park, Malta Place, Mons, Anzio, Normandy Drive. Hope thought it was a bit much. "It's all right to remember the war, but not to name your damn streets after them, not to remember the war every day." Curt used to talk about how some of the fathers in the neighbourhood were troubled by their war experiences. They'd drink too much, distance themselves from their families. I suppose now we would diagnose post-traumatic stress syndrome, but in those days, the veterans were just expected to carry on. I'm sure Hope was right. For these men, the constant reminders of what they had gone through can't have been very helpful.

Hope had a job as a switchboard operator for a telephone answering service—at a time when few married women worked. Earle was a bookkeeper for a company on First Avenue in Vancouver. According to Curt's cousin, Denise, he wasn't much of a family man. She said, "He was a golfaholic and an alcoholic. Hope would say something like, 'Well, let's do something as a family on Sunday.' He'd say, 'Well, all right.' She'd say, 'How about we go to Stanley Park?' He'd agree and then say, 'Why don't I get up early and play a round of golf and then we'll go to the park.' Hope would agree to that and then he'd show up at five o'clock, because he'd wanted to play a second round."

Earle frequently found fault with Curt, especially as he grew older. Once, angry with Curt for not bringing in the wood to fill the kitchen stove, he threw him out the back door. Hope, too, had a hot temper, which sometimes got the better of her. When Curt played at a construction site—against his mother's strict instructions—and came home covered in dirt, Hope got mad at him and yelled, "Take off that sweater!" He hesitated. She took the sweater by the hem and pulled it off over his arms. She jerked his arms so hard that she broke his collarbone. Hope told me, "After that, no one wanted to have anything to do with me. Didn't want to let their kids near me."

In all of this acrimony, Curt's grandmother, Clara, was a refuge. After separating from Stephen, she moved out to the coast in the mid-thirties. She bought a property in a rural part of Surrey and built her own house. Clara was not bound by sexual stereotypes—carpentry was another of her many skills. She established a farm; kept a cow and a few chickens. Curt liked to visit, coming most summers until his grandmother died in 1950.

In the early 1950s, Hope became involved with a religious cult called the Temple of the More Abundant Life, led by a man called William Franklin Wolsey. Denise said, "The cult gave Hope some desire to make her marriage work. Part of making it work was having another child. So that's why, sixteen years after Curt was born, Greg came along in 1953." (In 1959, the *Vancouver Sun* exposed Wolsey as a convicted bigamist, wanted on a series of charges in the United States. Wolsey fled and the church dissolved.)

Hope and Earle's marriage remained troubled. Ten years after Greg was born, Hope met Harry Pedrini, a lawyer. She finally divorced Earle and married Harry—a paunchy, dark-haired man who drove a Mustang convertible. The former mayor of Terrace, a community in northern British Columbia, Harry ran as a Liberal in the 1966 provincial election, in Vancouver East (winning only three percent of the vote). Denise said, "Harry was a jerk, too, a different type of jerk. He always had to be the centre of attention. We could be in Hope and Harry's living room. There might be eight or ten of us around, fairly crowded. And if Harry wasn't getting his share of the attention, which had to be fifty percent of the entire attention in the room, he would go and turn on the T.V. loud, and watch a football game and drown out everything else. But Harry seemed to make Hope feel desirable, attractive. And she was really happy with Harry. He treated her differently than he treated most people. I don't think any of us, except Hope, liked him."

But they fought, too. When I visited Hope's older sister, Clara Hague, at her apartment in Surrey, she told me, "Hope was a real feisty character. One day, Harry came to the table with no shirt on. Well, Hope was disgusted with Harry for that. So she came to the breakfast table with nothing on, too. I probably wouldn't even think of doing something like that. And if I did, I'd never have the nerve to do it."

Hope and Clara, 1945   PHOTOGRAPHER UNKNOWN

Curt nursed a long list of grievances about Hope—probably starting with the fact that she put him in a boarding school in order to flirt with men. But also on the list was the way she behaved when his father, Earle, became mentally ill. At the end of September 1978, Earle was in the Centennial Pavilion of the Vancouver General Hospital, receiving treatment for depression. Even though he and Hope were divorced, he asked her to visit, but she wouldn't. Earle locked himself in a sixth-floor bathroom, pried off a screen from the window and jumped to his death. Curt was away at sea when he got the message on his ship's radio. I know he thought it was a horrible, lonely thing to have happened.

The *Province* reported the story twice, once on Monday, September 25, 1978, and then again the next day, because a fellow patient did exactly the same thing. The headline read: "Did one suicide lead to another?" It was a distinct possibility, because of the striking similarity between the deaths. Earle's suicide was reported on the radio and the second man was an avid listener.

Earle had tried to commit suicide before, with a hose attached to the tailpipe of his car. His unhappy marriage and his drinking were probably contributing factors. Denise said, "He often came home really, really drunk. I think the police followed him home one time and said it was a miracle he hadn't killed himself and several people, the way he was weaving all over the road." No one I talked to had anything good to say about Earle, but Curt must have cared for him. Denise said, "I was aware that Curt was spending time with him. I was astounded, because of the way that old jerk always treated Curt. 'Why is Curt nice to him?' I wondered."

Much later, after Curt developed cancer, he intended to air his resentments with his mother. Greg tried to dissuade him; he didn't think it was necessary or appropriate to dredge up the past. Curt, never easily dissuaded, was determined to do it. When he got to Hope's place, however, something happened. He thought the better of it or his mood changed and he didn't have it out with her. But it was clear his feelings ran deep. I thought about those hard attitudes to women that Curt expressed in some of his letters. How much of his mother was mixed up in all that?

As I got up to leave Hope's room, I noticed a watercolour on the wall. I commented on it, and Sandra told me that it was one of Hope's, that a few years before she had taken painting classes. Hope asked me, "Do you know what this reminds me of?"

I looked at the painting of fruit. I saw familiar half oval-shapes meeting around a fibrous core with two winking seeds, pale flesh. The answer seemed obvious: "Apples?"

Hope flashed a big smile and said triumphantly, "Vaginas!"

Startled, I looked again. I saw what Hope was talking about. I saw something I had never seen before.

I was struck by how unconventional she was, how untamed, and how Curt was like this, too.

7. A wolf in the West End

"Fred," I asked, "what was that story about Curt and the wolf?" I remembered something—vaguely. Fred told me that a man who lived in the West End had acquired a wolf while he was in the Yukon.

"He got a wolf when it was just a pup and trained it as his pet.

"Or maybe he didn't have it as a pup because the wolf was wild. The wolf liked the owner. And it would tolerate Curt because Curt had lived with them. When I went there, the wolf lived outside. They had him tethered to a clothesline so he had the run of the yard but couldn't escape. Or they thought he couldn't. Curt said, 'Go out and give him sardines, Fred. He likes them and you'd get to be friends with him.'

"But there was no way I could get near him. It wasn't that the wolf was vicious the way a vicious dog can be vicious. He was wild. He'd back off into a corner to avoid me. You could see if I pushed him any further what he'd have to do. It was wildness, it wasn't viciousness. But he would tolerate Curt. This guy went away for a holiday or something so Curt was left to take care of the animals. But somebody must have complained because, one day, a policeman knocked on the front door.

"This cop said, 'I understand you've got a wolf here.'

"And Curt says, 'Oh, yeah, a lot of people think that dog is a wolf.'

"The cop says, 'Well, can I take a look at it?'

"Well, I mean, it was a fucking wolf. There was no doubt about it. Didn't have a dog's face. It had that funny wolf face.

"And he says, 'That is a wolf.'"

"Curt says, 'It's amazing isn't it? It really looks like one.'"

"The cop says, 'That is a wolf.'"

"And Curt says, 'Many people think it is. It's part wolf and part dog. It's amazing, though; you'd think it was a wolf.'"

"And it was a fucking wolf! Curt kept it up and the cop finally left.

"And then the wolf got away." Fred said, "And Curt phoned me up and he said, 'Fred can you come down and help me find the wolf?'

"And so I went down to the West End. Walking around the West End looking for a fucking wolf. What chance have you got? You could hear it occasionally." Fred imitated the wolf howling. "Arooooooo. Haunting, fucking wail." We went to where the wail was; I went one way, and for some reason, Curt went the other. And then he heard an old couple, sitting on a porch, speaking to each other. The woman said, 'George, I think that's a wolf.' And George responded, 'Martha, don't be ridiculous.'"

The wolf was finally found cowering in an underground parking lot and lured home with sardines.

* * *

Curt went much further on self-confidence than most people. One evening, Curt and Fred were sitting in the Alcazar, drinking and deep in conversation. A casual observer might have thought they were discussing the latest artistic trends, but no, they were hatching a plot—how to steal one of the large leather armchairs they were sitting in. Finally, the answer was obvious. They jumped up as one, grabbed the chair and walked decisively to the door. Their idea was to look as though they had a legitimate reason for doing this. However, one of the bartenders was not taken in and followed them. Curt and Fred walked a little faster. Another bartender joined in. The two friends began hoofing it. Soon they attracted a crowd of interested spectators. Curt and Fred realized they wouldn't be able to carry the chair and stay ahead of the parade. They abandoned it and fled down a nearby alley.

While Curt couldn't always pull off schemes like this, Jock Hearn was surprised by how often his persuasive inventions worked. He told me that, late one night, Curt was walking downtown and a policeman stopped him, wanting to know what he was doing. Right away, Curt noticed the officer had a marked British working-class accent, so he adopted a plummy upper-class English one. The policeman completely changed his attitude. Jock said, "He almost tipped his hat to Curt. 'Oh, yes, sir, whatever you say sir.' It was a manoeuvre on Curt's part. He saw right away what buttons to push. It worked so they let him go. He was very amused by that idea—instantly sizing up the situation and using that."

* * *

In the spring of 1960, after months and months of short rations, Curt's silver tongue played a large role in getting a decent job for Fred and himself. At that time in British Columbia, it was possible to make good money in the resource sector, logging or fishing. Fred told me that when he worked on a coastal steamer he easily earned more than $1,000 a month—then a princely sum. So the issue wasn't finding a job, but landing work that engaged the mind. Curt got the idea that the new Vancouver Maritime Museum might provide just such an opportunity.

Tom Wylie, circa 1960
PHOTOGRAPHER: FRED DOUGLAS

The museum opened to the public in June 1959. It had a spectacular waterfront location, a beautiful building designed by local architect Charles Van Norman and one magnificent possession—the *St. Roch*, a wooden schooner the RCMP had used to patrol the Arctic. But it had no other collections, nothing else for visitors to see. The *Vancouver Province* reported in September 1959 that the museum's new director, Tom Wylie, "is wise enough to know that it will take a great deal of time and effort to breathe life into the empty building but he is hopeful it will be open to the public with proper displays before next summer. First of all, he must build up a staff."

I don't know whether Curt saw that article or whether someone told him about it. In any case, he introduced himself to Tom, who thought he saw in Curt a man like himself. They were similar in some ways; both were intellectuals who had grown up on the east side of the city. After serving with the RCAF during the Second World War, Tom got a master's degree in anthropology with his veteran's benefits. He gathered ethnological specimens in central Africa and worked in a Saskatchewan Metis community before returning to Vancouver.

Curt, of course, was shy of formal credentials. He hadn't graduated from high school. He didn't know much about museums and hadn't taken any university-level courses in history or anthropology. Perhaps, in this case, those qualifications weren't the most important. Keith Ralston who was the curator at the museum from 1960 to 1964, later taught history at UBC. When I phoned him a few years after Curt died, he said, "It was a butt of jokes; the museum was completed and there was no collection." To create an exhibit in this situation, he told me, you needed "an ounce of artifact and a pound of setting." In other words, a little legerdemain was called for—something Curt *could* muster.

Curt brought Fred to meet Tom and convinced him that the two of them were just what he and his museum needed. Sometime in the late spring, Tom hired the friends to build and create displays. Tom had just enough budget for one position, so he let them share the job, which involved hand-lettering, drawing, photography, carpentry. The money was good and the idea of working half-time attractive.

The dispiriting poverty, the scraping-by, the rice-only-meals of the previous winter were over. Curt and Fred celebrated their good fortune by going downtown to buy new clothes—their first significant purchase in months. Foncie Pulice, Vancouver's well-known street photographer, took a picture of them on the occasion—one of hundreds of thousands he snapped from his spot on Granville Street near Robson. In the black-and-white image, Curt and Fred are walking at a pretty good clip, on what looks like a reasonably sunny day. They are wearing new-looking dark denim jackets and are carrying small packets.

* * *

The turn in their fortunes was especially welcome since by then, a third resident, a young woman called Gail, Curt's girlfriend, had moved into the Pender Street studio. At first, I got only snippets of information about her. She was described as beautiful, thin, ethereal, but also as Dionysian and dangerous. Some people told me she wore old-fashioned dresses, worked as a costume designer for the movies and came from Bamfield. I heard that she lived in London, or maybe Vancouver, or perhaps the Sunshine Coast. I didn't even know her last name. Did she use her maiden name, Phillips? Or a married name?

It took a while for me to find her, but eventually I spoke to someone who knew someone who knew her and, out of all the suggestive confusion, a phone number emerged. She was Abby Benjamin now and lived on the Sunshine Coast. When I called, she invited me to come for a visit. And so, on a Saturday in March 2011, I caught a ferry and sailed over. Abby, who had dark eyes and dark hair, wore a dress, although not a particularly old-fashioned one. Her house was comfortable, filled with paintings and situated on a large property. Abby told me the garden was glorious, although it was too early to see anything yet. During the course of an afternoon, over several cups of tea and a glass of white wine, she told me about her relationship with Curt.

In the sixties, there was no road to Bamfield, a small community at the end of Alberni Inlet, on the west coast of Vancouver Island. You could only get to the remote village by boat, either your own, or the sturdy *Lady Rose*, which made regular runs down the inlet. Abby loved living in Bamfield as a child, but when she became a teenager, she wanted to follow her older cousin, Linda York, who moved to Vancouver to study art. Abby's father, Geoff Phillips, said she could go, but not to study art. He gave her two options—becoming a hairdresser or a secretary. "My intention meant nothing. It was what my father was willing to pay for," Abby said. She went to Sprott Shaw, a secretarial school downtown. "I didn't last there very long." Linda began introducing Abby to the Vancouver scene—the grifters and drifters, the beats and bohemians, the artists and the wannabes, the poets and the dreamers, all one ever-revolving mix.

Abby met a man called Victor who wrote a poem about her. When he read it on a

CBC television show, he created a sensation in Bamfield. The village received only one channel—CBC—and everyone watched it religiously. Soon a delegation of angry fishermen made the long trek to Vancouver and arrived at Abby's door. They demanded to know where Victor was. Not only had he written a slightly risqué poem about her, but he was black. "They told me my name was mud in Bamfield," said Abby. "I was running amok and it was all my cousin's fault—she introduced me to these people."

Soon after Abby arrived in Vancouver, she met Curt, but she wasn't sure how. "It might have been at the Alcazar. I had a phony I.D. so I could get in. That's where everyone met everyone. Or maybe it was at a party." She remembered talking to Curt at a party when he'd just come back from a trip to San Francisco. "He said he was going around with a woman down there who had an incredibly long ponytail and someone cut it off. It was her pride and joy, this ponytail. Curt said that was the end of their relationship. Apparently she had a horrible time adjusting. Maybe that was when we met," Abby said reflectively.

Abby moved in with Curt and that, of course, meant moving in with Fred, too—in the ramshackle studio on Pender Street. Abby enjoyed Fred's company: "I found that living with Freddy and Curt together was much more fun than living with Curt alone. They were just such a couple." Mostly she enjoyed their crazy bantering. She recalled: "They were always going on about Jack Shadbolt, insisting that his wife was feeding him ground glass. I remember this Shadbolt story would go on for hours. They'd convinced each other that she would definitely do him in. They were very funny." But sometimes she thought they went too far. "I hated what they used to do when we were walking along the street. They would pretend to be spastics. I would lag behind."

"Curt had so many beautiful women, all so glamorous. Sometimes I wondered why the hell he picked me," Abby said. Maybe it was because, "I was the perfect person to try and educate. That's what they all liked about me. They gave me books to read. I had all the Virginia Woolf books, Sartre, all these depressing books. That was days of Ingmar Bergman movies, all these depressing movies. After seeing a movie, Curt would say, 'Okay, you have to tell me what the meaning of that movie was.' I began dreading going because I'd have to explain what it was about." Curt's friend, Jock Hearn, had ideas about Abby's education, too. In an email, Abby wrote: "Jock was a huge believer in Freud. Because I was terrified of snakes, he would take me to the reptile house in Stanley Park and insist I get really close to the glass. He would go on about the Freudian meaning and sexual trauma etc. He liked to play God and I found him creepy." Jock also took Abby to Essondale, where he worked as a psychiatric nurse. He wanted her to see the patients there. He didn't seem to consider the possibility that she was impressionable and young and might find it upsetting.

For several months, life in the studio took on a rhythm. Curt and Fred went to the museum where they built displays, took photographs, produced sketches and drawings. Paul Wolf said, "They spent a lot of time creating their own type fonts. They made some beautifully lettered signs." This also gave them a chance to trot out an old chestnut of theirs. Instead of writing: "No Smoking," they lettered: "Nosmo King" as if they were spelling out someone's name. I wondered how many museum patrons were baffled. But then in the fall, Curt did something I don't fully understand—he quit. Fred said, "Curt got tired of it and left without telling Wylie. Wylie was… it hurt his feelings. He was more than offended. He thought that he was being treated like nothing. He couldn't believe that somebody would do that. But Curt didn't think he'd done anything. They were never as good friends after that."

Keith Ralston remembered the sequence of events differently. "He and Wylie had a bitter disagreement, a blow-up, after the first show in October or November 1960. Tom Wylie was very unhappy with Curt's failure to deliver his portion of the exhibit on time— or at all. He certainly encouraged people with ideas and that's why he was quite bitter with Curt, because he didn't produce." It sounded like Ralston was bitter, too—*still* bitter, forty years later. Curt was dead, nonetheless, people were mad at him. I marvelled at the staying power of a grudge. Ralston said, "I was the one responsible for putting the exhibit up. I didn't have time to sit around and bullshit with Curt Lang for whom I had very little respect. And still haven't when I think about it."

So did Curt down tools and go without a word to Wylie? Or was he fired? I don't know. I think it's very likely he was bored. Despite what he and Wylie thought at the outset, the job wasn't a good fit. Fred, on the other hand, saw that it could open doors. This was the prudent way of looking at things—but not Curt's.

Fred continued to work at the museum. Later he told me the experience helped him get a position as a display technician at the Vancouver Art Gallery. Fred swore, "I would have never met Wylie, never have got that job myself. It made a huge difference to my life."

Curt and Abby (then Gail), circa 1960
PHOTOGRAPHER: FRED DOUGLAS

Then, as Abby wrote in an email: "Curt wanted to get married, and he proposed. He didn't want our parents to know until after the fact. I don't think it was anything to do with what people did then, as most of our friends were single except the older ones with kids. Maybe it was for shock value." Since Abby was under twenty-one, and since they didn't have the permission of her parents, she and Curt decided to go to the sheriff's office in Bellingham, in the United States. In December 1960, they drove down with Jock Hearn and Walter Langdon, who agreed to be witnesses. At the border, they discovered that Jock didn't have the right identification, and they had to go back to Canada. The next time, they actually got across, and into the sheriff's office, only to encounter a new obstacle. Abby was wearing pants, which the sheriff didn't consider proper attire. They returned to Vancouver a second time so Abby could change. Third time lucky. To celebrate, Curt took Abby to *North to Alaska* with John Wayne. She was furious.

Curt's sketch of Abby (then Gail), 1962
ink on paper, 10" x 8"

It wasn't the kind of movie she had in mind. Perhaps even more disturbing was his announcement that she wasn't allowed to go to any more parties. Abby said, "I thought, 'Boy!' But I did go to parties. It wasn't quite as bad as I thought it was going to be."

After the deed was irrevocably done, Abby called her mother and, as she was telling her about the wedding, the line suddenly went dead. To find out what happened, Abby called her aunt who lived next door. She went to investigate and then told Abby her mother had fainted and pulled the phone out of the wall.

A little later, Abby and Curt took a trip to Bamfield to meet Abby's parents. They went with Linda and Walter Langdon, who were a couple by this time. Abby's mother was apprehensive about the visit, intimidated by her worldly son-in-law, who'd travelled to Europe (and made sure everyone knew it). She would have greatly preferred Abby to marry a fisherman.

The Bamfield males came out in force to inspect Walter and Curt. Abby said, "Curt was just being outrageous. He leaned back in his chair and said in his best English accent, 'Do any of you like poetry?' They were absolutely stunned. They couldn't say anything. One of the Bamfield boys fell off his chair into the fireplace." Curt, Abby, Linda and Walter went to a dance only to discover that the local guys were spoiling for a little rough business with Walter and Curt, who didn't find it necessary to defend their masculine honour and hid in a boathouse. But Curt couldn't avoid his father-in-law quite so easily. A tall handsome man and highly competitive, Geoff Phillips was one of the best fishermen in the village—a "high liner." When Geoff wanted to find out what sort of man Curt really was, he suggested a little fishing in his boat, the *Juju*. The day they went out, just after Christmas, it was howling. Abby was surprised her father would think of going out. She said, "My dad was like that. A guy had to be able to squeeze a milk tin in half, with two fingers. That was a test for boys in Bamfield. I think Curt got seasick. My father ended up calling him a 'hothouse flower.'"

Curt and Abby made their home in the West End. First, they lived in a place on Denman Street over a laundromat and then they moved in with Walter and Linda, on the third floor of an old turreted Barclay Street house.

When I asked Abby whether she saw much of Curt's parents, she said his mother came to see them quite often. "Hope was something else. She was in love with Curt, absolutely dotty about him. Every event that Curt was at, she'd be there dressed to the nines. She was quite striking in an old-movie-starrish-looking way. I never really felt comfortable around her."

Curt's father, Earle, didn't come round. Abby said:

> He would never get out of his chair. He was just nothing. I couldn't for the life of me even bring his face to mind. Hope liked a good time, but I don't think Earle liked a good time at all. She would go to bars with a neighbour who was a friend of hers, to meet men; she was proud of it. I think she liked to shock me. She would show me all this sexy black lingerie that she bought—naughty, corsetty, like French postcards. I found it a bit embarrassing. I often wondered if Curt was embarrassed about her. I don't think he liked her that much. He could be very cold when he wanted to be, and he was with her. They certainly didn't hug and kiss or anything like that.

Money was a constant problem for Curt and Abby. Most of the time, they were flat broke. Evelyn Fertig, wife of the nonconformist painter George Fertig, felt so sorry for

Abby that she gave her a coat. Abby said, "I was always grateful." Occasionally Abby got dreary jobs—selling floor wax over the phone or flipping burgers. They didn't last. In the fall of 1961, Curt started a welding course at the Vancouver Vocational Institute. He received his ticket in March 1962. Paul Wolf told me that Curt saw welding had artistic as well as commercial potential. While learning the trade, he had time to spare at the noon hour, so he started making sculptures out of scrap metal. One of Curt's welded figures, evoking a samurai soldier, stood for years at the entrance to Mr. Mike's, a steakhouse in the 900-block of Granville Street. However, generally, he wasn't enthusiastic about the jobs he found and didn't work often.

Curt's sketch of Al Neil, 1965, ink on paper, 11.5" x 8.5"

Al Neil, a musician, whom Curt met when he started to going to the Cellar, a jazz club on east Broadway, remembered how poor they were:

> I didn't realize it was as bad as it was. He wasn't the kind of guy to talk about it. You'd kind of guess it. When he'd come over and I'd ask about Gail, he'd say she's not feeling so well and that sort of thing. She was actually starving. Depressed and starving at the same time. I was having my own problems. I was a junkie then. I had a wife then, too. He invited us over to his place for supper. I probably took over a cheap bottle of wine. We got there and all he managed to come up with was a very, very thin bowl of soup. I didn't comment on it at the time.

Abby told me her relationship with Curt began to turn sour while they were living in the house with the turret. One night, Curt went out and didn't come back until early morning. On his return, he said to Abby, "Guess what? I slept with Miss Australia!" He was so proud of himself. Abby thought, "You bugger." And then she got pregnant. They could hardly support themselves, let alone a child. They consulted some friends and decided to have an abortion, even though it was illegal. Afterwards, Abby went into a deep depression.

"Poor Curt, he didn't know what to do with me," Abby said, "I wasn't in my right mind. I don't blame him. He ended up putting me in some old people's home on Cornwall Avenue, of all places. The old people were horrified at this weird woman or girl who was in there." It was an act of desperation. Curt was insightful about many things, but not Abby's implacable grief and despair.

Hearing Abby's story, I was reminded of Larry Kent's film *The Bitter Ash.* Shot in Vancouver in 1963, it portrays a scene much like the one through which Curt and Abby moved. Two of the characters live in a broken-down wooden house across the street from the CPR yard and the Bayshore Hotel—near where Curt and Fred's Pender Street studio was. One of the women in the film, Laurie, waits on tables to support her playwright husband, Colin. She gets pregnant, but he refuses to look for a job because his play has just reached "a crucial phase." When Des, a typesetter, learns that his girlfriend, Julie, may be pregnant, he feels trapped. Birth control pills became available in Canada in 1960, but their use was restricted until 1969. Doctors could prescribe them but they had to invent reasons like "menstrual regulation." For women like Abby, Laurie and Julie, sexual liberation without easy access to birth control was a toxic combination. The fact that they were part of a social set who valued *male* artistic expression over remunerative careers, just exacerbated the difficulty.

Abby's state of mind did not improve in the seniors' residence, so her parents brought her back to their place. "I was just an animal then. I wouldn't keep my clothes on. The only person I would even see was my brother," she said. Abby's parents took her to a hospital in Nanaimo where she received "endless shock therapy." She saw a "ghastly psychiatrist," but also met a kind and understanding nurse who developed a real interest in her and helped her to recover. Abby's aunt in England, who thought a change of scene might be good, invited her to visit. Once there, she threw away the pills the psychiatrist in Nanaimo had given her, enrolled in the London School of Fashion and began building a new life. On visits back to Vancouver, Abby sometimes met Curt. He'd say, "You're still my wife," and when she asked him for a divorce, he refused.

8. The vault

I don't care how I look,
Just let me appear
        terrifying to all my enemies,
Irresistible to women,
Saintly and geniusly to myself,
Kindly and infinitely agreeable
        To my friends,
Innocent to the police,
And apart from that let
        me be a mystery
A deep blue fascinating
inscrutable mystery to the saucer
eyes of the world

—KURT LANG, 1964

The rumours persisted for years—of a mysterious eccentric man who owned a bookstore but wouldn't sell books. The shop was at 350 West Pender Street, on the southeast corner of Homer Street and Pender, part of a heritage building, the Victoria Block. When it was constructed in 1908, Victory Square, just a block away, was an important commercial and retail centre in Vancouver.

The Second Coming—A Century of Fine Furnishings occupied the same location when I visited a couple of years after Curt died. The owner, a woman with short blonde hair and a wide smile, told me that people still came in asking after the bookstore which was there so long ago and the man who wouldn't sell books. Sometimes they told her stories, but she only got scraps of information. I looked around the small showroom, trying to visualize it as a bookstore. I saw a pumpkin-coloured plaster wall, a heavy gold chenille curtain, a sign flashing the words, "Video Dreams," bar stools made of chrome and shiny blue vinyl, cushions covered in fake leopard skin, a red and gold Japanese silk kimono displayed like a picture...

Curt's Multiple Selves, October, 1964, ink on paper, 10"x 8"

I asked if the vault was still there. A thin man with long black hair said, "We don't take customers to the back." I looked at the blonde woman. She shrugged and said she'd show it to me. "It's not much to look at." I followed her through a narrow doorway where the walls changed to lime green. She drew back a printed cloth. I saw two doors, both open. The inner one had bars, like a jail, and the outer one was a sheet of steel with the words, "The Taylor Company," engraved on it. Beyond, I could see a walk-in vault about six feet by six feet. Not the sort of thing you would expect to find in a used furniture store.

"Pretty heavy duty security," I said.

"It sure is—for our pillows."

"Was this once a bank?" I asked.

The owner thought not. However, she had heard it was a jewellery store at one time and that was why the vault was installed. When the eccentric bookseller had the store, she told me, there were stories circulating about the vault—that he stored gold in it. So thieves broke in one night. Maybe there was no gold, maybe the thieves couldn't find it, or maybe they couldn't open the vault. Frustrated, they set fire to the building. And then there was flood or water damage. Maybe because of the sprinkler system or maybe because of the water the firemen used, hosing down the building.

"It's why we don't have a subfloor." She pointed with her foot at the black-painted boards under our feet. But there were other versions of the story, too, she told me. The fire wasn't set by thieves, but by somebody who wanted the mysterious man to leave. Some people even said the fire was set by the mysterious man himself—that *he* wanted to leave. And he did. After the fire, another bookseller took over.

"But that is strictly a rumour."

When I asked the owner for her name, she shook her head. "These are strictly rumours. Don't quote me."

We were talking about 1963–1964. After Curt and Abby split up, Curt decided to become a bookseller. He liked reading—the life of the mind and the idea of being an owner appealed to him. He could set his own hours and sell what he thought was important. He saw himself having long philosophical discussions with his clients, perhaps creating something like the City Lights bookstore in San Francisco—a cultural landmark. He borrowed about $800 from his family to set up in a shop previously occupied by McIntyre Books. Stephen McIntyre, the prior owner, was one of Vancouver's most knowledgeable booksellers, and not only did he sell Curt the stock he needed, he taught him about the trade. Curt changed the name of the business; optimistically, he called his venture "The Radiant Book Store."

But Curt grew increasingly irritated with the many details of running a business: tallying up the sales, bookkeeping, tracking orders, paying bills, answering the phone, serving customers. He *especially* didn't like serving customers.

Fred Douglas said:

> I used to go down there on Saturdays and sit around. Curt lived in the back. He had one of those old T.V.s with cigarette burns in the front corners. We'd sit on cushions in the back, sit around bullshitting. I remember one day this guy was in the front. A customer. There weren't very many customers. He must have been there fifteen or twenty minutes. He said quite politely, "Can I get some service?" He wanted to buy some books. Curt looked up and said, "Fuck off."

Curt retreated; he was *drawn* to the vault. He didn't just keep valuable books in there, or money. He lived in it, slept in it. He played music, sometimes on a flute, and sometimes on a saxello, a curved soprano saxophone, an unusual instrument that he found in a pawn shop. He painted the ceiling blue with stars and spent more and more time in the cell where no natural light entered, where the stars were not *our* stars, where a compass would not guide him. Peter Auxier recalled Curt's bleak frame of mind. Peter stayed over one night and the next morning, woke to find Curt in a sour mood. "I don't believe in humour," Curt stated. He strode over to the humour section of the store, picked up a shelf full of books, held them pressed between his outstretched hands and walked across the street to a competitor where he unloaded the lot. Curt stopped keeping regular hours; some days he didn't open at all. The display windows got greyer and greyer. The shadow in the vault was spilling out past the two steel doors.

Women came to visit Curt in the vault, even though he was poor and his business obviously on the skids. So many women came that sometimes he had one inside the vault while another waited outside. Greg coined a word for the metal room. He called it "the fornicatorium." Yet, because this is Curt's story it is multi-faceted, as my conversation with Gill Collins shows. She was a girlfriend of his then. I interviewed Gill and her husband, Mike Collins, also a friend of Curt's, in their comfortable Kerrisdale home. She met Curt in 1964, when she was sixteen, much younger than he was. She told me, "I had three older brothers. I was always more comfortable with an older guy than someone my age. I remember Curt wore a long green Second World War great coat. He had a kung-fu moustache. He was pretty beatniky, tried everything." Because Curt didn't have any money, their dates consisted of walking around the West End and ending up on a friend's floor for the night. "I really liked Curt," Gill said. "He was tender, affectionate. When we were walking somewhere, he wanted to hold hands." Gill went back east for a couple of years and, on her return in January 1966, shared a house with a man in Kitsilano. About four months later, Curt rented a room from them, too. Then in June, Gill and her housemate broke up, "I remember the night I moved out, Curt stayed around, made sure I was okay. There was a real kindness to Curt, he cared about me." But Gill and Curt did not become a couple. Later that year, Gill met Mike. He said, smiling broadly, "I was a different model. I had a job."

* * *

I left the furniture store and down the street found Criterion Books, up a long steep dark flight of stairs. In a room crammed with shelves and second-hand books stacked on the floor, I spoke to the owner, Lance McCaughran. He told me that he had heard about Curt. "He really was the Neal Cassady of Vancouver," he said. But McCaughran didn't know him, so I went down the long flight of stairs and wandered around outside, curious about what I might find.

In this commercial district at the margins of the economy, idiosyncrasy and eccentricity flourished. The Pender Grocery sold dairy products as well as ginseng and had a couple of large carvings in its window, wooden men about two feet high. Torrefazione Italia, an espresso bar, displayed a collection of boots: a thigh-high shiny black pair, another in a mid-calf style made of bright red suede and a short lace-up, pale-blue plastic number with translucent four-inch platforms. What was that, I wondered, a Cinderella slipper for a shoe fetishist? And what did boots have to do with coffee anyway? One poster advertised an artist's studio for rent and another asked in crudely printed block letters, "Why not?" I found a "blowout ladies clothing sale"—up to eighty percent off and a postcard in a window that read, "Adults Only. Blow-Up Farm Animals Desire You!" I walked into The B.C. Permanent Loan Company Building at 330 Pender, a solid structure of beige stone fronted by two pairs of thick columns two storeys high. Inside, hung a large Tiffany-style stained glass dome in tones of alabaster and ochre. In the back, a massive black steel door stood ajar. A receptionist told me that this was the door to a vault dating from when the Bank of Canada used the building between 1935 and 1966. She also said that, in the mid-fifties, the bank fortified the vault with machine-gun emplacements, but the present owner, a wholesaler of small tools, took them out in 1979. So while Curt was playing his flute in one vault, another, just half a block away, was bristling with armaments.

To find out more about Curt's bookstore days, I had to go much farther away, to Robert's Creek on the Sunshine Coast. I visited Don MacLeod who took over the shop from Curt. He died in 2008, so I'm glad I had a chance to chat with him. He lived in a cabin he constructed himself, a place filled with furniture he built from scrounged materials. We sat at a table with an old treadle sewing machine for a base and strips of mahogany wood on top. He got the wood from a local craftsman; it was packing for the stained glass he imported.

Wearing a checked flannel shirt, Don looked more like a retired farmer than a former bookseller. But his appearance was deceiving. He knew books, antiques, art, and though in his mid-seventies, still had a good eye. He said he had enough money to last him the rest of his life. "But once you've got that Jewsly buying and selling in you, you don't lose it." I flinched when he said that, but kept listening. He told me he routinely cruised thrift stores looking for bargains and recently found something very interesting in a local shop priced at twenty-five cents. He bought it because he immediately recognized what it was. A set of anklets attached to a chain, it was worn by slaves brought to North America from Africa. "This was a really old god damn thing." He took it to the Police Centennial Museum in Vancouver which specializes in macabre artifacts and sold it for $150. "I thought that was okay. Small profit. I was expecting more."

Don said Curt didn't pay the rent or the hydro. He was shut out of the store and the contents seized to pay his debts. Don noticed a sign in the window; the business was being sold. He decided to make an offer and borrowed $200 from a credit union to make the purchase. He couldn't believe his luck, although a friend was skeptical. "I remember telling Mac, 'I'm going to make a bid on that store down there.' He said, 'I wouldn't touch it. The wolves down there will get you.' I liked that idea that the wolves were going to get me."

"Why did you like that idea?" I asked.

"I felt I knew as much as they did."

Don was right. The store he named MacLeod's Books was profitable right away. On his first day, sales were $210. The very next morning, he astonished the manager at the credit union by repaying his loan. As well as books, Don sold antiques, art, vintage clothing, beaded purses. He even tried to sell the vault, but the owners of the building wouldn't let him. He hustled, visiting the Salvation Army thrift store every morning to see what might turn up. "Even if I had a hangover!" he said. His shrewdest buy was a 1620 edition of a book that he paid 50 cents for and sold for $5,000.

Second-hand and antiquarian bookstores did well on that section of Pender Street. So why was Don's friend worried about wolves? Maybe he was thinking about the fact that the Vancouver East Side, Canada's poorest neighbourhood, was just to the northeast, and Chinatown, not much better off, was a couple blocks away. But Vancouver's downtown and financial nexus was not far, the Alcazar pub nearby and the Vancouver School of Art, at the corner of Hamilton Street and Dunsmuir. They probably helped the business succeed.

Don told me that shortly after he took over the store, Curt broke into it through an open window in the back. He wanted to retrieve a parrot or monkey that he had left behind. Don couldn't remember which it was. The police spotted Curt and intervened. They asked Don whether he wanted to press charges, but he declined. Curt hadn't taken anything of value, only the pet that was his.

Something else of Curt's was left in the store. The police would have been interested in it, but Don didn't say a word about his discovery. He came across needles in the vault and curious, probed further with his screwdriver. Finally, he found it in the door slot— heroin. "It was a dangerous item to have," Don said. "I called Curt and gave it to him. He was talking all the hip gangster talk. He was saying, 'Yeah, I oughta get a ring out of that.' He'd use these baffling words." Don said Curt was using heroin with a jazz musician, Glenn MacDonald, whom he called, with his own baffling language, "a real snike."

Don had known Curt before he bought the bookstore. "I remember he and Freddy were running around like a couple of assholes, doing all kinds of weird things. They appealed to me. I liked their act." And when Don owned the place, Curt would drop in on him from time to time. He wasn't jealous of Don's success. In fact, he was rather pleased, because Don had made something of an opportunity he had recognized, as if this vindicated his judgment.

Curt would come in to talk and sometimes to borrow money. Once he needed $25 so that he could buy a corduroy suit to wear while presenting an idea to a businessman. Another time he asked for a loan to buy some equipment. He wanted to make what Don called "an assemblage of helium" so that he could fly. Curt didn't realize that the amount of helium you needed to do this made the idea impractical. "That was $25 I threw away," Don said, laughing. "I gave it to him, never saw him for another three months."

Eventually Don, too, sold the store:

> I bought my retirement with that. Did I ever! I had nothing. I was right off the street. And I just took over the store. I couldn't believe the absolute luck that I had. It was at a time when Canadiana was a big item. And I happened to get a lot of that. In the window, there was about four hundred dollars' worth of books. I could never understand why Curt sold the place, why he did nothing about it. If he had come to me and said I'll give you half ownership, you have to look after the store for a month or whatever, I would have gone for it.

Don Stewart, who bought the business from Don MacLeod, kept the old name, but moved to larger premises at 164 West Hastings Street. And there was, in fact, a fire. On October 9, Chuck Davis, the Vancouver historian, wrote a column in the *Vancouver Province* about Book Alley—the second-hand book trade in Vancouver. He recounted that Stewart's store was in the same building as the Enver Hoxha Communist Bookstore. In August 1983, someone who didn't like its books set a fire and burned everyone else out as well. Don Stewart started up again, at 455 West Pender, just across the street from Curt's original location, where he remains to this day.

Don MacLeod said, "I loved Curt a lot." And he asked, "How was Curt for laughin'? Was he good at laughin'?"

I told him that he was—right to the end. When he knew he had cancer, he was in the hospital for one of the tests that was supposed to reveal its extent. He said he was being investigated with a "bumscope." And when he was sitting in a small room in the standard hospital-issue backless gown, with those socks that never fit, that you can't get your toes into and that leave a useless triangle of extra cloth in front, he summoned a nurse. She came to see what was wrong. He pointed to the socks and asked, "Do you get many pixies in here?"

I also recalled, as he was really dying, how he told us all to smile. And his pain then was often terrible. As David Marshall told me, "Curt was in the hospital. He wasn't saying much. The nurse gave him something to eat. And she asked him whether he wanted anything else. He said, "You could give me a sweet push. I understood what he was talking about and I think the nurse did, too. But she didn't let on."

Don's question reminded me that when Curt said, "I don't believe in humour," how unlike himself he was. He was visiting the land of the shades, nosing about.

Don MacLeod, May 1999,
PHOTOGRAPHER: CLAUDIA CORNWALL

9. I could not send it out

POEM

I, bound with want-knots, cumbered with longing,
Set sail, year past, in a strange sea.
Unwounded by wakes but wind wound, wave wimpled,
Scented by cedar but land there never.
Maddened and luckless, losing a lifespan,
Spun on storm's tail, calmed then in glass,
But battered, blown, beaten, whelmed all under,
  Heartspiked, wasting
I'll fall to the Love-God Sea God.
  Ah never free, never from love's bad weather.

       —CURT LANG, 1957

Yarding Tug, North Arm Fraser River, 1971   PHOTOGRAPHER: CURT LANG

While Curt was living in the vault downtown in 1964, Fred was creating a bohemian oasis in North Vancouver. He married Evelyn Gilbert and moved to a house designed by Ron Thom, the architect who later went on to create Toronto's Massey Hall. In a quiet treed neighbourhood, Fred hosted memorable celebrations that often lasted days. He enjoyed creating a stir by serving unconventional exotic food—like bumblebees. Jock Hearn remembered eating about thirty of the insects on one occasion. "I don't think it did us any particular harm, though we got indigestion." During a particularly crazy party, bill bissett landed in the emergency room of the hospital when his jealous lover attacked him. After another, John Newlove lapsed into a mild hallucinatory state, fell asleep, muttering about how the tide had come in and washed away his shoes. Fred's gatherings were iconic of the era. Once the poet Lawrence Ferlinghetti, owner of City Lights Books in San Francisco, came. Another time, Leonard Forest arrived to gather material for his film *In Search of Innocence*, a documentary on the artistic scene in Vancouver. During the shoot, Fred drank copiously and couldn't be found anywhere. He passed out in his car and Forest had to postpone capturing a scene with Fred reading poetry until the next day.

Fred's home was also a refuge for Curt. "Curt had got into this very deep depression," Fred said. "This very real depression, not just feeling kind of blue. For a year or two, he didn't wash. He didn't have a place to stay. He wasn't interested in anything. He'd stay with us occasionally. Ev would make him give her all his clothes, and his underwear, to wash them. Because he stunk. Then she would let him stay. Otherwise he'd make the bedding stink. He was sleeping wherever he could, like a street person.

Sketch of Fred, circa 1963, ink on paper, 10" x 8"

"He was married to a very beautiful woman, Gail, and she'd left him... It was just like somebody whose guts had been taken out of them."

In Curt's papers is a notebook filled with simple line drawings of people. They're smoking, sitting in chairs with their legs crossed, bathing, sleeping on flower-patterned sofas, drinking coffee, drinking beer, sketching people drinking beer, reading. There is Fred—surely Fred, who else had such luxuriant eyebrows? Fred, painting, brush in hand, looking intently at an easel and again, lounging in an armchair, wearing boots, looking at a picture of a naked woman... And in the middle of the notebook is an undated letter addressed to Gail.

Curt wrote it in the Little Heidelberg Restaurant on Robson Street, having ordered kidneys and gravy. This was when Robson had so many German delicatessens that some people called it Robsonstrasse. My grandmother used to buy German newspapers there and my father would pick up spicy sausages called *debreziner* and *kommisbrot*, a type of rye bread. I have a memory of eating at the Little Heidelberg, maybe schnitzels. An image comes to mind—dark wood, a booth, beer steins—German kitsch.

It was raining the day Curt wrote to Gail, a green-grey sky on a Sunday, about half past four in the afternoon. Chess players and card players were talking quietly at other tables. The beatniks hadn't arrived yet. "I have eaten," Curt explained, "and I am trying to think how to say the truth."

"The truth of my desire is that we should love each other for I see something in you that goes to my best part. The truth of the time is that I have not loved you. Inside myself I loved you but I could not send it out. Not right enough or steady enough. What do you make of that?" Casting back for explanations, understanding, Curt thought about his family:

Memory of a Feeling 1, circa 1964,
oil on canvas, 18" x 18"   PRIVATE COLLECTION

Memory of a Feeling 2, circa 1964, oil on canvas, 16" x 23"   PRIVATE COLLECTION

When my dad came back from overseas in 1946, we went to the CPR station to meet him. My mother had had a couple of boyfriends when he was
away and she said to me before the train came in, "Don't say anything to
Dad about Jimmy—he wouldn't want to talk about it." So I remember him
coming up into the big waiting room and me feeling very awkward and
the greeting being rather cold and it was like he never came any more to
life for us than that. My mother didn't love him, he felt strange with me.
So for him to stay married was worse than anything. He should have left.
He should have lived. He stayed—why I don't know and wasted away. I
went through all this in an effort to understand why I trust no one and
can hardly open myself. I always had a fear of you, that you were sort of
using me or were going to change me to a kind of neutered animal like my
father.

Reading Curt's letter, I remembered a conversation I had with his cousin Denise
Goodkey. She recalled going along to the CPR station to meet Curt's father, too. She was

younger than Curt, about six. After Earle got off the train, they all went for coffee or a meal. Later, Denise grew to dislike Earle, to dislike the way he was with Curt. But then she wanted to sit beside him. In fact, she demanded it, and threw a temper tantrum to get her way.

Denise also told me about one Christmas in either 1961 or 1962. She was about twenty-one then; Curt, twenty-four. She, her mother, Clara, and other relatives were at Earle and Hope's for dinner. Her Aunt Pearl asked Curt's opinion about something. And he responded, as was typical for him, at some length. Earle was drunk and he started interrupting Curt, saying, "You think you know everything." Curt was quite patient. He said, "No, but Aunt Pearl asked me what I thought so I'm telling her."

Earle wouldn't stop. "Why do you think you're so smart?" he kept asking. "Do you think you know everything?"

And then Hope, who had been carving the turkey and had a knife in her hand, started screaming at Earle to leave Curt alone. "I'd like to kill you," she shouted.

"Come on, Mom, let's go out for a walk," Curt said, and Hope went with him.

This left the rest of the family sitting around the dining-room table, not saying anything, feeling very uncomfortable.

Earl said, "What's the matter with everybody? Why doesn't somebody talk? Why is everybody so quiet?"

When Denise reminded him of how he had been goading Curt, Earle shammed contrition. "Oh, I'm sorry. I'm sorry if I did that. I've been a bad guy."

There was silence for a minute. Then he looked at Denise and said, "You think you know everything..."

It must have been just two or three years after this that Curt was seated in the Heidelberg, writing a letter to Gail.

"Knowledge discharges like pollen from eye to eye if there is love." And then, "All my life I have felt on the run. Where can I stop and make a stand? I betrayed you because my own fear would not let me alone."

"I have memory of a feeling, some garden or trees where everything glowed, but I don't know where it was. I can hardly think for fear of lying to myself. I am afraid of being torn to pieces. I am afraid that harm will come to my genitals. I cannot look out of myself at the world, the people I see are as lost as I am. I want to be anybody but who I am."

It distressed me to think of Curt so alone and so unhappy on that Sunday after-noon, the rain running morosely down Robson Street. I thought about his memory of the glowing garden and wondered, as he did, where it came from. Curt painted a series of trees and houses at night; in the darkness, the windows of the houses shimmer with comforting light. Were they of this memory?

On the back of Curt's poem "Paris 55," I found a note Gail had written, in pencil, but still legible. "Dear Curt," she writes, "I waited a long time for you. I felt I wanted to see you again because I thought things and needed to talk with you. I don't know where you would be—will try your parents'—then go home and will be back Thursday. I really feel like staying with you because there is a lot of love about you. Take care of yourself, Gail."

After the letter, Curt's notebook has a sketch of a person in a sailboat. The sun is shining through clouds. Above the sketch Curt writes:

There is the truth of what I know is right.

I must remember it, and never pretend to it.

There is the truth of what I have seen.

I must remember it, and not deny it.

There is the truth of what I have done.

I must remember it, and live in it.

The next sketch is of a man and a woman sitting at table. The man's face is cupped in his hand. He seems angry and is not looking at the woman. He is looking down or maybe his eyes are closed. The woman's eyes are wide open. She is not looking at the man, but at the table. On it are plates, some cutlery, a salt shaker, a couple of small glasses, no food, though, and a few books. One has a title—*My Home by the Sea.*

Something was happening. An idea was gaining force.

* * *

My Home by the Sea, circa 1963, ink on paper, 8″ x 10″

Fred told me that Curt moved to a house on Burrard Street in Kitsilano. It was a big old place with an unruly backyard that no one was using for anything—a mess of long grass, boards and weedy tangles. It wasn't pretty, but it was available space. "And Curt decided to build a boat." Fred said:

> He'd always been interested in boats. He'd worked on the coastal ferries and on fishboats and really always loved the coast. I imagine just out of… just in this melancholy state, one of the things that seemed good would be a boat. And he said, "I'm going to build a boat, Fred." And I said, "That's interesting." And he said, "Yes."
>
> Then he says, "I have this theory that they overbuild boats. They don't need to be near as strong as they build them. The pressure of the water will hold them together." This fucking near made me cry because it was like himself. And I said, "Oh, yes." So he built this forty-foot boat out of D-grade, three-eighth-inch plywood and one-by-two's. But it would just flap around. It had no solidity at all. It was just flapping around. He could see that his theory didn't work.

So he built a twenty-foot boat. He made it smaller, little by little. Through doing this he came to realize he must find out something about boat building. So he went to the library. He ended up making an eight-foot skiff out of this material. But it worked. It floated. It was an accomplishment. He was pretty much out of the depression. You could see what happened. To me it was like a poem that he'd done. The whole activity was so poetic. It wasn't like somebody deciding to do boat building. It was like boat building as this myth of being alive. He says he doesn't remember much of that time. But I do. I remember that.

And as Fred spoke, his eyes filled with tears.

Curt didn't mail Abby his letter. But I did, when she said she'd like to see it. She emailed me back: "I've read the letter twice and feel like crying." A few days later, she wrote again: "I keep reminding myself it was half a century ago and we were just too young to help each other." Curt and Abby divorced in October 1966. They had not been together for some time. Abby's parents paid the legal costs which amounted to $700—"a huge amount of money in those days," she said.

Years later, when Curt told the story to Ruth, his second wife, he broke down and wept. Ruth recalled, "They didn't know what to do. Friends advised them to have an abortion. It was very painful for both of them. He said, 'I killed my child, I don't deserve to have children.'"

10. It was a blast

ONE MAY EVENING, standing on the shabby porch of a narrow Kitsilano clapboard house, I was filled with an equal measure of curiosity and apprehension, wondering what the man I had come to see would be like. He was an old friend of Curt's—Peter Auxier. I had come because I knew that he and Curt had lived together and collaborated on several construction projects in the mid-sixties. That's where the curiosity came in. And the apprehension? Well...

Don MacLeod said, "He's got wavy hair, a fairly nice face and he's a nice-looking guy. But he's... you're wound up in his torment, whatever it is." Jamie Reid, described him like this, "He looks like Van Gogh at the moment *before* he was going to cut his ear off." And Fred told me, "He's always, the fucking Mafia is after him, East Indian gangs are after him. He owes them money..." Then Fred remembered that once when he and Curt helped Peter move, they found dynamite under Peter's bed. "There was all this fucking dynamite. Curt says, 'That's really dangerous, you know, Pete. The nitro will have settled and that's really unstable.' Then Curt asks, 'What are you going to do about it?' Pete says, 'I'm just going to leave it here.' And he did. That's Auxier. Like he's just on the fucking edge."

I knocked, waited, straining to hear the sound of footsteps. Had he remembered? Finally, a bearded man with curly grey hair and blue eyes opened the door.

"Peter?" I asked. He looked normal. I had expected him to be more wild eyed.

He beckoned me into the living room, walking slowly and carefully ahead as if he had just come through an intense physical ordeal, as if every step hurt. The room was barely furnished—one couch, a coffee table, a T.V., no pictures on the walls, bare wooden floors, cardboard boxes in a corner. That was all. I sat down on the couch and then Peter disappeared. He didn't say anything. He didn't tell me to wait, that he'd be a few minutes, or tell me to come with him.

"Now what?" I thought. Maybe it wasn't sensible to have come.

After a few minutes, Peter reappeared and asked me if I'd like to have some cider. I said I would, and he went away again to get it, leaving me to worry if that was a wise thing to ask for. I'd heard that Peter had been hospitalized for alcohol-related problems recently. Maybe I should have asked for water. A few minutes later, he sat beside me on the couch and placed a couple of cold bottles on the coffee table.

I took a sip. "When did you meet Curt?" I began.

He was about twenty-two he said, and Curt a bit older, twenty-eight. Peter had graduated from UBC with a double honours in math and science, but had turned to writing poetry. He was an editor for TISH magazine. "Curt hated TISH," he said.

I relaxed. This was familiar ground—the thorny terrain of Curt's prejudices. I stopped worrying about gangs. Peter told me that he and Curt used to sit up all night and talk until four or five in the morning. They would talk about people they knew, about poetry—Gerard Manley Hopkins, William Blake—and philosophy. Everything seemed possible then. Curt would speak of his friend, Jock Hearn, who was born Catholic but became a communist, an anarchist and then a Zen Buddhist. The old order was dying. The old rigidities were melting away. It was a time of flux, of movement, of change. Peter said, "I had an open, scattered attitude towards life."

It struck me then that Peter might be the person who would know about one of Curt's more whimsical ideas. This was what Don MacLeod had called "the helium assemblage." He had lent Curt $25 to buy some equipment for it and then had never heard anything further. As far as I knew, the device was intended to help people move in great bounding leaps. You'd strap it on and away you'd go like a moonwalker.

"Do you know anything about a helium suit?" I asked.

"Ah," he said. "That was a too-late-at-night idea."

So he did know something about it. "Did you ever see it or try it on?"

"It was supposed to be a pyramid-shaped frame covered in some light, rigid material," he explained. "The base was going to be about ten feet by ten feet, tapering to a point about thirty feet high. I had calculated that you could get enough helium into it to lift a 150-pound man."

As I listened, I felt like I was watching a fantastic creature come to life.

Peter said that for three months he and Curt talked of nothing else. They imagined fleets of these craft being quietly deployed throughout the city and that when they were not in use, several might be tethered by their points to parking metres.

Briefly, I entertained myself with visions of the coloured balloon-like contraptions. An ancient dream—that we could fly around as free as birds—fulfilled. "What happened?" I asked.

Peter decided to buy a helium balloon to test the lifting power of the gas. Then he discovered that he had miscalculated by a factor of ten—or maybe a hundred. The pyramid would have to be at least 300 feet tall or more to lift a 150-pound man.

"I was crushed," Peter said. "It was completely impractical. I told Curt, 'I have some bad news.'" (Later I did some calculations of my own, with the assistance of Google, and discovered that while it may have been an impractical idea, it was not *quite* as outlandish as Peter thought. You can lift a 150-pound person with *two* helium pyramids ten feet square at the base and thirty feet high. If you just want an assist for a bounding leap, you could get away with less.)

I was quickly scribbling as Peter was telling me all this. He had asked me not to tape-record our conversation, although he didn't mind my taking notes and seemed quite happy to talk at length. "I've become a total chatterbox," he said, "though I wasn't always like this." Peter recalled that there were times when he would blush if called upon to speak. "I felt less sophisticated than the others, even though I had a college degree and had been an editor. I lacked the easy social graces of the others. They would always have a joke. I remember people would be standing around in someone's kitchen, the conversational ball passing from one to the next. Everyone would be making clever quips. To me it was almost like an interrogation. I was petrified."

He paused and said, "I began to have these unbelievable adventures. There were many Peter Auxier stories." He made it sound like a literary work, although Peter had abandoned writing by that time. He was no longer publishing poems in TISH or helping with the *Georgia Straight*, as he had once done. So he wasn't talking about his oeuvre. But

I think he had a kind of literary purpose, nevertheless—creating outrageous events worth commemorating. "I would tell Curt about them. He would nod. I knew he found what I was saying interesting." Peter paused again, remembering. "I wanted approval so badly."

I could imagine Curt's nod, his cool acceptance and Peter's eager wish to please, his desire to do something remarkable that would inspire a story. I sipped my cider, declined a second bottle and allowed Peter's words to carry me back…

In 1965, Peter was living in a ramshackle building at Seventh Avenue and Oak, not far from Vancouver General Hospital. Originally constructed as a residence for railway workers, the place had a distinctive covered walkway. Either because of the ambience or the cheap rent, it attracted a unique clientele—renegade contractors, drifters, dope fiends, madmen and—here is the salient detail—house wreckers. Half the residents were wreckers, mostly unemployed or unemployable. One, however, had some flair for language. Greg wrote me in an email: "Not sure if it was Peter, but I remember one of the loonies in the Seventh and Oak tenement had a company named Basho Demolition after the famous Japanese poet."

Somehow the wreckers got wind of a job at UBC. The university wanted to tear down some buildings. Prefabricated barracks thrown up during the Second World War in various locations around the Lower Mainland, were later moved on campus to provide necessary residences and classrooms for the influx of veterans. Students and faculty called them the "army huts." They were never supposed to be permanent and, twenty years later, the university was getting rid of about ten of them to make space for new construction.

The wreckers were convinced Peter was a shoo-in. They saw that he was somehow involved with the university and, to them, this meant he would have the inside track. Peter thought about the project for a while, talked to a professional wrecker, did some calculations. And then when a figure suddenly popped into his head, he fixed on that. His bid turned out to be $25 lower than the competition and he won the contract. So he hired about ten friends, an unruly bunch of unemployed poets and eccentrics, and started pulling the building apart in a conventional manner. But the work was hard and dangerous. A couple of the crew were injured and walked off the job. The remaining workers felt overwhelmed or got interested in doing something else; more drifted away. For one stretch, Peter himself worked four nights in a row, trying to get the work done.

Then he had an idea. And so, at about half past ten on a soft June night in 1965, a

Saturday, Peter, John Austin and a third man, whose name Peter didn't remember, drove to a small building on the northeast corner of the UBC campus. The evening was clear but dark; the moon had not yet risen. All day, Peter had been getting ready, stripping wallboard from the ceiling of the building and preparing the explosives, six bundles containing six sticks each of twenty-percent nitroglycerine stumping powder. His idea was to create a small explosion that would loosen the nails, making them easy to pull out.

Peter learned how much stumping powder he needed and how to array the bundles by phoning the explosives division of Canadian Industries Limited (CIL), the dynamite supplier, and telling them that he wanted to demolish a barn in Chilliwack. Following CIL's instructions, he inserted an electrical blasting cap in the middle of each bundle, wired them all together and hung the dynamite from the exposed rafters in a circle in the middle of the building.

Peter decided to detonate the dynamite with an electrical charge from the generator in his car. He and John parked a couple of hundred feet from the building. Then Peter instructed the third man to touch the wires, which led from the dynamite bundles to the car battery. John jumped into the car, gunned it to the max and yelled to the third man, "Now."

A loud boom ripped through the air. The walls of the building blew out, the roof lifted up and then collapsed. Only a little porch was left standing. Peter sailed into the air and landed unhurt on a patch of grass. A quarter mile away, a motorcyclist was picked off his bike which careened into a ditch. A huge concussive wave went out all over the city. A couple of miles east on Point Grey Road, windows rattled; across Burrard Inlet, residents were startled by the noise.

A play *In the Rough* was just letting out at the Frederic Wood Theatre on campus and, as the patrons spilled out of the glass doors of the theatre, some rushed over to have a look. "Please clear the area," Peter said, "There will be another blast in three minutes. Please clear the area." Then a group of students living in the theology college residence pulled on their shoes and ran out in their pyjamas to see what had happened. They asked Peter whether he thought anybody was in the building. He said, "I don't know, we'd better double check." Soon he had the students piling wood. Finally, one of them realized that there was nobody under the rubble. Peter said, "It sure is a good thing. Thanks a lot for your help, boys."

Meanwhile Peter began rolling up the wires and, when a police officer arrived, he was standing there with a fistful of them. "You know anything about an explosion here?" the patrolman asked.

Peter was not charged with anything. At the time, the campus was designated an unorganized territory and no laws against the setting of explosions applied. An anti-noise bylaw kicked in after eleven at night but Peter had detonated his blast shortly before.

The police were deluged with calls that night. The first one came from a homeowner in West Vancouver at about ten to eleven and the phones kept ringing until two in the morning. A local radio station issued a false report—the army at its Jericho base, just down the hill from the university, was testing new weapons and there was no reason to be alarmed.

On June 8, the *Vancouver Province* reported: "'We expect night blasting to go on for several days,' said a campus official, 'and we can't do a thing about it. The wrecking crew operated by Peter Auxier prefers the late hour to blast because there is no one around.'" The story offered a bogus reassurance. "Auxier, whose demolition business runs during the summer holidays only, has an experienced powderman during the blasting."

Peter did actually manage to fulfill the terms of the contract, without setting off any more explosions. Auxier Wrecking profited by $200 on the venture. For many nights thereafter, in the Alcazar and other bohemian watering holes, Curt and his friends regaled each other with the tale. Peter had created his magnum opus and, with it, earned Curt's coveted appreciation.

Peter told me that he and Curt co-operated on several building projects. One was a dismal reconstruction of a Vancouver warehouse on Franklin Street gutted by fire. They had proposed to salvage what could be saved from the wreckage and build a smaller one-story building out of the material. It was hard work—and dirty—dealing with charred lumber. I pictured them at the end of the day, looking like chimney sweeps, covered in soot. Another time, Curt was awarded a contract to build a small house. He brought Peter in to help but before the roof was on, Curt bailed, leaving Peter to finish it on his own. Peter said without any recrimination in his voice, "It was one of those beautiful summers..."

* * *

Curt on deconstruction project, circa 1965   PHOTOGRAPHER UNKNOWN

And then there was a canoe. Sometime in 1965 Curt moved in with Peter to a house he had on Third Avenue and Arbutus. By then, Curt was beginning a serious study of boat design. He was reading books on naval architecture and with Peter's help, decided to build an eighteen-foot fibreglass canoe. This would be his second boat, an advance on the first boat-as-poem which Fred admired so. "We started by using sand as a mould," Peter explained.

"Sand?" I asked, wondering how that would work.

"It turned out not to be very stable."

Next, they tried making a mould out of plaster and mesh. This was apparently a better technique, although it still took months to get it right.

Jamie Reid watched the canoe take shape:

Whenever I visited Peter, I would go down and look at the progress on this canoe. It hit many snags. Curt had no knowledge of how to go about it. He gradually accumulated the knowledge and experimented. Tried his own tricks. Succeeded in building a canoe. When you put it in the water, it floated. It could be paddled. It wiggled like a snake. It was peculiar. Irrespective of that, I was impressed. He had begun to do this with no expertise and had quite carefully planned it and worked it out and brought it to completion, even if it wasn't perfect. The imperfection was funny and entertaining in its own right.

Gill Collins remembered that canoe, too. "It was green," she said. "He came over to my place and we carried it down to the water. He paddled me across English Bay from Kits Point. It was a beautiful summer evening." Curt still had a lot to learn about boat building, but he was getting the hang of it.

An all-white cat with tail held high appeared in the doorway. It sidled alongside the coffee table. "She's the reason I had to leave the hospital," Peter said. "I had to keep her hidden. They didn't allow pets. I had to keep brushing cat hairs off the furniture so they wouldn't know. She's much happier here." I stroked her head. She jumped up onto the windowsill and stared into the dark night with patient watchfulness. I noticed that she had a pink collar—an unexpected note of ornamentation in that bare room.

It was getting late.

"Maybe I can come again sometime?"

Peter nodded. "Maybe I'll remember more about Curt, if you do." We moved into the hallway and towards the door. "You know, I think Curt was the most impressive person I've met. And I met Charles Olsen, Allen Ginsberg, the Jefferson Airplane—they stayed at my house once," he called after me as I walked down the stairs.

11. Dreaming in black and white

ROD GILLINGHAM HAD WIDE DARK EYES that slanted up a little, brown hair, a trim beard and a ready smile. A supervisor at Butchart Gardens, just north of Victoria, he had the ruddy complexion of someone who worked outdoors. He lived in the country, behind a tall fence with gargoyles carved into the top. When Rod opened the door of his house, two large terriers bounded out to greet me enthusiastically. I patted their brown heads as Rod tried to restrain them. Then he introduced me to his wife, Colleen, and we went into the living room. Native masks hung over the fireplace; a blue impressionist print on one wall. A Matisse I guessed. A Buddha stood in a small nook. Beyond the windows, Steller's jays swooped around a bird feeder.

"How did you get to know Curt?" I asked.

"We came here from California in 1970. It was shortly after that."

Rod told me he had been working in a gas station and studying photography at Langara College. There he met Joe Fahrni, a songwriter, or Joe Ferone, as he came to call himself later. Joe told Rod that Rhetta Grayson, a student at the Vancouver School of Art, was trying to get a group together to work on a documentary photography project that she thought a government grant might fund. After the three met a couple of times, Fred Douglas got interested. He told the group he knew someone who was not a photographer but would take really interesting photographs. That was how Curt became involved. Then Peter Thomas, another art student, and Nina Raginsky, a freelance photographer, joined in.

Curt 'n' Rod, circa 1972, gold toned gelatine silver print, 4⅛" x 6⅜"   PHOTOGRAPHER: FRED DOUGLAS

The seven called themselves the Leonard Frank Memorial Society of Documentary Photographers, in recognition of a man who moved to British Columbia in 1894 and travelled all over the province taking pictures. Leonard Frank's lens captured farmers, fishermen and loggers—especially loggers, often dwarfed by the immense trees they were felling. He snapped shots of buildings and crowds, railway yards, ferries and bridges. He was intrigued by work and economic activity of all kinds, partly the inspiration for the Memorial Society's project. According to a short description Rod handed me, the notion was "to take pictures of ordinary, everyday situations in an undramatic way." Fred had told me the aim was "a kind of depiction that wasn't likely to come out of the practices of news photography, postcards and advertising." Fred and Curt wrote a proposal describing what the group wanted to do and sent it to the federal government's Local Initiatives Program. In January 1972, they received an initial grant of $16,000. Then they asked for additional money, which they also received. Over a period of 18 months, the program provided a total of $38,000.

Leonard Frank Society photographers: Rod Gillingham, Fred Douglas, Nina Raginsky, Fumiko Greenaway, Curt Lang, 1972   PHOTOGRAPHER: TOD GREENAWAY

Rod told me that he and Curt went on several trips to take pictures—into the Fraser Canyon, out to the west coast, up to Prince Rupert, to Prince George. Rod said, "We made that trip to the Interior in an old Ford Falcon station wagon. We were only one day into the trip and the starter went. We were gone two or three weeks and we never replaced the starter. 'Fine, we can do without,' we decided. We couldn't afford to put another in it. We just parked on a hill for the whole trip through the Interior." He laughed.

Rod also recalled that Curt took pictures of an old building called the Englesea Lodge, near Stanley Park. Rod said, "He went in, knocked on doors and asked if he could photograph the interiors. They were absolutely beautiful." And then he discovered that the elderly people who were living there had evocative historical photographs themselves. So he broadened the scope of the project and started photographing their photographs, too.

Curt at Metlakatla, 1972   PHOTOGRAPHER: ROD GILLINGHAM

Then Rod showed me a photo of Curt in Metlakatla, a Tsimshian village, a ferry-ride away from Prince Rupert. "I really like this picture," he said. Curt stands on a beach with his tripod, behind about a dozen children and a dog. One boy stands in front of all the others, grinning widely, his arms outstretched, like a bird's wings in flight. I wonder what pleased him so. Rod had a few other pictures, too—one of a place Curt rented on Robson Street. You can see a camera screwed into a tripod—probably the one he had at Metlakatla, and behind it are a couple of shelves made of rough wooden crates. One holds several notebooks and books—*Suburban Souls, Bury My Heart at Wounded Knee*, a Minolta camera manual. Another displays a large model of a boat—maybe about three feet long. The sun streams in. It is so bright that in the photo, the flowered wallpaper behind the model is over-exposed. Rod said:

> I was like a sponge. I had just come out of service in Vietnam. So it was a
> totally different world with a huge cast of fascinating characters. Curt and
> I got on really well. He liked my wife at the time and the kids. He enjoyed
> that whole family situation. He used to come over to the house in West

Vancouver all the time. Curt never had a darkroom so he would come over to my place. I had set up one in my basement. He would come over and do his printing. We were dealing with big volumes of film so he started inventing ways of processing more film. Using plastic pipe and film developer, we could do sixteen or eighteen rolls of film at once. Figuring out something like that was not unusual for Curt. I was totally intrigued by the guy. He had so much knowledge, historical information about B.C.

I nodded, remembering how widely conversations with Curt could range.

"For me, everything was new," Rod said, adding:

> He used to bring over books to read, or Bach fugues to listen to. He'd bring *Woodsmen of the West*, a book that he insisted everyone should read—the story of logging on the coast, fishing. He thought it was a wonderful book. *The Secret Life of Plants*. He insisted I read it—a bizarre book. He gave me a bunch of L.P.s of Pablo Casals. He said, "You've got to have these— incredible pieces of music." The next thing I knew he was handing me the *Dictionary of the Chinook Jargon*.

"Yes," I said. "I've seen it." Actually, I had a copy. This was a softcover book, a 1972 reprint of a book, published in 1899 in Victoria. I bought it long before I knew Curt and then was surprised to discover he had something to do with it. The newer book was a facsimile edition, with no preface or introduction—just the thirty-five-page dictionary itself, in the typeface of the original and with the same advertisements. Chinook was a trade language of the Pacific Northwest and some of its words have now entered into English. Just think of "skookum" for "able or strong," "chuck" for "a body of water," especially in "saltchuck" for "ocean," or "mucky-muck" which has come to mean "big boss" although literally it is a "big banquet."

Much later, I learned how this book came to be. Howard White, publisher of Harbour Publishing, had unhappy memories of its inception—as he told me in an email:

> The first book I published that was not an issue of *Raincoast Chronicles* was a little reprint of an early Chinook dictionary that Curt talked me into.

Curt's taste in books, as in other matters, was highly esoteric. I remember thinking he'd used me and ripped me off at the time, though now I can't remember the details. He was one of the most brilliant, as well as one of the most unpleasant people I ever knew. Pete Trower also knew him quite well, before I did. Up to the time I knew him, his brilliance had mostly gone for naught.

Curt and the other members of the Leonard Frank Society took a vast number of photographs. When the project came to an end in 1973, the society turned the collection over to the Vancouver Public Library, where it remains today. The project aroused a modest amount of media interest. "Vancouver is on camera for five young men and two women out to provide a pictorial record of everyday life in the city," Aileen Campbell wrote in the *Province* in May 1972. She interviewed Curt, who said, "When I shoot, I feel I'm shooting for an audience thirty-five years from now." Four years later, in July 1976, she mentioned the project again when she described an exhibition of Fred's photographs, called *Durations*, at the Pender Street Gallery. She interviewed Ron D'Altroy, the curator of photographs for the library. Recalling the Leonard Frank Society, he said, "The taxpayer got his money's worth. These young people produced. There was no sloughing off. No lost funds. I'd stack them and their project against anything across Canada."

Curt hoped the work would eventually result in a publication. But at the time, it seemed there was little interest in the ordinary lives of ordinary people. A gallery on Lower Lonsdale Avenue in North Vancouver had a small showing, but then, none of Curt's photos were exhibited publicly or published until after he died. In 2003, Bill Jeffries, then a curator at the Presentation House Gallery in North Vancouver, organized an exhibition that featured eighteen local street photographers, including Fred and Curt. Later in *Unfinished Business: Photographing Vancouver's Streets, 1955 to 1985,* a book inspired by the show, the editors wrote: "The exhibition began without much fanfare. Nevertheless, the gallery saw a crush of visitors who kept coming for two months, with approximately 6,000 people viewing the exhibition."

Recently I spoke to Bill, who is now curator of the Simon Fraser University Gallery, about Curt's photographs in particular. When I asked him what made Curt different from the other photographers in his show, he said:

He just picked up the camera and did it. I didn't know Curt, but it's my sense that he was always looking at other people's work trying to figure out what he could have done better. He probably had been thinking about photographs for a period of time because he had seen other people's pictures—what was clichéd about them, that's my hunch. I've seen hundreds and hundreds of shots that he took during that one year. There's nothing clichéd about any of them. They're extremely direct. Several people during that period said, "I am the camera." or "I am a camera." That's how Curt seemed to see it. When he saw something that was interesting, he tried to take a picture of the thing that caught his interest. In some amazing way, he probably has something in common with people like American photographer Walter Evans. I think Curt knew that there was this language out there and, because he was a cocky guy, he thought he'd be able to make better photographs than anybody.

Much of what Curt photographed is gone now. I remember him saying that he would take a picture of a building or house only to discover a week later that it had been demolished. Leafing through his prints and contact sheets, what do I see? Curt had an exquisite appreciation of light, how it bends, pours, streams, glances and how the camera can capture the way it dances in and through the world. Later he would take this interest in an entirely different direction—inventing a way of measuring things using the play of light. But in 1972, he was an eye on the city. As I looked closely at his black-and-white images, details of a vanished place jumped out at me. Shambling wooden houses, succumbing to weeds and gravity. Many, *many* small corner grocery stores: Superior Fruit & Produce, Security Market, West End Grocery, Earle's Grocery, Julia's Market, Jack and Jill Superetta, McGill Groceries, Rob Roy Market, Ken's Market, Happy Vegetable and Fruit Market, Quality Meats and Produce, Sing Lee Fish Mkt.

Hard-luck cafés with their menus on signs: Deep Fried Prawns $1.75, De-Luxe Burgers 60¢, Milk Shake Any Flavour 40¢, Do Nut 12¢, Small Order Fish and Chips 45¢. Businesses of all sorts: the Manhattan Hat Service offers cleaning and blocking for Ladies and Gents as does the Leatherwear Dyers & Hatters, who advertise those services for $2. The Central Barber Shop cuts hair for $1.50, and the Central Hotel is a modest establishment with a tiny front door and five windows. Marble Rooms has two-room suites and sleeping rooms. Dr. W.J. Saunders is a "drain surgeon" who does plumbing. A Chinese herbalist asks, "Others gain health why not you?" and promises, "No matter with what you are afflicted, nor what you have tried and failed, or how long your case may be, you should try George Y. Lee." In its window, Bond's Books, est. 1932, has many volumes, including *Learning to Ride, Scarne's Complete Guide to Gambling, A Pictorial History of Wrestling, Flower Arrangements to Copy* and *Frontier Relics,* while Universal News sells pornographic magazines catering to a wide variety of tastes. *Male Sex Slavery, Leather Boy, The Abducted Wife, Cutey, New Ladies Tickler* are all available. You see the interiors of West End apartments, with their old-fashioned glossy dark wood panelling, exquisite stained glass, tidy rooms. And rain-slick sidewalks, shiny leaves. Neon reflections gleam on water-burnished Granville Street as the 14 Hastings bus eases past the Aristocratic diner and the Vogue Theatre. Curt, Rod Gillingham and the others were engaged in the photo project for about a year. Curt, himself, contributed about twelve thousand images, a remarkable collection. (A selection from Curt's 1972 portfolio can be seen following page 199.)

Curt's pictures show no derelicts, no down-and-outers, but no high flyers either. Here are people working hard to make a go of things at the margins. They carve out niches for themselves and provide the small but necessary services we rarely commemorate. Curt was interested in the things that are so much part of the texture of our lives we no longer notice them—the backsides of buildings, alleyways, parking lots, the places we *don't* regard as significant. He hated pretension and in his city no one is putting on airs. Curt achieved what he set out to do—produce a record of daily life. But there is more than documentation here—affection, sadness, humour and nostalgia suffuse these photographs in equal measure. They make you aware of Curt's deep connection with Vancouver—something that struck Fred, too. In a talk he gave as part of the *Unfinished Business* exhibition, he said, "Curt had a special sense of the kind of life that existed in the Lower Mainland. He probably devoted himself more intensely to the project than any of us." And then he added, his voice breaking with emotion, "The only way I can put it is, that it was as if he had been let loose to walk through his own dreams."

12. Stubborn as the buffeted birds

"THAT WAS A SKI BOAT—A JET BOAT," Rod Gillingham said, pointing to a picture he had taken. "We rebuilt it—for log salvaging." Curt started beachcombing in the late sixties almost as a game. He was living in a house along the Fraser River—building wooden dories because he liked the look of them, the elegant way they went together. He saw logs floating by and decided to grab a few and tow them in to his dock with his row-boat. He did it for the thrill of the chase, because it made rowing fun. Then he found out that salvaging was regulated. He got a licence and started foraging for saleable logs. Curt took out his first permit (L.S. 1386) in September 1968. It cost him $100 and gave him permission to range anywhere in the Vancouver Log Salvage District, from the Fraser River in the south to Cape Caution on B.C.'s central coast.

Curt invited Rod to join him log salvaging—when they weren't busy with photography. Sometimes he also asked his younger brother, Greg, to help. Greg was just fifteen when he started working for Curt. He had left home and was living on his own; Curt took him under his rather fierce wing.

In the early seventies, logs were pouring out of the B.C. forests—about 2.5 billion cubic feet every year, enough to girdle the globe with skid roads several times over. The coastal portion of this vast haul usually went to a mill by sea, loaded onto a barge or towed in a boom behind a tug. But the boom, particularly the type used then, the flat boom, was a flawed means of transport. It was just a single layer of logs bordered by more logs called "boom sticks" that were chained together. Sometimes, to prevent a boom turning from a rectangle into a circle, loggers connected the sides with swifters, logs driven across the top of the boom, or swifter wires, cables stretched across the boom. Still, waves, a boat wake or current action could roll a low floating log out from under a boom stick. And therein lay the foundation of a whole sub-industry. Log salvors scoured the coast looking for these escaped logs.

Mind you, they didn't always wait for them to escape. As Greg explained to me in an email: "Log salvagers are supposed to wait until a log is completely out of a boom before snagging it, but occasionally there is the temptation to 'help one along' if it is hanging halfway out of a boom. This can be accomplished by roaring by in a boat and throwing a big wake along the side of a boom, or by 'accidentally' brushing and bumping against the object of your desire until it pops free."

I remember Curt telling me about a salvager whose boat was designed to destabilize booms easily. It threw up a wake so large it sucked out the logs. Salvors like these gave the occupation a bad name. Just such a shady log salvager was a character in the popular CBC television series the *Beachcombers*, which ran from 1972 to 1990 and was set in Gibsons on the Sunshine Coast. Relic, played by Robert Clothier, would stop at

Log Salvaging, February 1972,
PHOTOGRAPHER: CURT LANG

nothing, including stealing logs, to beat his arch rival, Nick Adonidas, played by Bruno Gerussi. I don't know how many beachcombers fit this stereotype, but after spending a couple of hours in the library, looking at old newspaper clippings about the trade, I could see that the logging companies chronically regarded all salvagers with deep suspicion. They tried to prevent theft by regulating the salvors, who would inevitably resist any attempts to restrict their activities.

When Greg and Curt hooked a log, they first identified it as their own by stamping a number on the butt end with a stamp hammer. This was a short-handled sledge hammer with a four-digit number in reverse relief on the head. Marking the logs was akin to branding a cow, only the stamp hammer used pressure instead of heat. Greg explained, "The hammers would drive the fibres of wood way up into the log (maybe ten or twelve feet). It was like poking your finger into the end of a bundle of raw spaghetti. Even if a crafty thief were to cut off the butt with a chainsaw, a close examination could reveal the number on the new butt."

After collecting a small boom of their own, the salvors towed it into one of the receiving stations of the Gulf Log Salvage Co-operative Association, which sorted, scaled and auctioned off the logs. The salvors were paid out of the proceeds. Greg wrote in an email: "Some marginal logs were worth $30 to $40 while an exceptionally nice big fir peeler could get the salvager up to $1,000 (extremely rare—maybe one per year.)"

Curt taught himself how to salvage logs by doing it. He also used a small, obscure book, *Underwater Logging*, as a reference. Written by John E. Cayford and Ronald E. Scott, it described their experiences pulling pre-Revolutionary War oak logs off the bottom of the Penobscot River in Maine. Despite this rather esoteric subject matter, the text contained valuable information about equipment and procedures. A series of photographs explained how to identify logs.

In an interview at his house in Victoria, Greg remembered Curt's introduction to the trade:

> It came as a shock to him that log salvaging was so brutal. It was such a zero-sum game. If someone else gets your log, you don't have it. Curt once described being out there on the Fraser River, on a rainy, rainy, rainy, horrible foggy day. He's driving a dog, a ring with a spike on the end of it,

that you tie a rope to. He is driving a dog into one end of a log. He looks up, looks down the log and there is another guy in a boat driving a dog into the other end of the log. It's a tug of war. Whoever's dog pops out first, loses.

The sheer grit and struggle of salvaging also caught the eye of Peter Trower, a B.C. poet and novelist. Trower worked as a logger for about twenty years and wrote about the life, filling a dozen books. He said, "I met Curt in 1960 in the beatnik days. I was going to art school, before I decided to become a writer. At the time, Curt was writing. I saw him off and on. He was always hanging around that scene, the coffee houses. He used to play the flute in a jazz joint called the Espresso." (Owned by the musician, Neil Longton, this coffee house operated at the corner of Howe Street and Georgia.)

Peter Trower, 1972   PHOTOGRAPHER: CURT LANG

Trower told me that his "Poem Rower" was inspired by Curt. "It took place in front of the house around the bay in Gibsons, where I used to live." The poem, from Trower's award-winning collection *Chainsaws in the Cathedral*, starts like this:

No day for much
this glum grumbler sky full of dirty cloud
and a spasmodic wind
tangling in the antenna
making the images twitch.

The words are like a telegram from the past. Brief, they give no time, no place, no obvious pegs on which to hang the poem.

Better to sit indoors
by the seaward window
watching the lone beachcomber
stubborn as the buffeted birds
salvaging half-loosened logs
with a rowboat.

As I read, I grope for details. How would Curt have done this? Alone—with a rowboat? I know the principle of the thing. You wait for a high tide. That's what loosens the logs. Then what? Jump out of the boat and stand seaside of the log. In hip waders? Hammer in a dog while the log is shifting and turning in the wind-driven water? What did Curt do with the boat? Drag it ashore? Tie it to something and let it drift? And then? Jump back in the boat, the spray whipping across his face? Row and drag. Row and drag. How heavy was that log anyway? A couple of thousand pounds?

They say he writes poems sometimes
perhaps he is writing one now
of oarlock-creak
wave-slap
and the grunts of his dogged progress
to the last line of the tie-up float.

One afternoon, I visited Peter at his home in North Vancouver to talk about Curt.

Peter was in his early seventies then, and years of hard living had given him a rough raspy voice. "I guess Curt was really broke. All he had was this damn rowboat. That poem is very true. It was what it looked like, straining away, pulling the log," Peter growled at me. "I think he was just making a living as a beachcomber. I never could figure. It was such a funny jump from what he used to do, hanging around the arts scene. I did it the other way. I was a logger and then I came into the city."

Lane near Lonsdale in North Vancouver, February 1972   PHOTOGRAPHER: CURT LANG

But Curt hadn't been able to earn much of a living hanging around the arts scene. And while log salvaging was hard, at least there was some potential for making money. Not that he ever made a great deal of it—but that wasn't the main point, according to Rod. "It was about something other than making money," he said. "It was the lifestyle. It was about being on the ocean."

The jet boat Rod photographed was a major advance over the wooden dory Curt had been using. "It was a ski boat and we beefed it up," Rod recalled. A jet boat draws water into an internal pump and expels it through a nozzle at the stern. Because it doesn't have a propeller that can strike rocks in shallow water, it is highly manoeuvrable. Curt's craft was wedge-shaped and well adapted to pulling logs off rocky shores. It had a 454 Chrysler engine and dramatically increased Curt's ability to bring in logs. Rod said, "We went anywhere we could find logs. We'd go along the Sunshine Coast, up the Fraser River, around Vancouver, over to Howe Sound and into Deep Cove, sometimes up to Lighthouse Park, Point Atkinson, near Bowen Island."

Rod told me that occasionally the salvaging was so good that he and Curt would collect more logs than they could comfortably handle on their own. Then they teamed up with Dave White, a teacher from Roberts Creek turned beachcomber. Dave had a tug, the *Paul C*, with a much bigger hauling capacity than Curt's jet boat. When they had about four hundred logs to tow, they called on Dave for help. They'd bring in Dave's logs and their own and sell them all to the salvage co-op.

But the activity was inherently risky because it was weather dependent—it depended on the weather being *bad*. That was the best time to go out because that's when the booms broke up. Rod explained:

> I remember going out in the worst, most torturous weather in the middle of winter. We'd go up, and I'd be dusting snow off these logs. You'd look at them on the beach to see whether they were worth taking or not. We were always desperate to get logs.
>
> Once we hit really fierce weather where you go across by the Lions Gate Bridge. It was so snotty that we thought we'd lose the boom. We tied up at Ambleside. Because of the particular lay of the weather at that time, we could get in there and it looked like the logs would be okay. We came in and walked up to our house at Ambleside and expected to go down the next morning when the weather had calmed down a bit. And when we came down, the logs were gone. They had taken the whole boom—three hundred logs. You're talking about thousands of dollars. Curt was infuriated to the point of tears. There was nothing we could do. It was open season if you were stupid enough to leave your logs. We got our gear back though. Somebody phoned us and told us it was in North Vancouver at the dock at Mosquito Creek. Probably the salvager who stole the logs trying to be

ethical in some way: "I'm taking your logs, but leaving your gear." So we went down and retrieved what gear there was. That could have been a month's work.

One big trip with Dave was particularly memorable. They were coming down from Sechelt and got caught in a stiff wind. Rod said:

> I thought I was going to die. I didn't think we were going to make it. After crossing Howe Sound, we came out around Gambier Island. We had the whole boom, the jet boat and the *Paul C*. We pulled out into this thing— the storm. It was just blowing. We were all in the *Paul C* at that time. I remember the prop on the boat being out of the water and spinning in the air. Everybody was just hanging on for dear life. I remember Dave White was glugging rum like some old seaman. It was a heck of an adventure, I can tell you. Scary. It was just so awful. We decided to try and beat the weather, which was the wrong call. It was usually Curt who'd say "Let's try." Testing his mettle.

On a map, Howe Sound looks protected. But when a notorious arctic outflow called a Squamish blows up, it can go from dead calm to forty knots in fifteen minutes, transforming the inlet into a churning mass of whitewater. The locals maintain the worst spot is Hood Point, on the north east corner of Bowen across from Gambier Island. The wind hits the point, bounces back and whips the water into a vicious chop. Some say a boat can get swallowed up there. Rod explained:

> We never had any intention of bringing the boom back in bad weather, but we just got caught. We decided to make the final run even though the weather was turning on us. We came out of the lee of Gambier and we just got hit. As soon as we got out there, we said, "This was a mistake. We shouldn't have done this." But you have no choice at that point. You have to carry on.

One time, when Rod and Curt were cautious and sought shelter, the wind won anyway. Rod said:

We ran into bad weather. We took the boom and tucked it into Snug Cove on Bowen Island. Seemed like the safest place. Either we came back in the boat or took the ferry back. We were sitting in West Van for a couple of days; it was too awful to go out. When we got the courage to go out and deal with that boom, it was just a mess. That dog line was totally trashed. I remember Curt standing on the front deck and he had tears running down his cheeks. He was just so frustrated by the whole thing. It was going to take us days to sort it out. We lost so much stuff. I remember looking at him and he was just totally incensed by the whole thing.

I asked Rod how Curt had learned to make booms. He said, "In my perception, he read about it and thought, 'I can do this.' It struck me that Curt would take an interest in something and learn it." Rod told me that Curt had taught him how to splice rope and he remembered how they used to sit a whole day splicing rope and making hundreds of dog lines. These were sixteen-foot polypropylene ropes with an eye spliced into each end, attached to a dog. Later Greg told me that when you gathered ten to fifteen logs on dog lines, all fanning out beside each other, you'd have a string. Several strings could be towed one behind the other by tying them at intervals to a long tow rope.

I read that in the seventies, about four hundred beachcombers were working actively in and around Vancouver. You could make a decent living if you were diligent and paid close attention to the weather and the tides—provided, of course, nothing went wrong. But frequently it did.

One night a west wind came up while Curt's jet boat was tied to a dock. Greg said, "And the little bit of fetch across the middle arm of the river just lapped into the boat, a cup of water at time. As it got lower, the boat was taking on a quart, then a gallon. Finally, when we got to it in the morning, it was just hanging, a dismal sight, hanging at the end of its mooring lines. It's like the feeling of 'Oh, shit.' At least it was fresh water. The engine had to be taken apart."

Another of Curt's boats sank when its mooring line got wrapped around a spike in one of the pilings on the dock. When the tide came up, the rope held the boat down and it filled up with water.

* * *

Even what looked like an ideal salvage arrangement turned bad. One year, Curt made a deal with the Port of New Westminster to clear the debris under the Annacis Island Bridge. This was a wooden railway bridge that ran from the top of Lulu Island over to Annacis Island. During the spring melt, all sorts of junk—logs, dead cows, barn doors—would build up around the pilings on the upstream side of the bridge. An operator had been keeping the waterway clear by using a crane to grapple the rubbish, swing it around the bridge and drop it on the downstream side. But it was expensive for the port to maintain the crane all the time.

Curt offered to keep the river clear if he could have an exclusive right to the log salvage. On the face of it, it looked like a good agreement. It meant that, instead of having to hunt for logs, Curt could wait for them to come to him. And rather than fighting other salvagers for them, he would be in the enviable position of having the sole rights to the logs. Greg said:

> So he and I lived in a horrible little house on the top of Lulu Island—up from the Queen's Hotel. Pretty rough neighbourhood, Queensborough. We had this cold, uninsulated wooden house. He and I once again lived in spartan conditions. I can't understand why I wasn't goofing around with my little friends. Nonetheless.
>
> At the beginning of the freshet, whenever a log would go across the gap, we would pull this debris and ram it through roadways underneath the bridge. We'd send this crap floating on its way to the sea. Really it built up much too quickly for us. We could only be there for twelve or sixteen hours a day. It always had more time than we did to build up. Honest to God there were dead animals, gates, whole trees that had fallen off the bank. I've never been in such good shape. I had a big long pike pole. And I'd run back and forth along the top of these railway ties, hopping from tie to tie, jabbing these things and trying to steer them through the hole while Curt would be running the dozer boat.
>
> To my shame—it was partly my fault and partly not—the dozer blew a seal or something. All the oil drained out of the engine into the bilge. And I had the choice of floating off downstream in this thing or running

it to the dock. I made the decision to run it for five minutes to the dock. In that time, I cooked all the bearings. This is like thousands of dollars that we didn't have to go into rebuilding this Perkins diesel. So that was a nightmare.

One February morning, I drove over to Lulu Island out of curiosity. I found the railway bridge Curt and Greg worked to keep clear, now no longer made of wood but of turquoise metal girders. I walked across and on the Annacis Island side saw a vast car park for new vehicles that were being unloaded from the freighters in the river. Hundreds of Hyundais, white plastic sheets taped to their roofs and trunks, looked like identical accident victims patched up with giant bandages. I also saw something that struck me as a relic of the past—an old-fashioned flat log boom tethered to a few pilings just downstream from the bridge. The waterway was free flowing that day, but then spring melt was still several months off. There were no dead cows, uprooted trees or barn segments requiring removal.

I crossed back to Lulu Island, with the intention of finding 68 Duncan Street, where Curt and Greg had lived. I located 61, home of the Fraser Shipyards and Industrial Centre, a collection of weathered wooden buildings once painted blue. I saw a sign, "Patrolled by Guard Dogs, Aggressive K-9 Services," and behind a chain-link fence, a man in a forklift moving scrap metal around. But number 68, which should have been on the other side of the street, was gone. Even when Curt and Greg had lived there, it was barely habitable. Greg wrote to me in an email: "The house was definitely cold and stark with peeling paint, gapped plaster, holy old linoleum, stained sinks, cracked windows—like Sluggo's place." I thought about the gruelling life Curt was leading. Why had he chosen it—was it the price of freedom?

That mild morning on Lulu Island, there was warmth in the sun. I took off my jacket and walked closer to the river. It was smooth, benign. A tugboat steamed west towards the sea. A half submerged log drifted downstream. At the extreme top end of the island, I came to a townhouse development, the Royal Port. It was a fifties fantasy, handkerchief-sized yards, picket fences, lace curtains, tricycles on walkways. The odd thing was, I saw no one. No face looking out the windows, no child playing in the street. It was empty—a Potemkin village.

The salvaging business started to change as more logs were transported on barges or in booms made up of bundles of ten to twenty logs held together with wire or metal banding. These booms were better for the logging companies because individual logs couldn't slip away as easily. But they reduced the opportunities for beachcombers. Not only that, the price of logs dropped. At one point, Gulf Log Salvage wasn't even buying cedar. Rod said, "It certainly wasn't profitable. It wasn't worthwhile. It was so much effort." Eventually Curt would let his log salvage licence lapse.

Greg has run his own software business for several years, but he occasionally gets nostalgic about working on the boats. "You remember beautiful sunrises and healthy hard work and coffee conversations in the dark wheelhouse ranging from euthanasia to cannibalism to guitar playing, but then you remember the glove frozen to your hand and the rusty jaggers poking you and the near-death experiences and you come to your senses."

Greg Lang, circa 1972   PHOTOGRAPHER: CURT LANG OR FRED DOUGLAS

13. Always winging it

I have watched the mornings
White with promise.
The sun hanging like a great electric fuse
Burning the mist away.

—CURT LANG, 1956

A MODEST HOUSE IN EAST VANCOUVER. It looked slightly odd to me and I couldn't figure out why at first. Then I realized that, though it had a peaked roof, it had no eaves. This made it seem vulnerable, exposed. Like a person walking in the rain without a hat or umbrella. The curtains were drawn. There was no bell; I knocked. No one came to the door. I knocked again. Still no one.

I was looking for the *Whalebird*, a fishing boat Curt built and named after Antarctic petrels that followed whalers to feast on blubber and oil. I had found the current owner's name and address in the Canadian Shipping Registry, but no phone number. None was in the phone book either. That's why I ended up on a door stoop, hoping to meet him in person. I walked away, disappointed to have missed the connection with that storied craft.

Fred spoke about Curt's first canoe being mythic. The *Whalebird* was perhaps even more so. Curt constructed it single-handedly and then created a new life—following the fish, learning their invisible ways, how to intuit their movements forty fathoms down. He travelled much farther than he did log salvaging, and stayed away from Vancouver for much longer periods. Curt used to talk about how he worked to the limit of his strength when he was fishing—how the sheer exhaustion of it threw simple pleasures into high relief. Once he came upon a floating restaurant, a café on a barge, went in and ordered an apple pie. When the waitress brought it, he was flooded with intense gratitude. Life on the *Whalebird* was life writ large.

Curt taught himself boat building. He figured out how to work from a table of off-sets—measurements that specified a series of points determining the size of a boat—and the lines—a drawing indicating how those points should be connected. He mastered the art of lofting—turning the small-scale lines into full-size templates or patterns needed for the hull. The skill gave him great satisfaction.

In 1965 and 1966, Curt built a couple of small wooden dories, a few dinghies and a fibreglass canoe for his own entertainment. Starting in 1967, he began making and selling larger work boats, including six small steel tugs. Fred took a picture of Curt perched on a saw horse in front of one of these boats. It looms behind him in a cavernous space. The hull is finished, its metal skin gleams darkly. Curt, who is smiling just a little, clearly

Curt with steel tug, circa 1970   PHOTOGRAPHER: FRED DOUGLAS

looks chuffed by what he has wrought. This was no canoe that wiggled like a snake.

With his can-do, damn-the-torpedoes attitude, Curt took on more risk than most people—and courted more failure. In 1972, with Dave White, Rod Gillingham and Greg as partners, he started to build a fibreglass boat for beachcombing. He gave it one of those bird names he liked, *Turnstone,* after a shorebird which searches for food by turning over stones and other small objects. As Greg said, "That again was a very seat-of-the-pants operation. Dave and I would go log salvage and Curt and Rod would build the boat. The idea was to build a log-salvage boat that would make us all money." They managed to finish the hull, the deck, the cabin and the tanks—a part of the construction that Greg remembered vividly. "Curt, Rod and I glassed plywood baffles into the fuel tanks, which ran across the hull behind the cabin. We all had our heads stuck down in the tank, no masks, no ventilation, all giddy from the resin, all lustily singing chorus after chorus of 'Skippy, Skippy, Skippy the bush kangaroo; Skippy, Skippy, Skippy a friend brave and true.'"

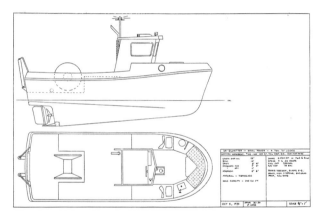

Curt's fishing boat design drawing, 1975

The high spirits didn't last. The group couldn't get enough money together for the engine or the wiring. Log salvaging was supposed to finance the venture, but opportunities for beachcombing were drying up.

Rod and Curt argued about who owned what percentage of the unfinished boat. The *Turnstone* was hoisted on blocks at a place Rod owned in Ladysmith. Confusion and disappointment about the wasted effort reigned. "The last I heard of it, it was just coming apart. That was a drag," said Greg.

In October 1974, Curt began working at Advance Mill and Marine in New Westminster. The company, which made large storage vessels, had just added a new marine division. Curt's task was to hustle up boat-building contracts and oversee construction. In his new job, Curt drew lines for tugs, cruisers, longliners, trollers, gillnetters, salmon boats, halibut boats, research vessels as well as barges. His plans bristle with nautical language—bollard, bulwark, lug, deck, topside, trawl, port. They also include figures—pounds of deadweight, cubic feet of volume, tons of working load capacity, feet of length, feet of beam, inches of freeboard loaded and unloaded. Files detail fittings—engine and gear, drive shaft, rudder stock, fir joists, tanks, windows, doors, berths, bilge pump, pipe and head, cleats and bow post, steering, controls, Morse, vents, propeller, lights—and prices to supply and install. A man Bernadette once described as *"trop négligé sur la question d'argent,"* could no longer be cavalier about it. He had to master the binary discipline of money—plus-minus, black-red.

I found a purchase order, dated September 21, 1975, for a $170,000 yarding tug to go to Inlet Tug at Tahsis, in the heart of Nootka Sound—"subject to financing." Then on October 5, a Sunday, Curt drew a 28-foot gillnetter with a hold capacity of 245 cubic feet, a top speed of 20 knots, capable of sleeping a crew of 3. And that was it. No more drawings. What happened? Did the deal with Inlet Tug fall through? Did the financing fail? Were there no other sales? Curt gives the gist in an undated memo: "During the 74/75 recession the Canadian forest and mining industries ceased expansion overnight. Many projects were cancelled. My company (Advanced Marine) was hit hard." On October 20, 2 weeks after drafting his last boat for Advance Mill and Marine, Curt took out a loan from the Royal Bank for $12,426 (principal, $9,000; interest, $3,426). His collateral consisted of two boats, *Boom-a-day* and the *Turnstone*. With the money, Curt started building the *Whalebird* in a complex of rental bays on No. 2 Road in Steveston. Working by himself, he cut and welded sheets of aluminum—the most difficult metal to fuse because of its low melting point. Welders have to take great care not to burn away the plates they intend to join; Curt was an ace.

When Curt finished, he had a solid working boat. The *Whalebird* was 35 feet long with a top speed of 11 knots. It weighed 5 tons unloaded, about 11 tons full. "It was fine looking," Greg said, "It had a whaleback bow and a sunken deck with a hatch in it. The cabin was in the stern so it looked like a phone booth in a bath tub. There was a very narrow walkway around it, very utilitarian. Built like a hammer. And about that much regard for creature comfort." Curt's aesthetic preference was always to cut away anything extraneous. You might recognize a thread leading back to the messianic idea promoted by the Austrian architect, Adolf Loos—that ornament is excrement.

The *Whalebird* was unconventional in one respect. Greg explained:

> All the framing was on the outside. It had box beams built on the outside and a smooth inside. So the fish hold didn't have any internal frames in it. It was all like a smooth bowl. So you could easily sluice the fish around. Curt had firmly held ideas about hull design. And he seemed to think that these external frames that were being pushed through the water had very little effect on fuel consumption or speed. If Curt were here, he'd explain it all to you.

In December 1975, Curt bought a ten dollar "C" class fishing licence to harvest groundfish—but not the coveted salmon. Though Curt knew how to handle boats, he had little experience fishing—about a month of work on a salmon boat when he was twenty years old. He taught himself, which is what he always preferred anyway. When he wanted to paint, he didn't attend art school; when he became interested in photography, he just picked up a camera; and when he wanted to write poetry, he didn't study it at university. "That seems like a form of death," he wrote to Jim Polson.

Forging ahead, Curt rigged the *Whalebird* for longlining—a method of catching halibut, rockfish and dogfish that involves laying lengths of baited hooks on the ocean floor. From September to December 1976, Curt landed 14,212 pounds of mixed ling cod, red cod and rock fish, as well as 9,312 pounds of littleneck clams.

I remember Curt telling Gordon and me that the native fishermen nicknamed him "needle watcher." They were amused by the way he navigated. Whereas they were guided by experience, he calculated his way around. You can see it in his water-stained log book: "Sept. 21, 1976. Point Washington to Victoria 31 nautical miles. Estimated time of arrival at 6.5 knots is 4.77 hours. Actual time 4.5 hours, corrected speed estimated at 6.9 knots." It was the same with the fishing. He had to build up the detailed lore that more seasoned men had. Curt was famous for talking; now he had to listen; there was no other way to get the information he needed.

His notebook is full of conversations: Heinz, skipper of the *Rolano*, told Curt about gathering herring roe on kelp beds for "some high figure per pound." Ott advised Curt not to clean cod on the grounds "as they get full from eating their brethren and the day's fishing is shot." Geoff from the *Drag Queen* spoke about squid on a shelf twenty fathoms down just outside Ucluelet. Hughey from Ahousat, a native village on Flores Island, said that Hesquiat Harbour was full of large dogfish. The captain of *Galley Bay*, Ed Hanson, said that Ramsay Arm, just east of Bute Inlet, was good in July, though the weather could change dramatically. "Fly at the first sign of southeast ripple," he warned. From Edy on *Freja*, Curt heard about squid shooting around on the surface at night, attracted by her boom light. She mentioned that "draggers catch quite a lot of them." According to another fisherman, named (or nicknamed) Crabber, there was octopus on the west coast of Flores Island between Rafael and Yates Points and also near a big rock on Mackenzie Beach south of Tofino. Peter Frank's uncle informed Curt that he could longline for cod, "in the deeps, forty to sixty fathoms down, outside Hotsprings Cove." There was a sweet spot for cod jigging at Clark Point, fourteen fathoms down—"grandma country," said Otto Botel, skipper of a Canadian Packers' vessel. He also described hitting very heavy snapper over the hundred fathom hole in Quatsino Sound just east of Restless Bight and talked about feed so heavy it was "a continuous cloud at forty to fifty fathoms" in Klaskish Inlet just north of the Brooks Peninsula.

* * *

Curt did not fish alone. Usually he had a crew; sometimes they were good and sometimes not. I remember once over dinner he spoke about a man he came to loathe. When he couldn't bear the idea of one more day in his company, Curt headed towards a wharf and tied up. He braced himself for a fight, and told the man to get off his boat, and not to come back—ever. As the man spluttered and asked what he had done, Curt handed him his pay and the money he needed to get home. Then Curt pulled away, leaving him dumbfounded on the dock.

Joe Ginger, by contrast, was a deckhand who worked out well. He was a native from Hesquiat, northwest of Hotsprings Cove. Curt told us that he worked in the computer industry after his spell of fishing, but I didn't know where. Would I be able to find him? I began phoning band offices on Vancouver Island. Finally, from the Nuu-chah-nulth Tribal Council Office in Port Alberni, I got a phone number in Seattle.

"Ah, Curtis," he said, when I called. "I always wondered what happened to him." Joe told me that he'd been a computer operator *before* he met Curt, which made him one of the original mainframe guys. He'd wanted to take a break, and so when Curt pulled up to a wharf, looking for crew, he decided to go with him. Fishing was a breather, he said. He was happy fishing. He had done it when he was fourteen, in Kyuquot Sound, with his cousins. He still looked on the experience fondly even though in many ways it was difficult. He liked working on Curt's boat:

> He was fair, a hard worker—independent. We got along. I was a reader and he was a talker. We were in Kyuquot for a few days. We had some harbour days at the end of February on our first trip. He was talking to all the natives, figuring out where all the halibut beds were. He always went out and talked to people about where the good spots were. He was pluralistic before "pluralism" was a big word. He was so engaging, that he talked to everybody.

When Joe began as Curt's deckhand in 1976, he was longlining:

> It's pretty gruesome—up there with crabbing. Like fourteen-hour days in March, April. Snotty part of the year. Doesn't get nice until May, June, July. Still winter up there through April. You're up before dawn and you're cutting bait after you're done. Pretty physical, demanding. We were after cod, snapper, halibut. But halibut was the primary focus. The season wasn't long. The best halibut beds were near Prince Rupert, and we stayed up there until the season was done.

Then Curt decided there was better money in cash buying. Joe said, "It was a piece of cake after longlining. Curt bought Double A for the export market. He offered top dollar. On the Fraser River, the gillnetters weren't very good about cleaning fish. They weren't good at processing it for the Japanese, who treated it like candy." Curt bought the best fish he could and Joe cleaned the fish, just the way the Japanese wanted. The two worked up and down the coast, from the Gulf of Georgia to the northern tip of Vancouver Island.

In March 1978, Curt got a contract with Quality Fish to buy herring. Quality Fish provided the boat, the *Walter M.*, which at fifty-five feet was considerably bigger than the *Whalebird*. Curt took Joe and another man, Ray Breckner. At the time, herring and herring roe were fetching astonishing prices. Joe said, "When we went up north, Curt probably had between $200,000 and $250,000 on him. If a herring fisherman had a good catch, he'd pay out $10,000 to $15,000. And that would be just one morning's customer."

On March 15, a storm warning flashed over the radio. Joe said, "It was always snotty in February and March. It could turn on you real quick, go from sunny to forty-five in an hour—get crappy real fast. Fishermen pushed the envelope. They'd bite it. Back then, it was more dangerous. Now I think the government is more concerned about safety issues, survival gear. I don't think we had survival suits. Life jackets, rafts, that was about it. If you went in, you had fifteen minutes."

It blew like hell. Winds reached 75 knots, Force 9 on the Beaufort scale, a strong gale. The *Walter M.* was solid, a classic as far as hull design went. Going 6 knots, it slipped through the water without any disturbance, with no more wake than a canoe. But it was built in 1925, and it was wooden. Its top speed was 9 knots, less than what Curt was used to getting in the *Whalebird*. At three in the afternoon, one seiner in the fleet, the *Ocean Invader 1*, sent out a distress signal. Towering 40-foot waves were threatening to swamp the boat and the visibility was less than a quarter of a mile. It was foundering. Then its radio went dead. The manager of the fishermen's co-operative in Port Simpson, just north of Prince Rupert, kept calling and calling the boat, but got no response.

"It was touch and go," Joe recalled. "We were one of the last boats in. As scary as it ever got for me. The next day you could hear how close we came to being victims of the storm."

On March 16, the *Ocean Invader 1* was still missing. On March 17, rescue crews found it overturned and damaged off Cape St. James, at the southern tip of the Haida Gwaii. Six fishermen, all from the Parnell family, had drowned.

Curt got his herring—a hundred tons of it. The *Walter M.* turned south. It was still windy though not quite as bad as it had been. Joe was sleeping up front, exhausted. When he woke up, Curt said, "I was really concerned, when we hit those big swells, about whether the bulkheads would hold that big load." The bulkheads were partitions that kept the cargo evenly distributed. If the bulkheads broke, the fish would begin to slosh around in the hold, making the boat much more unstable.

"Well, Curt," said Joe, "I never thought of that."

* * *

I found Ray Breckner. who'd been on the *Walter M.* with Curt, in a farming community close to the U.S. border. I went to visit him, and found myself sitting in a roomy kitchen overlooking fields. Outside on a deck, three large dogs dozed in the sun. I settled back with a cup of coffee and was startled when a small green bird landed on my shoulder. Then it swooped onto my notebook and began pecking at it.

"Shoo her way," said Ray, a lanky man with slicked back dark hair.

I tried—ineffectually.

He got up and found a piece of newspaper with which to distract the bird. I suspected this wouldn't be nearly as appealing as my notebook, and it wasn't. "Okay, Molly," Ray berated the bird. "You'll have to go in your cage."

I pulled a beige piece of paper out of my bag. It said: "Union Boat Clearance. Date: March 4, 1978. Vessel: Walter M." Under a column titled "Name," it listed three people—Curt Lang, Ray Breckner and Joe Ginger.

"This is why I wanted to talk to you," I said.

Ray scrutinized the piece of paper. "I remember what that was. We were somewhere tied up to a dock up the coast over Tofino. A union organizer came and said, 'We want you to join the union.' And I said, 'I don't believe in unions.' He went and got a bunch of guys together to storm the boat. They were going to beat us up so we phoned back to the office at Quality Fish and they said not to cause any trouble. So we joined the union. It's the one and only time I've had anything to do with a union. Quality Fish wasn't a union company. Maybe the guy didn't like me or us."

Ray Breckner told me that he met Curt while he was building the *Whalebird*; he had a shop in the same complex. When Curt got the contract from Quality Fish, he asked Ray to join him as an engineer. Ray was not a fisherman. "I was more nuts and bolts, building things," he said. But the seventies were boom years for fishing in British Columbia. The lure was great. As Ray recalled:

It was like a gold rush. All this crazy, haywire wildness. It probably got rolling about '73. The big year was '78–'79 and then it fell apart. Dropped back to something more realistic. They were paying $5,000 a ton for herring at one point. It was unbelievable. All these fishermen with the little skiffs, herring punts, they had their own boats to live on. They might spend 2 or 3 weeks in a spot. So they had a salmon gillnet boat and they dragged the punts behind. They had a seiner that wasn't licensed and that's where they lived. So they had all these communications. They'd get on the radio. "What are you paying?"

"Well, I'm paying $2,200."

"Well, I'm paying $2,300." You could hear all this. It was wide open. People were offering the stupidest, wildest things. This guy here had a couple million bucks. This guy there had five.

"You got any money?"

"I don't know if I can spare… my plane's coming in tomorrow. I'll give you half a million."

"Pass it over."

A plane would come in the next day and drop off four or five million bucks. And away you'd go.

Guys would come in with ten tons. They would give you bogus numbers. They would have numbers painted on the side of the skiff. But they would give you bogus numbers and some haywire name. Like Deep Throat. Deep Throat 1234. If you wanted the fish, that's what you put on the ticket. So there was no record. And you paid in cash. I remember guys who had never seen a thousand dollars in one place with a hundred thousand dollars in their pocket and absolutely incensed if we had anything less than a hundred dollar bill. Because where are they going to put it? Crazy. They've been working long hours. They're tired. And they're goofy anyway.

Guys were playing in the bars. A thousand dollars a bet. Right out of the Wild West. Airplanes flying in with more money. Money was a commodity. If you didn't have any money, you couldn't play, so get money.

Curt's strength was that he knew the Indians. He had been up with the Whalebird clamming. Trying to organize the natives is difficult. He was able to wade into that and not get as upset as most people. He understood it to some degree. We expected to get quite a few deliveries from the natives.

Ray was a no-nonsense guy, an inventor who developed a fish pump to transfer fish from one location to another and who had a number of other patents to his credit. Yet as I talked to him about fishing, a Homeric cast of larger-than-life characters rose before my eyes. There were heroes and villains. One man was a Jekyll and Hyde. When he got behind the throttle of a boat, "the fangs grew." This was war and he was going to win. He was so hated that people would slap him in the face when they passed him on the dock. Once, a fisherman went full steam for the side of his boat. Hyde was on the radio to the whole fleet, saying: "I'm in full reverse, I'm going as hard as I can go. I'm about to be rammed." He was broadcasting it to everybody. Hyde regarded fish as a finite resource. If someone else got some, there was less for him. He often ran interference so that other people couldn't get theirs. When another purse seiner set out a net, he would manoeuvre his boat inside the net, so the fisherman couldn't close it and get his fish.

Ray said that one time the same man was using a seining technique called "beach tying." Instead of having a skiff hold the tail end of the net while the boat formed a loop with the rest of it, he had a crew member row ashore and tie onto a tree. Then he hit the throttle with such force that he pulled the tree down. He sent a fellow in to tie onto another tree. The same thing happened. This was in cottage country, not a remote bay up the coast, so people could see what was happening and they started to throw rocks at the man on shore. Didn't bother Hyde at all. Ripping out trees? He didn't care, he was catching fish. He regularly made a million dollars a season.

And then there were the heroes. Ray said:

> Edgar Arnett was famous. You're talking about a real pioneer, no radios, no nothing. I think he may have been in the *Walter M.*, way up to the Bering Sea with quite a large crew. They got into trouble and the propeller

shaft broke. There was no way to repair it, up in the middle of nowhere. They were drifting around. They were all going to die. They would try this or that. Then the old man had an idea. He just kept it quiet until everybody spent all their enthusiasm and haywire ideas. He presented his idea, which was incredibly stupid. But it worked. He chopped down the mast, cut v-notches in the bulwarks of the boat and ran the mast across. They ran some ropes around the capstan and around the mast. They fixed pen boards from the fish hold and made a paddle wheeler. They would run for a few hours, something would fly off, they'd fix it. They came back to port like that.

Ray also remembered another man, a west coaster who rescued the crew on a sinking freighter. "The ocean was carrying water across the freighter and he knew every so often you would get a large wave, every ninth. He went in on a swell. He hit the wave, landed on the deck, got two or three people in and got off on the next one. No ordinary person can do that," he said, then looked at me and asked, "More coffee?"

I nodded. Ray went on:

You know, there was a bunch of beachcombers, fishermen, towboaters, logger-type guys. All proficient with boats and knew what they were doing. Curt was not in that group. He was not as capable as they were. He would have been there at the coffee shop, but he would have been slightly out.

The boat was different. It wasn't the way you built a boat. In Curt's mind, there was an advantage to doing the boat this unusual way. Not in many other people's minds. If you talked to some of the guys, they'd say "What a piece of shit!" But Curt made it go. It was Curt's way. It didn't matter what anybody else said.

I sat back in my chair, cupping the hot drink in my hands. "So was he chasing the pot of gold at the end of the rainbow or was he just in it for the ride?" Ray asked.

This was an easy question. "The ride," I said. Ray thought about it a minute and then responded.

You know, I made some money, so if I could do it, he could do it. It doesn't matter what you do, the game is the game. You have to be honest. You have to put your heart into it to be long-term successful, but the goal, not the goal as the object, but the goal as scorekeeping is the money. If you're winning, you're making money. If you're doing it but not making money, you're not winning. That's how it is. That's what it's about. Fact of the matter is, you like to look in the mirror and say, "I'm a winner." And the mark of a winner is the money.

For Curt, money was not the object, nor the way he kept score.

As I said, it was the ride, and the thing about Curt was that he didn't always know where the ride would take him. That trip through Seymour Narrows, for instance, when Curt was cash buying with Rod Gillingham—this time in his own boat. A plane had flown in with an attaché case full of money. Curt had counted it and Rod, too. It was more cash than Rod had ever seen at once. He felt like a high roller.

Curt got on the radio to alert fishermen in the area that he wanted to buy fish. At first, there were no takers. But finally, Archie, a native man in a big seiner responded. He had a boat full of salmon. They met in a nearby bay and Archie loaded Curt's boat. After he had delivered the fish, Curt's boat sagged under the weight. There was hardly any freeboard left.

The next thing they knew the Department of Fisheries was on the radio. The fisheries officers wanted their location.

"This is problematic," said Curt.

Archie, who had heard the broadcast, came over in his seiner.

"You follow me. We'll shoot through Seymour Narrows. This is the wrong time to be doing this. But we'll shoot through the narrows and get through the other side. And I know the fisheries boats won't come through there."

Seymour Narrows is just north of Campbell River between Vancouver Island and Quadra Island. Its riptide is notorious. Until 1958, a huge killer rock, called Ripple Rock, right in the narrowest part of the channel, added to the navigational nightmare. Captain Vancouver had described the Narrows as "one of the vilest stretches of water in the world." By 1953, the Rock had taken 114 lives and the Canadian Department of Public

Works decided to blow it up. It took five years, a 3,000-foot tunnel under the sea, 1,375 tons of explosives and one of the largest non-nuclear explosions on record. Ripple Rock became Ripple Shoal, but the passage was still treacherous on account of its extreme turbulence, whirlpools, standing waves and 14-knot currents. In 1984, a cruise liner, *Sundancer*, attempted to power through an ebbing tide, but failed and ran aground on Maude Island. No passengers died, but the ship was a total loss.

Curt trusted Archie's knowledge of the hazards. So he took him up on his offer and followed. Archie struck a course through the shallows. The tide was running exactly the wrong way. Curt tried to stay with Archie but his boat was less powerful than the big seiner and was slowed down by all the fish in the hold. He lost ground against the tide and became afraid of smashing onto the rocks. He manoeuvred to the centre of the channel, deciding it was his safest option. When Curt and Rod looked over the side, they could see whirlpools that were twelve feet across. Huge logs were being sucked down. Curt was at the wheel trying to hold on, going nowhere, without the power to get beyond the rapids. Rod was at the front of the boat, gripping the rail, his knuckles white. They spent an hour like this without making any progress. Then the tide turned slack. Curt headed straight for Vancouver.

When Rod told me the story later, he said, "It was really scary, really scary, really, really scary."

Rod said he thought that Curt fled the fisheries officer because his licence permitted him to buy gillnet fish only, not seiner caught. But when I look at the licence Curt had for cash buying, no restrictions like that are mentioned. I suspect the trouble arose because Archie was not supposed to sell them anything. Although many native fishermen had commercial licences, if Archie didn't, he would only have been allowed to fish for his band. A deal with Curt would have been illegal.

Curt sold Archie's fish on the Campbell Avenue wharves. But his wild fishing days were coming to an end. When Curt first got his "C" class licence, it allowed him to harvest halibut as well as groundfish. However, in 1979, Canada's Department of Fisheries began requiring that commercial fisherman who wanted to take halibut have a new "L" class licence. Further, it was only going to give out 435 licences. When Curt applied for one, he was denied. He appealed and, on May 18, received a telegram from Romeo LeBlanc, Minister of Fisheries and Oceans: "I regret to inform you that your appeal has been denied. Unfortunately, the necessity to limit this fishery has precluded your receiving a licence."

Quite eloquently, Curt appealed again. He said that his income, though modest, was growing: $5,000 in 1976, $10,800 in 1977 and $21,686 in 1978. His financial commitment to fishing was significant; his debt for gear and the boat amounted to $50,576. He wrote: "Many other boats granted 'L' licences have 'A' (salmon) and herring licences. I do not. Some of the other boats have prawn gear and freezers. I do not. Some of the other fishermen own income property and have other investments. I do not. I have one 36' [foot], ice-packing longline boat, 1,500 hooks/snaps and that's it."

On May 22, Romeo LeBlanc sent another telegram. "I am pleased to inform you that your appeal has been granted, and you may purchase the 'L' licence you seek. Please accept my sincere good wishes for a most successful season."

But debt was crushing Curt. Interest rates had skyrocketed. The bank was sucking up every penny he earned at sea. On September 23, 1980, the Royal Bank repossessed the *Whalebird* and Curt came ashore.

* * *

I was walking with Gordon at the Cleveland Dam near our house. On the north side of the dam was the lake, silent, calm, gently lapping on the shore and, on the south, water foaming over the spillway, rushing, abundant, its energy released. We looked both ways, as we usually did. I told Gordon some of the fishing stories about Curt and said that, when he rigged the *Whalebird* for longlining, he'd actually had very little experience fishing—a summer working on a salmon boat, maybe not much more than that. Gordon laughed. "It was the same with computers. What Curt did was so audacious and desperate. It was bold; it was hard. And he was always winging it."

A few years ago, I made another attempt to find the *Whalebird*. It was still there on the registry, only it had been sold, to a gentleman in Prince Rupert. I was able to find his phone number and rang him up. Yes, he told me, the boat was still plying the waters. He sent me a photo. The box beams on the outside are clearly visible, running down at an angle from the gunwales. The *Whalebird* is backlit with puffy white clouds behind, the water slightly rippled. As I looked at it, I thought about what Gordon had said. Yes, it was true, Curt *was* always winging it. But that meant he did actually fly.

14. Take the money and run

"I WOULD BE PLEASED TO TALK TO YOU," went the message on our answering machine. The man's voice appealed to me and I remember telling Gordon so. He had applied for a programming job with Western Softworks and now Curt Lang, the president, was inviting my husband to come for an interview.

On a sleety evening in November 1986, Curt and Gordon met for hot chocolate, in a café at Lonsdale Quay in North Vancouver. About fifty and somewhat stocky, Curt was a talkative, expressive man. His short, clipped hair was still blond; he looked fit. Gordon was about ten years younger, tall and slim, with curly brown hair and a beard. Always a bit reserved, he was in a wary mood that day.

A month before, Gordon had quit his job with Krieger Data, which had been an emotional roller-coaster ride. Ralf Krieger had decided to take his fifteen-person company public, announcing to Gordon, "One day, Krieger Data will be bigger than IBM." 'It will take more than *saying* so, to get there,' thought Gordon. Ralf was deeply committed, but going public was time-consuming, frustrating and expensive. He was squeezed for cash. Gordon wrote in his diary: "The company sells $30k per month, but spends $60k—yet Ralf refuses to make cuts." The promoters helping Ralf offered bridge financing to tide him over until the public financing came through—*if* Ralf gave up his voting rights. He was on the ropes; he accepted. Gordon's heart sank. Ralf was a serious, intelligent man, beguiled by a dream. Gordon wrote in his diary: "Dreams that are strong are like strong lenses—they colour and distort reality." He was grateful to Ralf for giving him a chance (his first job, fresh out of a crash programming course) and he felt disloyal for leaving. But as he wrote in an essay, "Curt Lang as Technologist," he worried the company was "going down in flames, victim of management *naïveté* and VSE scam artists. I wanted something more straightforward."

While Gordon and Curt nursed their drinks, Gordon appraised him cautiously. Curt said that Western Softworks was a service company doing contract work. He was looking for someone to build school scheduling software for Columbia Computing Services. It wasn't exciting, but Gordon thought it sounded sane—low budget, low overhead. Western Softworks had a small office on Crown Street, near the Second Narrows Bridge in North Vancouver. Curt told Gordon that he would charge out his time at $40 an hour and pay him $30. This was good money in those days, and Gordon liked that. He was fed up with schemes only tangentially related to reality; this seemed like a perfect antidote.

Gordon didn't know it, but Curt had just come off a string of business reversals himself. In 1979, he invented a device to make longlining easier by automating the baiting of hooks. He patented the AutoSnapper and sold his first prototype for $2,000. When he gave up fishing in 1980, he struck a deal with Shields Navigation in Vancouver, to promote and sell his machine. But Shields' main business was delivering fuel and equipment up the coast; the AutoSnapper was a side venture. Nothing much came of it. When I recently spoke on the phone with Mike Shields about the device, he said, "It worked just fine, but it needed someone who could promote it and was interested in it. It needed a champion and some tweaking it wasn't getting. It died on the vine."

As Curt's hopes for the AutoSnapper faded, he left his long engagement with the sea. The gleaming promise of computers took its place. Curt's friend, Tod Greenaway, wrote: "Curt was immensely curious. He was curious about how a dish had been made: he would question the cook until he understood. He was curious about language: he made it his business to investigate the syntax of classical Greek. He had read up and remembered the laminar flow of water over dolphin skin." For a man like this, computers were an irresistible intellectual challenge. Curt was an "early adopter," a person who eagerly embraced new technology. He first used computers to help with boat design—to loft the lines. Then he began to think about other possibilities.

The world of computers was a new frontier where fortunes were easily won *and* lost.

Companies sprang up, grew explosively, then divided, spawning new ventures. The players changed constantly and formal qualifications didn't count for much. As Mike Collins, a friend of Curt's from the early sixties, observed, "it was made for people like Curt, people who had skills and intelligence, non-conformists. The entry-level, and the credentials that you needed, weren't defined. You could just show up with your raw talent." High-school kids, dropouts, autodidacts commanded respect—if they had a clever idea.

Curt met Lynn Richards, a software entrepreneur, at a presentation she made in Vancouver. Described as an "opinionated dynamo" in an article in the *Vancouver Sun*, Lynn gave Curt his first job in the computer industry. She was a graduate from UBC's computer science program and the proprietor of the Software Store. She hired Curt as a salesman and systems analyst for her company—not actually a "store" per se, but a start-up in the basement of her house. Very little off-the-shelf software existed at the time, so the Software Store filled a need by developing programs to order. Curt landed one contract with Western Stevedoring, a supplier of longshoremen and marine equipment, and began mapping its data flow. Then he got another with Sydney Development Corporation to create a program aimed at real estate agents.

Despite Curt's successes, he lost his job after about a year. Jeff Chow, then a programmer at the Software Store, said, "I think they were tired of him. He took it bad. I talked to him that night when they let him go. You could tell his feelings were hurt. I tried to make him feel better." Shortly afterwards, Sydney Development hired Curt as a software designer. The company had just made a shrewd deal with Don Mattrick to market his video game *Evolution*. It rapidly sold more than 400,000 copies, turning the 17-year old inventor into an instant celebrity. Later Sydney made a disastrously ambitious move. It launched Sydney Learning Stores—envisioned as a North America-wide chain of 360 outlets where people could learn how to use computers. In September 1984, after establishing just 4 stores, the company had spent $16.7 million, with little to show for its effort. The president, Tarnie Williams, admitted to the shareholders that Sydney Development, Canada's first publicly traded software company, was in trouble.

Meanwhile, Gil Johnston, a manager at Sydney, was starting his own venture, Evergreen International Technology. Unlike Sydney, which offered the gamut, everything from games to accounting, his company was going to specialize. "Our research thrust," Johnston announced in a February 1984 release which went out on PR Newswire:

"is to develop new computer-based learning systems that will speed the learning process." Jeff said that while Sydney spiralled downwards, "Curt and Gil got talking. Then Gil hired Curt." To create software learning programs, Curt, in turn, hired Jeff Chow; his brother, Greg; and a friend, Jerry Pedersen. He found a company in California that was already writing good courseware and, to speed up development, persuaded Evergreen to buy it. Curt insisted on clarity and brevity and fought fiercely with his colleagues at Evergreen when he thought they were going to overcomplicate things. He brought to programming the same aesthetic, elegant and spare, that informed his boat designs. Soon Evergreen had software that could teach people how to use several popular programs of the day—DOS, Lotus 123, WordPerfect, Word, Easywriter.

Gil was a ruddy-faced former alcoholic whose avuncular manner concealed a couple of unfortunate business instincts. One was, Greg said, "never to leave any money in your client's pocket. If he knew there was another nickel floating around in your jeans somewhere, he wasn't going to feel right unless he had it. He would work on getting deals up to one step away from completion and then he'd ask for more." He also spent lavishly— outfitting the office with marble tables and a cappuccino bar, and taking business trips on the Concorde (at $10,000 a pop). By 1985, Gil could no longer afford to keep Curt. He didn't lay him off, but he stopped paying him. Curt stayed for almost another year, hoping, I suppose, to cash in when he sold his shares. Then Curt and Gil disagreed seriously about the nature of those shares. Curt believed they were free-trading, Gil maintained they were not. In 1986, Curt left in disgust.

No wonder simplicity had such great appeal for both Curt and Gordon. No investors. No gambles. No $100-million business plans. Gordon could see, however, that Curt was not just motivated by the bottom line and that spoke to a deeper part of his nature. In the course of a (wide-ranging) job interview, Gordon was surprised to discover that Curt had read the logician Alfred Tarski (who changed twentieth-century logic by his work on the concept of truth) and the linguist Benjamin Whorf. Gordon, who had studied philosophy, was intrigued by Whorf's idea that language influences and constrains thought. This inspired his thesis "Other Worlds," which argued that there can be alternative conceptual frameworks. Gordon was happy to meet someone who, like himself, was interested in the power of ideas.

In that two-hour conversation, many things were not said. Gordon didn't get around to mentioning the novel he'd written (about a future so technologically advanced that people could get what they wanted by wishing for it). Curt didn't talk about his writing either. He was no longer trying to publish poetry, but still wrote it occasionally. Nevertheless, the ex-novelist, ex-philosopher and the not-quite-ex poet, were drawn to each other because of their mutual recognition of the wider possibilities of life. Sure they both needed to make a living and, for various reasons, contract programming looked like a good way of doing that. However, it would never be completely satisfying for either of them. This was a beginning, not an end.

Gordon started to work for Western Softworks in January 1987. At first, he was a little dismayed by just how bare bones the operation was. Tables were doors on sawhorses and contractors were expected to supply their own computers. But the money was decent, and Curt was a fair, albeit somewhat eccentric boss (as his unusual job interview style suggested). At lunchtime, he led freewheeling seminar-like conversations. One day, the topic might be relational database design—how to organize information to minimize redundancy. Another time the subject might be the principles of lofting and ship design or Hypatia, a fourth-century Alexandrian woman and mathematician. "This would derail the afternoon work program," Gordon wrote.

Curt and Ruth, circa 1981   PHOTOGRAPHER: DENISE GOODKEY

Curt quickly became a friend. Gordon and I met his wife, Ruth, a dark-haired and kindly woman, who was studying horticulture. They had married in February 1981, and she told me, "We fell in love when I was twenty-three. He was working as a fisherman. In the fall, he would harvest clams. He asked my sister and me to help him sort clams. We fell in love over the clams." Gordon and I met Fred and Ev Douglas who lived around the corner from Curt's place in Lynn Valley. Over good food and wine (almost always Pinot Noir), we discussed books, history and literature. Like the lunchroom conversations, you could not predict where these might go—Curt's seagoing days, the Northern Crusades (struggles around the Baltic Sea in the name of Christianity), or current politics (where Curt and I were often miles apart).

Curt also filled a kind of father figure role for Gordon. He said:

> Curt was eleven years older than me and certainly a mentor. From him, I learned these basic things that help you get on. Probably the first lesson was, "Cut the scope: make it simple." If you're feeling overburdened, look for something to cut. Another thing was, "Listen to your stomach." Many times Curt would ask in a business situation, "How do you feel about this person? Or how do you feel about this deal? Is the stomach happy or is it not happy?" The head can say, "Yes, it makes sense; let's go ahead. There's no reason not to." But the stomach doesn't always agree. It's more defensive and self-protective. It asks, "Can I digest this?" It says, "It's not very appetizing. I think it's off." Curt gave me lots of good advice. It was a helpful steering relationship.

At Western Softworks, Curt had two principal customers, Western Stevedoring (from his time at the Software Store) and Columbia Computing Services. Curt's cousin, Grant Foss, looked after Western Stevedoring and Gordon led a small team for the Columbia project. Dave Dieno, a talented recent computer-science graduate from Simon Fraser University, worked in the office at Crown Street; a few other programmers operated from their own homes. The group began churning out reports about DINCS (discipline incidents) and DACTS (discipline actions). And then, because all of this was running reasonably well, or because Curt simply could not resist the temptation of starting something new, he launched two more companies: Textworks to provide desktop publishing and 4GL Systems to offer relational database design. Georg Hoevel, who had just completed an information technology course at Capilano College, answered Curt's small ad in the classifieds and was hired on at Textworks. Peter O'Brien, a programmer with an accounting background, joined 4GL Systems. Both Textworks and 4GL Systems struggled; Western Softworks did better. Gordon wrote: "Curt turned down no jobs. He never seriously questioned whether his team had the necessary qualifications. He summed up contract programming in the phrase, 'Take the money and run.' Despite this entrepreneurial attitude there often wasn't enough work to go around. Some people quit to work for proper companies, but I stuck it out because I liked Curt."

Then Western Softworks ran into an unexpected headwind. In October 1987, Robert Maxwell, the British billionaire media baron, announced he was moving into the education industry and planned to acquire Columbia Computing (valued at $18 million). By 1988, one of Maxwell's companies owned ninety percent of it. With the shift in ownership came a shift in policy; development would be done in-house. Western Softworks was cut loose and Curt and Gordon suddenly scrambled to find work for everybody.

Gordon called up a man he met while working for Krieger Data, Haroldo Borges. He was a bright, flamboyant Brazilian. His family back home was well-to-do; half his relatives were generals, the other half communists. This made for lively family dinners, his mom desperately trying to keep the peace by steering the conversation away from politics. Haroldo was entrepreneurial, a hustler, who usually managed to negotiate favourable contracts for himself. He used to say, "Money is oxygen." When Gordon spoke to Haroldo, he was managing a project for Health Care Systems, a Vancouver company which supplied software to hospitals. Haroldo was coordinating development of a new accounting system; it was a major undertaking and Gordon thought there might be opportunities for outside contractors. Western Softworks bid to develop three modules of the system and was awarded one contract, worth about $130,000.

In the summer of 1988, Gordon began working at the client's site and soon Georg Hoevel and Peter O'Brien came to join him. "It was a project from hell," said Gordon. "The really hellish thing was that the tools (chosen by the client) didn't work. They were raw and new, really buggy. The system crashed all the time. You'd spend days of effort on something and then have to give it up or develop elaborate workarounds." The job took much longer than expected; at times Gordon wondered whether they would be able to complete anything at all. Curt successfully negotiated an additional payment on the grounds that faulty tools were to blame for the delays. Finally, in the fall of 1989, Western Softworks delivered a fixed-asset management module that was reasonably bug free. The stress and uncertainty took its toll on everyone who worked on it—even the normally ebullient Haroldo. When he found himself staring into space for long periods, unable to recollect what he had been thinking, he quit.

* * *

All this time, Curt had been thinking. Another idea was being born—probably Curt's boldest yet. I don't know exactly when or why it came to be. But I do know that on September 27, 1987, Curt wrote in the daily business journal he was keeping: "ranging and 3D digitizer for architecture." He was exploring the possibility of a system that measured an object at a distance. It would project a series of dots or stripes of light onto it, take multiple pictures of the projections and then analyze them with a computer. The result would be a scan or range image that represented the object's shape. From this you could derive measurements. Curt's first thought was that architects who were asked to renovate buildings, for which no accurate plans existed, would be able to scan them inside and out and generate drawings. He wasn't overly concerned about the market; the idea was so entrancing, he wanted to make it real regardless. Moving fingers of light would quantify the world. Curt's old interest in light was resurfacing, though for technical more than aesthetic reasons.

As the months went by, Curt made more notes and started sketching his ideas—on April 12, 1988, drawing a house caught in a V of light beams. He began involving other people—a catholic mix. He talked to Don Lawrence, an art student, who had studied illusion and built an illusion box. He consulted Doug Beder, a University of British Columbia physicist whose field was optics. He phoned Simon Fraser University and the B.C. Institute of Technology, searching for more local experts. He began wondering who would fund research. He called the B.C. Science Council and the National Research Council. He started asking questions about the Vancouver Stock Exchange. On May 14: "Which brokerage houses have a good reputation? Any?" He worried: "Wild bull markets get everyone thinking they will get rich easily so they aren't interested in operational things (design, manufacturing, marketing). We are taking a long position; we will be very illiquid for a time."

Curt discussed his ideas with Dave Sloan, bearded and professorial-looking, but a rock star among Canadian physicists. An aerospace pioneer, he was instrumental in getting MacDonald Dettwiler and Associates into the satellite business. Then, at Mobile Data International, he played a key role in creating B.C.'s wireless data industry (currently worth more than $1 billion a year). Dave Sloan said he would participate "if it was fun, if it felt good." And it did, so *he* did, at the end of 1988—a stunning coup for Curt. Next he approached Mike Ryan, the well-connected former president of the Vancouver Stock Exchange and analyst with Leith Wheeler Investment Counsel. "Jan. 24, 1989, Mike Ryan says he is interested in being chairman of a couple of companies and thinks our venture is interesting," Tall and wealthy, Mike was an éminence grise in Vancouver's business community, frequently interviewed by the local media on financial matters. Mike had invested in Columbia Computing, earning handsomely when the company was sold. This whetted his appetite for more tech investments. It also meant that Western Softworks' good reputation with Columbia's management carried some weight with Mike. Six months later, on July 4: "Mike Ryan will act as chairman." Curt's fledgling company was taking off.

Gordon wrote: "Curt dreamed up something new. He decided to become a product company; not just software products but hardware, too—electronics and stepper motors and cameras and lasers, which nobody in Western Softworks was remotely qualified to deal with. Curt wanted to do three-dimensional shape capture. When I heard about this, I thought, 'Great!' and I understood why I had stayed with him. I also thought, 'Holy shit, how are we going to do this?'"

Greg remembered the genesis vividly. In March 2011, he wrote me an email:

> I went for dinner with him (Isadora's) about this time, and he was incandescent on the general subject of range perception, and how it could be applied to such fields as architectural restoration, undersea robotics, machine vision, on and on and on and on. He was (that evening at least) about as enthusiastic and rantatious as I ever saw him. I guess he had been brewing these ideas in isolation for a few days or weeks or months, so he

was emitting them with considerable pressure.

He talked about how a ROV [remotely operated vehicle] could use range information to figure out where to grab something underwater (like a loose rope). He talked about the basic ideas of parallax and triangulation. He swatted away questions and interjections as though considering them might cause him to step off the visionary path he was on and tarnish his wonderful shiny idea.

So that evening, my girlfriend and I didn't have to say much. Just chewed and listened. Very stimulating to hear such strong ideas so well put, but also alarming in a way.

The change in Curt's focus split Western Softworks. "The sensible people decided to stick with contract programming," Gordon wrote. Curt asked Haroldo if he was interested in taking over this business. He was, and so the two, together with Georg and three other shareholders, established Western Softworks Consulting. Curt got a forty percent stake in return for handing over customers like Western Stevedoring and helping to drum up consulting business. But his real interest now lay with the alluring new Range Vision Incorporated, or RVI. Gordon joined Curt, seduced by the sweet siren song of wider possibilities.

15. The high-tech heartache blues

THE OFFICE WAS NONDESCRIPT, a second-floor walk-up in North Vancouver. The carpet was worn, the furniture basic. A resident cat prowled the warren of small rooms, lobbying for attention. The only real clue to what was happening was on the walls. They were covered with printouts: scans of people, chairs, office bric-a-brac. When Gordon returned to work at Crown Street, Curt, Dave Sloan and Dave Dieno had already put together a couple of prototype range cameras using lasers and parts salvaged from old hard drives. Now they were experimenting, playing with them—giddy with excitement about the progress they were making. Sometimes at lunch hour, they'd be in such high spirits they'd shoot each other with mouse-driven laser beams. Gordon wrote in his diary: "The technology was like a baby in 1989. The apple of our eyes, adorable, incompetent." Still, nagging doubts tugged at his mind. The scans weren't accurate, the shapes distorted. Later Gordon wrote: "We need to calibrate the system. How do we do that? Who can help us? How much money will it take?"

In the six weeks leading up to Christmas 1989, there were no paycheques, but the group wasn't worried. The money would come. Curt was driven, flying high. Mike asked a friend, Ian Adam, to invest and join the board. They raised $150,000 and Curt secured a $100,000 loan from the B.C. Advanced Systems Institute, a non-profit foundation with a mandate to help new technology companies. In 1990, Curt rented workshop space in a windowless storage area on the ground floor, and hired an expert Swiss tool and die maker, Rudy Voser, as fabrication guru. The team designed three more prototypes,

Models 3, 4 and 5. Gordon wrote: "Every couple of weeks we'd have a breakthrough and I'd yell down the stairs, "We've made scanning history again!" Curt and Gordon went on expeditions, scanning a cliff face on the Sea to Sky highway, an old mining tunnel at Britannia Beach, the stone lions in front of the Vancouver Art Gallery.

Scan of lady, 1990

Curt worked the phones, looking for companies that needed accurate measurements but found conventional ways of getting them slow, expensive or dangerous. He wasn't looking at one particular industry or type of subject. Anything would do, as long as it kept RVI afloat. In March, he heard Rick Clark, president of the Ontario company, Custom Industrial Automation (CIA), give a presentation about the mining industry. Rick said mines were looking for a convenient way to survey the excavations (called "stopes") from which they removed ore. They wanted to be sure that, when they created these large caverns, which could be four hundred feet high and many hundreds of feet long, they hit the richest seams. This piqued Curt's interest. He buttonholed Rick after the meeting and told him his company, RVI, could measure tunnels. Rick was also intrigued. CIA was just a start-up, with no customers. But if Curt's technology was as good as he said, Rick could see opportunities. The two men agreed to keep talking.

In May, Curt spoke to Bill Swindall at Highway Products. Also an Ontario company, it made road videos. These were not road movies like *Easy Rider* or *Motorcycle Diaries*, but tapes of roads, hours and hours of asphalt and concrete rolling by. Human viewers (who must have had a high tolerance for boredom) noted and located defects. Swindall wanted an illuminator to cast a very even light over the road surface and make it easier to spot cracks. He wondered if R V I could build one for him. Why not? thought Curt.

In the summer, I played a small role in another positive turn of events. Always looking for story ideas, I thought a piece about a trip on B.C. Rail might be fun. At the time, it took passengers from Vancouver to Prince George, through some of British Columbia's most breathtaking scenery. My pitch to several magazines went nowhere, but while preparing it, I learned something potentially interesting for R V I.

B.C. Rail gave me a stack of company newsletters and, in one, I read about some innovative technology, a rail-grinding machine. This heavy train inched along the track, correcting the shape of worn rails with grinding stones. An iron behemoth that spewed showers of sparks, it often ignited fires along the wayside in hot weather. Nevertheless, it extended the life of rails and improved the ride and safety of trains. Since careful measurements were needed to determine where and how to grind, I passed the article on to Curt. When he developed a range camera, he didn't have railroads in mind. But never a slouch about following leads, he phoned Doug Allen at B.C. Rail's engineering department on July 11, and took notes about how rails develop washboard or corrugation—one of the deformities grinders correct. On July 15, Curt optimistically sketched a scanner that could measure the shape of rails. Then he didn't know about the slow sales cycle endemic to the industry. Railroads, even relatively small ones like B.C. Rail, were ponderous. Decisions to buy—especially new technology—could take years.

Because Curt still didn't have a solid order, he had to keep all his prospects alive. On July 17, he wrote: "Rick Clark, still hot, Falconbridge, Inco, Noranda." Later that summer, Curt flew to Sudbury with a range camera and met Rick at Inco. They donned hard hats, headlamps, boots and protective suits. With a guide, they descended about 3,500 feet down a mineshaft into a dimly lit stope. Curt was intending to scan it, but ran into an unexpected problem. The range camera needed 110-volt power, but there were no wall sockets 3,500 feet underground! "No problem," said their guide, who produced a portable generator. Rick later said, "It delivered an unknown amount of power at an unknown speed. When Curt plugged it in, he toasted the camera. It went up in smoke. Only a small inexpensive part, a serial card, was blown, but the demonstration was aborted. Remarkably, Rick was still convinced Curt's device had potential.

In August, Curt took RVI's first order from Highway Products, for a road illuminator. Though it wasn't what he set out to build, by this time Curt was thinking, "A sale is a sale." RVI was surviving on loans: one for $50,000 from Western Softworks, Curt's old company, a $40,000 grant from the federal Industrial Research Assistance Program, another $100,000 grant from the B.C. Science Council and a trickle of private investment. On Remembrance Day, Gordon wrote in his diary: "The company has a lot going for it. But it's spread too thin—too many projects, too few resources, too little money. A lot of interest from potential customers, considering the small effort that's been made to entice them. What will happen? The company doesn't feel doomed (yet I often fear its demise). Curt is inspired. A lot of brilliant ideas are being born. We are incredibly loose, yet we seem to make progress." When Gordon grew anxious about falling behind schedule, Curt said to him, "Forget the project plan!"

By the end of November, Curt's relationship with Rick Clark showed new promise. Rick discovered another application for which Curt's cameras might be ideally suited— the inspection of coking drums. Oil refineries use these large vessels to extract coke from petroleum distillates. Over time, the drums develop bulges in their walls, often six or seven inches deep, and associated with dangerous cracks. If the cracks are not repaired, the oil can leak and cause fires or explosions—hence the need for periodic inspection. Curt described the drums in his journal: "Colour rusty steel, some flat black carbon deposits (dirt); pitch black inside; 26 feet diameter, 65 feet high and one 3-foot manhole in top center; atmosphere is air, no dust, occasional steam, humidity high after steam cleaning; hand portability necessary, go up catwalk and lower down; inspect sides only, no top or bottom." The vessels were toxic, but the only way the refinery could check them was to send a crew in. While breathing poisonous fumes, the inspectors erected scaffolding, climbed it and looked for bulges using straight edges and rulers. Although they worked around the clock, the drum was out of service for about a week, a long and expensive hiatus.

Dan Torres, at Atlantic Richfield's (ARCO) refinery in Cherry Point, Washington asked Rick if CIA could come up with a better way. After reviewing half a dozen technologies, Rick concluded the best solution was to lower an R V I camera into the tank. No one would be exposed to toxic chemicals, and the job would be finished in a matter of hours, not days. Curt had no experience with coking drums, but he was adaptable. The drums were an easier target than the underground caverns he and Rick had been considering. They were much smaller and their shape was a standard cylinder. Curt told Rick that, if A R C O wanted C I A to do an inspection, he could deliver a camera.

At the end of 1990, Curt relocated the company to a new five-thousand-square-foot building on Graveley Street in Burnaby. There was no longer a resident cat, but much more space. Here the team developed Curt's favourite instrument, the Model 6, a close-range, three-dimensional scanner based on slide projector technology. Gordon wrote that it "produced beautiful scans, smooth as butter." Unfortunately, the projector bulb would burn out after a couple of days of use, so Gordon suggested putting a strobe lamp in it. It would be much brighter and last a long time. But the strobe lamp made a noise. Gordon wrote: "It went pop-pop-pop. A strobe flash is an arc of electrons, like a miniature lightning bolt. Curt hated the idea of putting a strobe in the Model 6. He said, 'It would be like taking a can of spray paint and writing *Shit* all over it.' He loved the quiet light of the Model 6." This was Curt, more artistic director than businessman. I was reminded of a comment from his friend, the poet Jamie Reid, "In the final analysis, Curt's motivating force was aesthetic. Whatever he undertook, he wanted beauty to be implicated in it in some way. That's what made him interesting. He pursued it not on a superficial level and not in the way that anybody else would."

Early in 1991, Curt, who had been phoning B.C. Rail off and on for about six months without results, got lucky. On March 27, he wrote: "Norm Hooper, starting as new maintenance manager. Sounded enthused about *Rangecam*." Though the railroad could extend the life of the rail by using a rail grinder, eventually worn rail had to be replaced. Norm was sure B.C. Rail could save money by doing this in a more rational way. In those days, maintenance personnel walked the track, measuring wear with hand tools, a time consuming and subjective process. Since it cost the railroad a quarter million dollars to replace each mile of rail, Norm thought such a valuable asset should be managed more scientifically.

A capable man who became chief engineer at B.C. Rail in 1998, Norm now runs his own consulting company. We spoke recently on Skype while he was on holidays; palm trees swayed in the sun behind him as we talked. He said, "My sense was, we weren't really sure, when we were changing rail out, whether we got the full life out of it. If we measured all this stuff, we could get ahead of the curve, wear the rail longer and tell management what we needed and when we needed it." Norm believed Range Vision's technology could give him the information he wanted. Two cameras (one for each rail), mounted on a vehicle travelling up and down the track, would provide more consistent measurements, more quickly, than human beings with manual instruments. "I had a strong feeling," Norm said, "the equipment would pay for itself rapidly."

Norm remembered Curt as "a visionary who talked the big picture." And he liked the team Curt had assembled. "Mostly what they needed was cash and somebody to take a risk on them." Norm had seen competing systems; Canadian National Railway used one called Orian, but Norm wanted more accuracy than it provided. Since Range Vision was local, he could work with it to get exactly what he needed. He decided to push for the purchase.

Despite these encouraging developments, Mike was growing unhappy with Curt as president. He told me, "A high-tech start-up has to have a president who is able to convince people with money that it's worth investing in it. Curt was useless at that, to the point where you had to stop taking him to investor meetings. He offended the investment people badly. We were turned down by everybody in town. One of them phoned me and said, 'Mike you've got to get a new president. No way you're going to get any money.' Because they saw in Curt this wild-eyed promoter with no idea where he was going. Didn't even understand what the words 'business plan' meant." I thought Mike was being unjust (although I freely admit to bias). After all, Curt had managed to get *Mike* to invest, so he had some ability on that score. I think Mike didn't understand how difficult it was to make plans and projections while creating new technology. When I told Gordon what Mike said, he responded grumpily, "Some people should stick to investing in floor wax companies."

Mike began searching for a new president. At the steam room at his club, he mentioned his quest to an acquaintance Ron Stanford who said, "I might be interested in something like that." Ron had sold his family business, West Coast Woollen Mills, to Joseph Segal's company, Mr. Jax, and was looking for something else. He had many qualities Curt lacked. He was well-dressed, suave, affable—he knew his way around

Vancouver's best restaurants. He didn't have Curt's passion and imagination, but was part of Mike's social circle and comfortable with persuading people to invest. I am pretty sure he had never been penniless at the side of the road somewhere in Europe, hoping his luck might turn.

The board—Mike, Ian, Curt, Gordon and Dave Sloan—discussed the new appointment. Dave expressed skepticism about Ron's qualifications—he wasn't technical enough. But Curt did not stand in Mike's way. If Ron was a better public face for RVI, Curt was for it. He saw no sense in hanging on to power for its own sake. But Dave was right that a background in tartans (West Coast Woollen Mills' speciality) was a poor preparation for RVI. So while Ron took over as president, Curt stayed on as senior vice-president of product development. He would help Ron, compensate for the gaps in his understanding.

By June 1991, Range Vision's burn rate had increased. It had an administrator, Peter Adams, as well as more help on the hardware side: Barry Rowland, a protégé of Dave Sloan's; Scott Roberts, a young mechanical engineer; and Doug Kirk, an electronics technician. Caught in a cash crunch, RVI missed its mid-month payroll. When Doug asked Gordon for money, he shook his head. Later he wondered whether he should have given him the $20 he had in his wallet, whether that might have helped. On June 18, Range Vision got the news that a purchase order from B.C. Rail was imminent. Gordon was elated. Ron shook his hand. But on June 21, there was still no money. Gordon worried that people would quit at this crucial juncture. On Monday, June 24, he put the arm on Ron for an infusion of cash. Ron waffled, then agreed in principle and went for lunch. When he came back, he was resolved to invest, provided he got a commitment from Mike for enough capital to make the company fly. He met Mike two days later, and cheques were distributed. Gordon wrote: "Everyone felt better, except possibly Ron."

On Thursday, June 27, the B.C. Rail purchase order (for a system priced at $249,900) crackled through the fax machine. This was good, but Curt was feeling the accumulated pressure of the last couple of years, the long hours, no weekends and never, ever enough money. They'd raised a million dollars so far, and they were still on the brink. He had been trying to hold it all together, telling everyone this was breakthrough technology, that it would dramatically reduce costs for many businesses. But people were losing heart. Dave Dieno quit, went over to Haroldo at Softworks.

Ruth wanted Curt to take a holiday:

> He pushed to the limit. I told him he needed more balance. He said when the business was going we would have lots of time for holidays. It was always later, later. I wanted to have fun now and I knew Curt was capable of it. But he said, "I want to build something that lasts." He knew he was getting older. Time was running out. He was obsessed. That's how he was. When he was fishing, he would fish night and day. He wouldn't sleep for a week. And then he would come home to his house in Strathcona and sleep for days.

Ruth began telling Curt that she felt lonely, that he wasn't there for her. He asked, "What do you mean, I'm not there for you? We sleep together, we eat together, I'm here for you." And she couldn't explain why that wasn't enough. They were starting to think about separating.

To fill the order from B.C. Rail, Range Vision had to stretch, do things it had never done before. Norm wanted to tow the range cameras behind a Chevy Suburban hy-rail—a hybrid vehicle adapted to track and road. RVI had to build a trailer on which the cameras could be mounted. The system needed to record the exact locations of 1,200 pairs of rail profiles per mile, in mountains and mudflats, along the entire 1,821 miles of B.C. Rail's line. It had to store a vast amount of data, digest it and produce usable reports that busy engineers could read quickly. And then there was Norm Hooper's demand that the system be accurate to within a thousandth of an inch. He wanted to verify that the rail grinder did its job properly and brought the rail to within a thousandth of an inch of the ideal shape. This was a challenge. The cameras weren't operating in a pristine lab. They had to contend with dirt, mud, rail grease, snow, frost, ballast (gravel) between the rails that sometimes piled up, obscuring the view, and sunshine, reflected from mirror-like rails, strong enough to blind the system. And the cameras were always moving, at speeds of up to thirty miles an hour.

When Curt started RVI, he didn't know his company would have to become expert in metrology, the science of measurement, which no one at RVI had studied. Developing this arcane knowledge required a lot of experimentation, plus, said Gordon, "an anal-retentive fixation on accuracy." All sorts of things could interfere with accurate measurements—the world eluded definition. The RVI team had to learn about laser speckle—interference patterns that distorted reflected laser light. One day, Dave Sloan announced "We have been naïve about cameras lenses." He discovered that even the most expensive cameras were plagued by slight distortions from true. If you photograph a rectangle, you will *see* a box with straight lines in the picture. But in fact, the lines in the photo have a wow in them—ever so minor. In photography this doesn't matter, but RVI could not ignore it when the aim was one thousandth of an inch accuracy.

Railway tracks, Prince Rupert, 1972   PHOTOGRAPHER: CURT LANG

How can you accurately measure something with a camera that is itself inaccurate? You have to measure its inaccuracy and then compensate. The team converged on the idea of "doing it in software." This involved taking several pictures of a special target, printed with four hundred dots, mounted on a granite slab (for stability). Using sophisticated software RVI had developed, the computer could analyze the pictures and determine the exact location of the dots, while characterizing the lens distortion. The method was computationally heavy; it took all night to crunch the numbers and calibrate the camera, but it worked well. And temperamentally, it suited Curt—solving for all those unknowns, seeing what you can do by yourself, from first principles, with a minimum of information supplied.

After B.C. Rail placed its order, RVI immersed itself in the universe of trains and railroaders—its language and culture. Gordon said, "It was a very big subject." Curt sketched rails, and labelled their parts—field face, head, gauge corner, flange, web, base. He learned how locomotives sometimes spin their wheels and melt the rail head, how rails develop corrugation and how curves affect rail wear. The team learned that on the railroad, a mile is not a mile. The railroad may take out a bend, reducing the distance between Milepost 90 and Milepost 100 to less than 10 miles. Mileposts, which didn't measure real distances but nominal ones, were a source of major headaches, because it was so important to pinpoint the exact site of rail wear.

Curt searched for other railroad prospects. Canadian Pacific Railway, Norfolk Southern and CSX seemed interested and, among suppliers to railroads, there were Sperry Rail Service, Loram Maintenance of Way and Pandrol Track Systems.

Though all of this was good news, Mike and Ian insisted the railroads were a niche market that wouldn't give them a big-enough payback. They wanted to add other applications. Curt had something up his sleeve. In November 1990, he had written in his diary: "Model makers and pattern makers could be buyers of a range camera for reverse engineering. They could build a model by hand, then scan it and make a data version." A car designer at General Motors (G.M.) told Curt that he first produced a clay model, then measured it and created an electronic "blueprint" or CAD (computer-aided design) model. But this process was laborious. Curt wrote: "A big problem is refitting local changes to the CAD model; 'merging is biggest pain in ass.'"

In November 1991, Gordon, Curt and Ron took the Model 6, to the General Motors Research and Development Center in Warren, Michigan. They were hoping to prove Curt's intuition that model makers might find a range camera useful. So here they were inside the brain of the many-tentacled beast, then the world's largest automobile maker, with yearly sales of more than a hundred billion dollars and more than three hundred thousand employees. Not only the maker of cars and trucks, G.M.'s reach extended to telecommunications, aerospace, defence, finance and insurance services. In its technical centre, people invented the future, creating technologies to keep the company thriving for decades to come. Curt and Gordon set up in a lecture theatre surrounded by lawns, trees and reflecting pools, more like a university campus than the grounds of a corporation. Forty engineers were assembling for the demonstration. Many had flown in from G.M. facilities scattered across North America and the room buzzed with greetings. While the engineers settled, Gordon hooked up cables, linking the various parts of the device. However, what should have been routine and easy, was not. The instrument was infuriatingly inert. Its only activity was the error message on the monitor. Gordon wiggled connectors, trying to bring it to life.

Curt stood up to speak without letting on that anything was amiss. But he was thinking, "Yeah, right Curt, here you are talking to a roomful of G.M. engineers about range cameras." These were the elite of the elite, with PhDs, scholarly papers and years of research behind them. Watching Gordon with that stricken look on his face, fiddling with the machine, what could Curt do? Drag things out, delay the moment of truth. Curt could converse with almost anybody about practically any topic. Presented with a theme, he could riff on it like a jazz player. So that's what he did—he went on and on about the company and the history of its innovation.

Gordon really didn't know what was wrong with the machine. Haunted by the thought that he would have to stand up and admit to technical difficulties, he nervously tweaked this and tightened that. Then, without any warning, the camera shutter started going at its top speed of seven frames per second. It was alive—and out of control. "If I shut everything down and reboot…" Gordon wondered. He held his breath. It worked.

The instrument was glowing quietly and ready to go. Curt concluded his speech without missing a beat. He didn't act relieved. That frantic activity was just the way they did things. Stripes of light passed over three objects in succession: a flat, white metal plate, a rounded automobile part and a target Curt contrived to show the system's ability to resolve the thickness of a single piece of paper. The data was lovely, smooth, gapless. Curt relaxed. He looked around the room, taking in the approval. It was amazing what an underfunded band of fifteen dedicated people could do with a little ingenuity. He had skated back from the edge.

Dr. Paul Besl, one of G.M.'s leading researchers, promised to test the data and forward the results to Vancouver. A few days later, Gordon took his call. He invited Gordon to call all the G.M. groups who were holding off ordering until he, Paul Besl, had seen the data. He said to tell them it was good. When Curt heard that his baby, the Model 6, had wowed them in Detroit, he was pleased that his faith was validated. The technology was performing. But the business was not. In July 1992, Gordon forestalled another late payroll by pleading for money from Mike.

In August, Ruth left Curt. Their differences had deepened—particularly on the subject of children. Ruth explained:

> When we first got married, Curt said, "I don't want children." I was twenty-four, and that was fine. I didn't want children either. But when I was thirty, I really wanted to have children. I had all sorts of tests, even a laparoscopy. Everything was normal. The doctors said we should just have sex more often. I started to watch my cycle. Curt didn't like the pressure. He wouldn't have any tests. He just wouldn't. He said, "This is your thing." And when I suggested an adoption, he was adamant: "I don't want to raise another man's child."

So Ruth moved out to the Fraser Valley to establish a nursery business and Curt bought a condominium in North Vancouver. Ruth tried to keep their relationship friendly. She said to me, "I would call him about every two weeks. He never called me." Curt was still pouring everything into RVI.

At the end of the summer, CIA ordered a coking drum inspection system, a sale Curt had been nurturing for two years. Without his enthusiasm and persistence, it wouldn't have happened. Nevertheless, Mike was dissatisfied. He blamed Ron because the company wasn't turning a profit and began searching for a new president—again. This time he looked further afield than his club's steam room and found Don Wilkie, an executive with Xerox for twenty-two years. Don took over in October, supported by *two* former-president vice-presidents. Ron stayed in charge of marketing, and Curt directed product development.

You could hardly imagine a person more different from Curt than Don. Curt compared leading Range Vision to guiding a polar expedition, a small group trudging forward in the teeth of the gale, never sure whether the ice would hold. And every so often he would look around and see one of his snow-blind men wandering off in the wrong direction. Curt accepted risk. It was his element. It was not, however, Don's. He even declined to serve on the board, because that would expose him to personal liability.

One of Don's first moves was to rent additional space (for $1,800 a month) across the street for the executives. He'd just arrived at RVI and he was already setting himself apart. The rest of the RVI staff took to calling the new place "World Headquarters" and Curt spent little time there. Don also retreated from the company's lifeblood—its customers. Gordon recalled, "I was talking to Don and he had a question for Ron who was in his office with a client. Don ignored the customer, asked his question and left without introducing himself. I was shocked." Don drew up charts that showed how the company should be organized when it grew. They showed five vice-presidents and three administrative assistants reporting directly to him. But he had no idea how to run a start-up or how to make it flourish. Gordon was sure Don was a disastrous choice and had lunch with Mike to tell him so. Mike didn't do anything, but Gordon felt he had planted a seed.

In December 1992, the B.C. Rail system passed its acceptance tests—a year and a half after the order was placed. The investors had no idea it would take so long. Ian said to Gordon, "We thought all you had to do was slap a coat of paint on it." However, now that the B.C. Rail system was finally running, RVI could sell more of the same. And indeed that month, Sperry ordered a copy.

In May 1993, CIA got its scanner and used it for the first time at ARCO's Cherry Point refinery. It completed the inspection in a few hours, a vast improvement over the week needed for manual inspection. RVI's range camera turned out to be an elegant solution to the oil refinery's problem. Using it, Rick Clark eventually built a very successful drum inspection business. He said, "If I hadn't met Curt, I probably wouldn't have been aware of what a range camera could do. It wasn't well publicized outside of British Columbia. Twenty years later, we still believe that this technique is the best one, and it all came about because of Curt."

In June 1993, Sperry got its delivery; production was speeding up a little. In July 1993, Norm Hooper published a complimentary article about Range Vision in the trade journal *Railway Track and Structures*. He told me that not replacing rail that wasn't worn out "saved us a fortune." He also "found a bunch of stuff that actually makes your hair go white." This was bad rail that the hand inspections had missed, so weak from wear that it could derail a train. He said, "The investment was paid for in the first year, probably five times over." Don hired a sales manager, Gareth Jones, an Englishman who had worked at Apple Canada. Despite this positive activity, for six months there were no new orders. A June 1993 business plan blue-skyed sales of seventy units in 1996, and projected revenues of $16 million. But in the short run, RVI was staring down a long empty pipe.

RVI on track, 1993   PHOTOGRAPHER: NORM HOOPER

Curt didn't know what to do. He was marginalized in his own company—Mike no longer respected him. Years later, I could hear the contempt in Mike's voice when he said, "That was totally lacking in Curt, the ability to get something done and be organized, pursue a goal and stop flannelling around, chasing every dream that passed his desk." And Don? A crabbed man with no vision. He was the kind of boss Curt would have walked out on years ago. Curt's friend, the sculptor David Marshall, remembered when Curt was welding a pipeline, "It was hot midsummer, really miserable working there welding upside down and everything. Curt had had enough and he wanted to get out. And this boss came along and said something about Lang had to be more productive. And Curt thought, 'Now how do I articulate this, so this man will understand?' He looked at the guy and said, 'I ain't gonna.'" Saying, "I ain't gonna" wasn't an option now. He'd invested so much time, energy and love in Range Vision, although Curt probably wouldn't have used the word "love." But he did love the technology—the beauty of it, fingers of light quietly moving across surfaces, measuring, detecting tiny imperfections invisible to the human eye. Don and Mike didn't care about the technology the same way; for them it was only a vehicle for making money. And now they were in charge. They could do with it what they wanted—maul it, sully it in ways that turned Curt's stomach. He took to playing *Castle Wolfenstein*, a video game in which the object is to move through different levels of a castle, kill Nazis, find the secret war plans and escape alive. It was his way of saying, "I ain't gonna." Or maybe he was trying to figure out how to get out alive.

Curt started to distance himself from Range Vision. It still owed Western Softworks about $28,000 and Curt had been receiving payments in dribs and drabs. But suddenly he wanted it all back immediately and decided to take legal action to get it. He couldn't be on the company's board and sue at the same time. Therefore, on September 1, he resigned as director, although in his letter, he made a point of saying that he was not stepping down from his position as senior vice-president. On September 2, he served a garnishing order to RVI at its lawyer's office.

Shortly after that, Don fired Curt. By stepping down from the board, Curt had relinquished his power. Don announced the fact at a weekly project meeting, saying to the group, "Curt was out of control." Gordon remembers Don saying to him, "You and I will get along just fine." But Gordon told me, "From then on, he was my enemy."

Although Gordon and Curt no longer saw each other at work, we often had dinner together. I remember answering the doorbell when Curt arrived; he'd be standing on the front porch with two bottles of wine, one in each hand, and grinning broadly. Then he'd head straight for the kitchen to see what we were cooking. Despite all that had happened, the trouble with Ruth and the trouble with the business, he was surprisingly cheerful. You never had to worry about awkward silences when Curt was around. One evening he came over and, by chance, an elderly American friend was also having dinner with us. I wondered what they could possibly find to talk about, they were so very different. I needn't have given it a moment's thought. Our other guest was from Indiana and a history buff. It turned out that Curt knew quite a bit about the founding of her state. As they chatted happily, I was astonished.

When we went to Curt's place, he usually cooked fish. He was fussy about where he bought it and how it was prepared. As Rick Clark said later, "He was a purist in many ways." We'd bring our children, Tom and Talia, and he'd ask, "How are the short people?" When they quarrelled about who got to sit on one particular square foam cushion they coveted, Curt shook his head disapprovingly. But he often rented movies for them, a treat, since we didn't have a T.V. We usually stayed long past their bedtime and they'd be fast asleep when we drove home.

Gordon and Curt, circa 1993   PHOTOGRAPHER: CLAUDIA CORNWALL

On those evenings, we talked about the book I was writing, the stories I was learning about my grandparents—what it was like for them to live in Austria in a time of madness before and during the Second World War. We talked about the book Curt was writing with Jeff Chow, his friend and colleague from the Software Store and Evergreen Technology. We talked about a renovation we were planning. He had ideas about how to simplify it and I could see why "Cut the scope" was one of his business maxims. Sometimes we talked about the kids—problems we were having with Tom, his unhappiness at school. Though Curt didn't have children, he took the responsibilities of fatherhood seriously. Ruth had told me, "Once at a party, the daughter of an artist approached

Curt. She said, 'Oh, you know my father.' He said, 'Yes, I know your father.' She said, 'If you see him or speak to him, please tell him I want to see him.' Curt couldn't understand why anyone would behave this way with his own children."

Of course, R V I was always a running theme in our conversation. Curt wanted to know what the latest problems were and proffered solutions. I was amazed to discover that he thought Mike would somehow pull the rabbit out of the hat and make the company go, even with Don Wilkie as president. "He's got a plan," Curt said. By that time, I was skeptical. But Curt declined to criticize Mike. I felt like shaking him, like he was in some kind of unseeing torpor. I said, "You are too much of a gentleman, Curt." He was taken aback. It was the only time I ever insulted him.

In March 1994, Gordon invited Mike to lunch again, to express concern about Don Wilkie—his third attempt. At last, Mike acted. He fired Don, and promoted Gareth Jones. Gareth, R V I's fourth president, at least had talent with customers. In May 1994, Advanced Rail Management ordered a system and, in December, Los Angeles Transit and the Hungarian State Railways ordered as well. At the end of March 1995, annual sales totalled $1.1 million and there was a net loss of $150,000. It was R V I's best year and Gordon was buoyed by the performance. But soon the company was poised over the abyss—again. There were no new orders. Gordon wrote: "R V I seems to be going down the tubes." In August, he went to Budapest to install a system for the Hungarian State Railways, but in September, he quit, convinced R V I had no future. He took to singing, "I got them high-tech heartache bluuuuuuuuuuues."

In October, Gordon joined Haroldo's company. It was now called Softworks Consulting, and Curt was no longer involved, having sold his shares to Haroldo. Once again, Gordon was a contract programmer. It felt like defeat.

16, I am I

THIS IS WHERE IT HAPPENED in the spring of 1997—in the office Gordon and I share at home. Curt was really at the top of his game then, starting something, fighting, negotiating, thinking hard. Earlier, I felt he was slumbering, but he'd shaken that off. He reminded me of Odysseus, coming back to Ithaka, killing his wife's suitors who had been plundering his estate. "You yellow dogs, you thought I'd never make it home from the land of Troy," the old warrior shouted. That was Curt, come back to seize his technology.

On an afternoon in early April, Curt and Gordon went for a walk. They ended up in our office, scribbling notes on the whiteboard. Ideas about strategy. How to do it right this time. Stay in control. The white board is still on the wall behind me. But it is blank now. Faceless.

That April afternoon, the sun streamed in through the sliding glass door, warm and bright. Curt was combative and forceful, telling stories. He was like Odysseus in that, too. Homer called Odysseus "skilled in all ways of contending," but also said he was "the teller of many stories." That can be a way of contending, too.

Curt recounted how he had lunch with a family of Spanish grandees, the relatives of two brothers to whom he had taught English. He described how surprised he was when these seemingly dignified old men started a bread fight over lunch. He thought they did this to make him feel less constrained, more at ease. He drank too much wine and went shooting with the grandees afterwards. I imagined them as thin and white-haired, odd-looking gentlemen with goatees, wearing black. Decadent, immature aristocrats. I don't know if Curt gave any physical description of them. They walked through fields to a stone tower on that hot Spanish afternoon. A servant ran ahead and banged on the tower's iron door. A flock of pigeons burst from openings in the top of the tower and swooped around in wild, loopy patterns. Curt shot two of them. Later he found out that the grandees had ordered their servant to clip the wings of the birds so that they would fly in crazy ways. It was unusual to hit two, the grandees said. The story was entertaining; perhaps more important, it also served as a reminder that Curt could sometimes nail the nearly impossible. Could he do it again?

After being forced out of RVI, Curt kept innovating. He and Jeff Chow published their book *Data Base Publishing on the Web and Intranets*. Curt revived his old interest in boat building by modifying a canoe in a couple of original ways. Once he gave it long, scull-like paddles. Another time, he turned it into a pedal canoe that whipped across the water. Curt demonstrated its speed when we were out with him in Vancouver harbour, Gordon and I in a conventional canoe, and he in his pedal canoe. When a young man in a nearby kayak challenged him to a race, Curt said calmly, "I'll win, of course." The young man wasn't deterred, but Curt knew his craft. To the chagrin of the kayaker, Curt beat him easily.

Curt in pedal boat, 1997   PHOTOGRAPHER UNKNOWN

Curt also struck up a friendship with a Russian woman, Irina Borisova, who lived in St. Petersburg. She was a writer, a matchmaker and a boiler-room operator. She wrote me recently in an email: "Many St.P writers worked as gas boiler operators in St.P as it was possible just to stay there and do what you want (write of course), and monitor the boiler, not much work (if any) in reality, but an average wage was paid, not so bad in 90-ies." Irina maintained a website for Western men seeking wives in Russia and posted a story there in English about her experiences as a matchmaker. An email friend of Curt's forwarded it to him and, he liked it so much that he emailed Irina and encouraged her to write more. He offered to edit her stories and act as her literary agent.

However, Curt never lost sight of RVI. If there was a way for him to get it back, he would find it. By March 1997, it was in its death throes. Each of the three presidents Mike Ryan had appointed after Curt was to echo Tolstoy, "unhappy in his own way." Now the company was down to two employees and Mike was giving up. He wanted to sell it. The decline of RVI was not only a hit to Mike's pocketbook, but also a knock on his reputation for picking winners. It was an embarrassment that he wanted to put behind him as quickly as possible. And though Curt was the founder of RVI, Mike felt no special obligation to him. His intention was to get as much money as possible for it from anyone who was interested. At the very least, he wanted to pay himself and Ian back for their loans.

At CIA, Rick Clark, who bought a coking drum inspection system from Range Vision, seemed surprisingly keen on acquiring the company. Gordon wrote that he was "sniffing around, talking to Mike, trying to figure out how he could get it all." Curt's relationship with Rick had been mutually beneficial in the past. But the idea that Rick would own his invention was like salt in a wound.

Bob James was one of the two remaining employees. A brilliant programmer, he stayed with Range Vision for seven years, developing and refining the software. Taciturn and reserved, he poured his soul into writing code, achieving a standard of clarity rare in the software industry. To him its technological promise was sweet. But he was deeply angry and bitter because he thought his efforts had been wasted. The management of the company had squandered them. If something could be pulled from the ashes, that would give him satisfaction.

Gordon kept talking to Curt, who was hammering out his plans to rescue the technology. But he didn't know whether to join Curt's new venture or not. He had been working for Haroldo at Softworks Consulting for the last year and a half. The experience was an unhappy one; it left him subject to depression and anxiety. He wasn't sure whether he was up for another big gamble.

When I first met Haroldo, he was charming and amiable, expressive in an agreeably Latin way, a lively raconteur. Running his own company brought out another side. At the time Gordon joined Softworks, fifteen contractors worked there. Then one of them, Richard Macdonald, who was heading up a team on a project for Canadian Airlines, decided he no longer needed Haroldo. He staged a palace coup—seceded, took his group with him and started a new company, AeroInfo Systems. It captured Canadian Airlines as a customer and with it, three-quarters of Softworks's revenues. Haroldo rode his remaining contractors hard, scrounged for more work and tried to establish a branch office in Seattle. He said things like, "Success is the only option."

Meanwhile Gordon's project at Softworks was behind schedule. The look and feel of the program he was developing gave him trouble and his decision to support languages other than English in the user interface cost more time than it should have. So he went to Haroldo to discuss these issues. He'd been working hard, felt tired and undermined by grumbling co-workers; he was emotionally vulnerable. Somehow Curt came up in the conversation. Haroldo said, "I don't want to hear *any* comparison between Softworks Consulting and the *old* Western Softworks. Curt wasn't good at making money, he wasn't a success." He went on and on in this vein, badgering Gordon to agree that he, Haroldo, was a better businessman. Finally Gordon conceded the point, but left the office feeling as though he had betrayed Curt. Afterwards, he thought he should have thrown his keys on the desk and told Haroldo to go fuck himself. More recently, Gordon said, "That meeting wasn't about solving any problems, it was all about stroking Haroldo's ego."

Gordon knew he had to get out. And in 1997, on the Ides of March, he quit, undecided about what to do next. "Fear has an unholy grip on me. I feel like I'm in a fog," he wrote late that month. Going with Curt was clearly risky and Gordon wasn't sure whether he was up for more uncertainty. "Is Curt going to succeed? Is he going to get anything off the ground?" he asked in his diary. And he asked me, "What happens if this fails? Then my heart would be really broken."

And there was me, looking to my past, too, mining it for guidance, for insights. I was urging Gordon to join Curt. I talked about my grandfather, who at fifty-seven, fled Nazi

Germany and got a new job in Shanghai. I talked about my parents who came to Canada on a visitor's visa after the Second World War. When it expired, the immigration department issued a deportation order. My parents managed to have it stayed temporarily and then started a business with the threat of expulsion hanging over their heads. I told Gordon I wouldn't be alive if my family hadn't taken risks.

Curt decided to make an offer for Range Vision's intellectual property, the code and engineering drawings, not the company. He considered taking over the business. But it wasn't an attractive proposition. Because it already had shareholders, they would have a claim on any gains the company made under Curt's leadership. New investors would have to share with them. This was probably unappealing enough to deter anyone from coming on board. Curt's early discussions with Mike about getting the intellectual property were cantankerous and angry, and he worried that Rick was getting the upper hand.

Then Curt thought of something that could tilt the negotiations in his favour. In Range Vision's dying days, Gareth, the president, had taken an order from Rick and a $45,000 down payment. Though Range Vision started to build a second drum inspection system, it never finished it. Mike felt he owed Rick an instrument or, at least, his money back. But that $45,000 was long gone and Mike had no way of completing the delivery. If Curt offered to do it for the balance owing, it would get Mike out of a jam. At the same time, it might remove one of Rick's reasons for wanting to buy Range Vision. If he got the equipment he needed, would he really want the headache of another company?

Everyone would get something if Curt started a new business. It was all win-win. Bob and Gordon agreed to be his partners with substantial share holdings. On April 4, 1997, Curt, Gordon, Bob, Mike and Ian had a meeting and more or less reached a deal. By noon, it was down to bargaining over a percentage point. Curt was getting a licence to use Range Vision's intellectual property in exchange for a royalty on all product sales for three years. Curt called his new business Industrial Metrics Incorporated or IMI. When you said "IMI," it sounded like "I am I." Curt told Gordon, "This will be my last company." Later we wondered whether he had a premonition of what was coming.

Curt had one order in the bag—finishing the system for CIA. There was also a possibility of another coming from Advanced Rail Management. It wasn't a lot, but it was enough. More sales dribbled in, first, some maintenance and repair on the systems RVI had sold. Then Gordon closed a sale for software upgrades with B.C. Rail and Advanced

Rail. Curt, however, did not think that railroads would sustain the company in the long run. There were too few players. He wanted to make a range camera for manufacturing inspection—a much larger market. Companies that forged or cast precision parts often found measuring them slow and difficult. After making a number of phone calls, Curt found that makers of turbines, fuselages, engine blocks and the nozzles on jet planes were receptive to his ideas.

In August, he took a trip down the west coast of the United States to visit manufacturers in the aerospace industry. He wanted to identify prospects and determine exactly what kind of scanner would be useful for them. Last time round, he had a technology that was chasing customers. This time, he was going to find the market first. He came home with a long list of contacts, tapes of his interviews with them and even a trio of potential investors in Los Angeles who had been involved with rapid three-dimensional prototyping—manufacturing directly from CAD models.

In October, Jeff Chow joined IMI. "So now our strength has increased by one third!" Gordon wrote cheerfully. He liked Jeff; he was good humoured and sensible. Jeff also had more experience with electronics than either he or Bob did, so was a valuable addition. In January 1998, Gordon wrote: "This has been a very good year." By April, the IMI partners raised $110,000 from their friends and family, and added $50,000 of their own money, to get the venture off the ground. They began talking in earnest with angel investors, who could put more money into the idea.

On the Labour Day weekend, Gordon and I went canoeing in Desolation Sound with our children, Tom and Talia. On September 4, I wrote in my diary:

> Okeover Inlet, Cochrane Bay. This is clearly the site of an Indian midden. In the forest behind us are mounds of dirt mixed with shells. The forest was noisy last night. Trees creaked. There were bustlings and rustlings of creatures. Leaves moving in the wind. A great sighing above us. A breathing world. The water lapping, and gently rolling stones. A place hugely alive with its own purpose. I feel we have once again entered that magical zone that I only know through canoeing on the coast. I feel the world has embraced me.

That Labour Day weekend, Curt didn't take a holiday. He stayed in the office, working with Fred Kaufman, a consultant who was helping him with a patent application that would be the foundation of the new company. Fred was painstakingly careful, detail-minded. Though normally Curt would be quite prepared to answer Fred's questions at length, this day was different somehow. Exasperated, he said, "I'm feeling stretched beyond my limit and I think we should end this meeting now," he said emphatically. In the afternoon, he worked by himself on developing the arguments for the patent application. He felt better, calmer, although he had a headache. That evening he went to old friends for dinner, Tod and Fumiko Greenaway.

Tod Greenaway and Curt, circa 1970   PHOTOGRAPHER: FRED DOUGLAS

Driving home towards North Vancouver, Curt started to see double. This had never happened to him before. He pulled over to the side of the road for a moment, and the disconcerting illusion went away. When he started to drive again, however, his vision separated for the second time. The white lines on the road were veering off in different directions; the oncoming traffic seemed to be heading towards him from all sides. Then Curt figured out that if he closed one eye, the sensory confusion stopped. He drove across the Second Narrows Bridge towards the mountains. The next day, he checked himself into Lion's Gate Hospital.

On Monday, September 7, Gordon and Jeff were working in the office. Curt called and asked to be put on the speaker phone. He said he'd just learned he had a tumour in his sinus—most probably malignant. The biopsy would tell.

17. Dead man's chest

WE VISITED ON MONDAY, SEPTEMBER 7, as soon as we heard. It was a warm, caressing evening, the summer heat not yet dissipated. Curt looked remarkably dashing in his room at the hospital, where he was waiting to have a biopsy. He didn't wear a gown, but a green fleece jacket and khakis. His black eye patch made him look like Moshe Dayan, the Israeli military leader and politician. Like a soldier, he didn't talk about being afraid. When he described the hallucinations he was having, he said they were beautiful—geometrical patterns swirling up from water and fern-like shadows playing over the curtains. I'm sure I would have been terrified.

Curt's room was Command Central. He was still working on the patent application. He had a phone, a laptop, his briefcase—he seemed in charge, in control. The nurse who came to take his vital signs asked, "Should I come back later?" As if what she had to do was somehow incidental to what was going on in the room. Curt was reading a thick cranial anatomy text he had borrowed from the hospital library. He said he might have to make some tough decisions—whether to sacrifice an eye or part of the brain. And for some reason, he also wanted to read John Buchan's novels. His brother, Greg, and I both descended separately on a used bookstore on Lonsdale Avenue looking for copies. I think the bookseller was astonished at the sudden surge of demand.

Curt joked about having limo-therapy, driving around with pretty girls drinking martinis. And since the hospital rules stated that in this ward only relatives could visit, he began musing about how to pass Jeff Chow off as a member of the family. He said he was going to explain to the staff that there were two branches to the Lang family—the Scottish branch and the Kowloon branch. Jeff, of course, was from the latter. Curt laughed at his ruse. (In actual fact, the hospital didn't seem to bother enforcing its rules.)

When we came on Thursday, Curt was fairly cheerful. I was surprised by his high spirits and wondered how long they could last. Were they an effect of the drugs he was taking? Was he in a state of denial? After our visit, he walked us out to the elevator, just as a solicitous host would. He seemed fully vigorous, talking loudly about Rebecca West's *Black Lamb and Grey Falcon* in which she described her travels throughout the Balkans just before the Second World War.

The next day was not so good. Curt finally had his biopsy but it made him uncomfortable. The packing around his sinuses meant he couldn't breathe through his nose. He'd fall asleep, his mouth would close, he'd start to smother and wake up again.

When Curt recovered somewhat from the procedure, he went to Victoria to stay with Greg and wait for the results. The medical reports were confusing. Curt called Gordon to say that his doctors did not know what kind of tumour he had, but it did not appear to be malignant and it was not in his brain. Three days later, he told Bob that his tumour was "galloping." Gordon wrote in his diary: "Curt's message to us—said softly but I hear it clearly, is that we are going to have to carry the company. 'Got them ol' high-tech heartache blues again, momma.'"

Curt's emotions were very close to the surface, exaggerated. His voice broke with feeling when describing a silly T.V. comedy show. We had dinner together on Saturday, September 26, and Curt told Gordon that it was Bob's support that convinced him to start IMI. The next day he worried that he had offended Gordon. On Sunday, Curt tried repeatedly to reach him by phone and apologize. Finally on Monday, he got through. Gordon said not to worry about it. On Tuesday, Curt phoned again to say he was sorry about what he said. Gordon told him he was okay and thought how unusual it was for Curt to be so emotionally hyper-sensitive. "Perhaps I was bit miffed," Gordon wrote in his diary: "but no more so than by many things he says."

Curt informed us that the doctors were still not sure what his best treatment option was. Apparently, six oncologists reviewed his case, and two favoured not treating him at all.

Curt's last visit to IMI, 1998   PHOTOGRAPHER: GORDON CORNWALL

Despite these worsening reports, Gordon, Jeff and Bob were carrying on at IMI, still arranging demos. They set up a meeting with Karl d'Ambrosia from Exotic Metals, a contact Curt made on his trip down the coast. Curt attended part of it and the discussion went well. Karl wanted to see more, and have a group from IMI visit his factory in Washington.

There was one thing that happened in September, that Curt didn't know about, and I didn't either, until much later, when I met Abby. She didn't remember the date exactly, but said it was in September. She was working at the Lions Gate Studios in North Vancouver. Everyone had gone out on a shoot. She had finished her work and was waiting for the crew to get back. "I began thinking about Curt. I always felt there was something unfinished about our relationship. I wanted to have one nice talk." She hadn't seen Curt or spoken to him since 1981, when he and Ruth decided to marry. He had called because he didn't have a copy of their divorce papers, and he needed them before he could marry Ruth. Abby looked up Curt's number in the phone book and rang it. "He answered," Abby said, "and then I got cold feet." She hung up and they didn't have a last talk. When Abby told me the story, she said it was so strange that she had called just then, when he started to get sick. I thought so, too.

Early in October, Curt's doctor recommended surgery, to be followed by radiation. Curt wanted confirmation that this was the right way to go; he arranged to see a specialist in Seattle for a second opinion. But the American physician had no other suggestions, so Curt decided to have his surgery at the B.C. Cancer Agency, as planned, on November 4. Things didn't go well. After an extensive sixteen-hour investigation, the doctors decided surgery wasn't possible. Curt might die on the operating table because of the tumour's involvement with the carotid artery. But he could proceed with radiation.

Curt made a point of acting like a person who was going to live. He insisted that Gordon bring him a new wastepaper basket and he bought himself new cutlery with translucent blue handles. He said he was going to give up drinking and spoke about getting back to work. "I don't know what to think," I wrote in my diary.

On November 12, Curt had his first radiation treatment. He was euphoric afterwards. He left a message on my answering machine. "I have a very strange message for you. This is not related to me. You can smile, laugh, take it however you like. You can do what I tell you. Today is the day. This will sound very funny. The great witches of Ireland have won in their eternal contest with the great witches of England. It happens in cycles. If you dance for half an hour in honour of the witches of Ireland, you will be bringing magic in the world. I'm laughing as I tell you this."

Later, what he imagined or dreamed, inspired him to write:

A POEM IN PRAISE OF PAGAN WOMEN

They were old.
They were young.
They were children.
They were good.

My tribe had golden hair in braids;
They were the witches of England.

The others had black hair that stood up in shocks;
They were the witches of Ireland.

There was no malice in any of them.
They lived to grace the world.
They gave life and love to men.
They made us.

Each year they contested
To be the most giving,
To be the most useful,
To be the most blameless.
They were noble.

Each year they honour each other.
The contest is eternal.

This year the black haired ones were best.
For one half hour the gold haired ones danced to honour them.
Then for one half hour they danced a loud dance to honour themselves.

See these honourable women in the sunlight.
Gracing the world.
Dancing in long rows.
Making the world.

I didn't dance as Curt requested, and I felt guilty about that. But perhaps his poem brought magic into the world by itself. On November 19, he was at the point of tears when he told Gordon that he and Ruth were reconciled. She was going to come and live with him for a while. And to Ruth he said, "When I look at you, you remind me of my own soul."

The news kept getting worse. On November 24, Curt told us he had liver cancer. There was now a Plan C—to add chemotherapy to radiation. Curt was all for it. As Greg said, "He wanted to be like Nelson and go down with all guns blazing and the burning mast breaking over his head."

Gordon dreamed there was a black, grisly monster in our house which he defeated after a great struggle. He woke feeling deeply refreshed, with the thought that it was Curt's cancer. He told me this and I wrote in my diary: "I wish."

Curt's cognitive function was starting to fall off. He had trouble with his computer and phoned Gordon for help. He wanted to fill out a signature block for his email. Gordon walked him through the procedure step by painful step. On November 29, Curt couldn't find his poetry and asked Jeff to come over and help. I wrote: "It seems so sad—for him to be ill and then to lose his poetry, too. Must everything be taken?" But Jeff was able to locate it and, on December 1, Curt wrote a reminder to himself in his diary: "Poems are now to be found in C:\poems\poems.doc. They are in the 3.5–5.0 DOS format that prints directly from my old printer." The next day was his last entry: "Phrase, 'Sleep Deeping' an inverted neologism that conveys that sleep can take place in many ways." By this time, he was no longer writing; he was printing. And his hand must have been shaking, wavering, the lines of the letters look like they are vibrating. The great engine of his mind was slowing down.

I had a nightmare that night. A slug-like creature turned into a quickly moving small furry beast with sharp fangs. Squirrels fled in terror when they saw it and so did our cat, Alex. Then the slug beast changed into a small vicious dog. When I told Gordon about the dream, he said that Curt described the cancer in his head as a slug.

Curt started his chemotherapy on December 5, but on the tenth, Ruth called Gordon to say that he didn't have long to live. He had been hallucinatory for a couple of days, albeit with a moment of lucidity. That was when he called Gordon, wanting him to draft a letter of explanation to his Los Angeles and Portland contacts. He was calm and made perfect sense.

Curt never said he was dying. But when we saw him on twelfth, after he was readmitted to the hospital, he said something about "this other issue." He told Gordon he was finally catching on. I said, "After all these years, he's finally catching on." Curt smiled. Everyone laughed. Then Curt said, "Smile." His eyes were closed and Gordon told him, "We're all smiling." My cheeks were wet with tears.

Yet even there, I heard a story about Curt that I hadn't heard before. Ruth's dad, Ken Gordon, recalled building a ship in a yard on Granville Island. He was hammering a large piece of metal that needed shaping. The hammering made a loud, ringing noise. Behind him, Ken heard someone asking, "I wonder what that would sound like if you recorded it and played it backwards?" He turned around. Curt had just started working at the shipyard. This was the first time he'd met him. Ken laughed. I laughed, too. But my feelings were in turmoil.

I remembered that Curt always worried about dying alone, as his father, Earle, had done. But Curt need not have worried about himself. Friends and colleagues filled his room and overflowed into the hallway: Fred and Ev Douglas, his brother, Greg, who came with his partner, Daphne Wass, David Marshall, Tod Greenaway, his co-workers, Bob James and Jeff Chow, who visited with his wife, Iris Kobayakawa, several women who were fond of him, Noriko, Sadi, Anna... This was where I met his cousin Denise, for the first time. She was just three years younger than Curt and her family and his were always close. When she came to the hospital, the cousins recounted the old stories, that he told her the first dirty joke she heard—something about a Scotsman wiping his bum on a leaf. And what happened when she was about three or four, and fell off her tricycle. She hit her head on a sharp rock. Curt was close by and carried her home. He was sobbing and sobbing. Denise's mother came to the door and said, "Curt, it's okay, don't cry, it's okay." And he said, "You'd cry, too, if somebody was bleeding to death." They both laughed at the memory.

And here I first met Curt's mother, Hope. She was wearing a bright blue coat and fuzzy hat to match her large blue eyes. Somehow I had expected her to be a bony, rangy woman, a bit formidable, like Curt himself. But she surprised me by being pretty and feminine and soft.

On December 15, Curt moved to the palliative ward. He was wheeled over in his bed, along several corridors and through a long tunnel under the street. Curt smiled and laughed, delighting in the speed and the motion. I marvelled at his capacity for enjoyment, how he was able to wring the last drops of pleasure from life. I knew he was dying, but in some irrational way, I also thought this turn of events might still be reversible. Curt was such a fighter, he had me half convinced he could fight this, too. My mom, the eternal optimist, said, 'Maybe there will be a miracle.' I was thinking that, too, but I told myself I shouldn't, that it wasn't realistic. "Don't *hope* any more." I admonished myself in my diary.

The next day, when we came by, Ruth told us that Curt's memory was failing. He asked her what his occupation had been. This was actually a difficult question, since he had done so many different things! What was she to say? Poet? Artist? Log salvager? Fisherman? Boat builder? Author? In the end, she said he had been an inventor, that he and three other men developed a range camera, a device which uses light and lenses to measure things. Then he started talking about lasers.

Gordon told Curt that he had sold his van. Curt opened his eyes, but they were milky, unseeing. Then Gordon said that he liked Curt's beautiful poem about the witches of England and the witches of Ireland. He didn't respond, and that night Gordon wrote in his diary: "He is falling apart. Scattering to the four winds, to the minds of those who love him. He is scattered now, more in us than in his body, more in his notebooks, more in IMI, more in Ruth, Anna, more in Fred, Tod, Greg, Daphne. More in his business associates, in Fred Kaufman, Norm Hooper, others I do not know."

On December 17, Gordon drove to the hospital alone. It was raining, hard sluicing rain that ran down the streets, that filled the gutters. Rain that oozed into the ground, oozed and oozed until the earth could hold no more.

The ward was quiet. The lights in the halls muted. Gordon's leather shoes clicked on the polished floors. He came to the room he was looking for. That night its door was almost shut. Slowly, tentatively, he pushed it open. Inside, Curt lay on the bed, his body covered with a comforter. His eyes were closed. Ruth was sitting with him. She looked at Gordon and told him Curt had a violent seizure and after the neural storm passed through his body, lost consciousness. His breathing became agonized and laboured. When Greg visited he said, "Go, Curt go." Still he hung on. Stubborn as ever. But then, even he could resist no more, and slipped away.

Gordon took his hand. It was warm. He and Ruth talked for a long time. It was quiet in the small room, and the two felt companionable as they thought about Curt and what he meant to them. Ruth talked about what might have been, about the children she wanted. "But he never wanted children," she said. This disagreement was a large part of the reason they had separated. Now she wished she had not left. She regretted the pain she had caused. She remembered how angry he always seemed when she called him, how she could hear it in his voice. She told Gordon she would have liked to grow old with Curt.

Gordon talked about what had been. He went back to the beginning, telling Ruth a long complicated story about Curt's dreams. The dreams had followed Curt to the hospital, in his notebooks. They were ordinary blue notebooks, spiral bound. He insisted that Ruth bring them, even to the palliative ward. After December 2, he didn't add any new entries. But he read his old ones from back in July and August and printed comments about them in the margins. "Go slowly and carefully here," he wrote about one potential customer. "Or whatever you and Bob want them to be," he wrote concerning some notes on the patent claim. He was trying to help his partners carry on with the dream that had so possessed him.

Ruth already knew part of the story Gordon told her. She had seen the conflicts—she had seen how hard Curt was working, how stretched he was, how exhausted. She had sometimes tried to persuade him to take a holiday. But he didn't want to, not until the company was on a more solid footing. There was so much to do, so much to think about.

When trouble ate away at Curt's dream, he didn't tell her. He didn't tell her that he lost the presidency of RVI. He didn't tell her when Don Wilkie took on the position. And he didn't tell her that when Don said he had to go, he was powerless to do anything about it. Instead, Curt said to Ruth that he had decided to take some time off, to think things over. She thought that was odd—she had never known Curt to "take time off," when she was living with him. However, she didn't question him about it. Now that Ruth understood, she was overwhelmed with sadness. Again she began thinking about what might have been—what might have been if he had told her. "He never wanted to admit to a weakness, especially not to his mother or me," she said.

Gordon had dreams, too. It was partly why he and Curt were friends. They recognized this about each other. Gordon knew what it was like to lose your dreams. The last time he followed Curt, he was afraid. He asked, "What happens if this fails? Then my heart would be really broken." Gordon knew very well how hard it was to admit that a dream was gone, to stand naked in the world without it. But still he became angry thinking about what had separated Curt and Ruth. He began thinking about what should have been.

"Curt, you should have told her!" he said. And he pummelled Curt's chest. Ruth smiled to see herself so defended. And Gordon smiled, too. Why was he pounding the chest of a dead man? Gordon said, "I still wanted to communicate, but I couldn't."

And yet, Curt continued to affect those who knew him. On May 22, 1999, Gordon wrote in his diary:

> I miss Curt. I dreamed last night that he wasn't dead. He had the tumour, but was alive and lucid and I could talk to him. So it wasn't quite, as Bob said, just up to the three of us. I felt so relieved! And I thought maybe he won't die. I woke up a bit, to the point where I realized it was a dream, but I still thought that Curt was alive, and I felt better. Then I woke up a bit more and realized he was dead. The weight fell back on my heart. In this time of great uncertainty and anxiety I miss him the most. I know that if I could talk to him, he'd have good ideas and some plan would come out of it and I'd feel better. But he is not. I can never talk to him again. I have this recurring fantasy that miraculously Curt comes back to life and I get to tell him everything that has happened. That would be such fun.

The fantasy, said Gordon, recurred for years:

> I'd be sitting at IMI and I'd imagine Curt just wandering in the door, having been resurrected and not knowing what's going on. I would bring him up to date and take such delight in showing him where we were and what we'd done and amazing him with the events of the world. Like 9/11. I'd imagine typing "9/11" into Google and going to the website and seeing the towers collapse. He'd say, *"What? The World Trade Centre!'* He missed that. That was one of these events that changes your whole view of the world. I wanted to bring him up to date and show him that and experience it with him. I wanted to say, "Look, Curt, look what's been happening." His response would be interesting and worth hearing.

Curt's influence was profound. As Gordon wrote in "Curt Lang as Technologist," "Another thing I learned from Curt: we have free will. We can keep going the same direction we've always gone; but we don't have to. We can turn ninety degrees. We can decide to shoot up then decide to build boats then decide to run a technology company then decide to write a poem. All it really takes is the courage to say, 'I am free.'"

On November 27, 1998, a few weeks before Curt died, he wrote about himself: "I write occasional poetry—not as a career—but as an activity that makes me feel that I am a free man and can exercise my free will." His life shows us the power of choice.

This is not the end

RANT

If think you then
This be an end
Of anything that I have said
Or done then you are wrong.
There is more wine and some more red
That had not been to water wed
And in this night each voice burns long.
Who cavils now that we are led
Into some pasture of the dead?
Oh let him fall who will not burst
Into some wilder, fairer song.

—CURT LANG, 1956

As about so many things, Curt was right about this. He touched many people and started many wheels in motion. When he died, the people remembered, and the wheels he spun continued to turn. His life was like a great wind that blew through Vancouver, a great mocking, laughing wind, and even those people who did not know him, remembered the wind, seeing the leaves scatter.

Curt was a catalyst. Though he did not always profit financially by what he instigated, others frequently did. The patent application Curt was working on was successful. It was granted to Gordon, Bob, Jeff and Curt (posthumously). Nevertheless, IMI had a rocky start. While Curt was dying, Bob, Gordon and Jeff decided to move out of the big building at Graveley Street. They no longer needed so much space. Oddly enough, when they looked for a new place, they found an old one, the office on Crown Street where Curt founded Western Softworks. After Curt's death, the trio did not hang together. Jeff left first, and then Bob. Like Curt, Bob wanted to take the business in a new direction, but Gordon did not. He thought it best to stay with railroads; he felt he was making headway and was tired of looking for new markets. The business was down to one. I wondered if its name, IMI, was prophetic. Gordon stopped making hardware, and concentrated on software. Railway engineers all over the country opened his program, called *Rangecam*, to the opening screen shot, Curt's picture of a Prince Rupert rail yard. IMI grew slowly. In 2004, Gordon hired Belinda Lui and, in 2007, Igor Markhvida. In 2008, Gordon sold the business to the Holland Company in Chicago, which had become one of his best customers. He no longer works there but occasionally does some consulting. The IMI group still operates out of the same office on Crown Street, joined by Rui Zhang and managed by Bob Tuzik. Bob James moved to eastern Canada, and Jeff is still in Vancouver where he creates whimsical art and writes software for libraries

Gordon writes fiction and philosophy which you can find on the website *The Phantom Self.* He said:

> There's something Curtish in what I'm doing now, starting all over again, starting something new. A lot of guys my age play it safer than I'm playing it. They retire, take up hobbies, get a sailboat, play tennis, travel, pick every weed out of their lawns. I'm not doing that. I'm entering the domains of philosophers and writers. At my time of life, I risk losing my gravitas. I could have stayed longer with IMI. I could have cultivated the possibilities of consulting in the railroad industry, kept going at a senior respected level. I was a little tired of all of that. I wanted to get back to what I started

when I was young and had to leave. That's what I'm doing—being an apprentice and putting up with everything that entails. Essentially I'm starting at the bottom. Curt always did that.

Aeroinfo split off from Softworks Consulting and in 2000, The Boeing Company bought the breakaway group. In 1997, Softworks Consulting became known as Yaletown Technology Group. Haroldo eventually sold his share and went back to Brazil. In 2005, California-based FileNet bought the Yaletown Group for $11 million. Georg Hoevel, its president and one of its principal shareholders, said, "I wouldn't be sitting here as a retired entrepreneur if I hadn't met Curt. If I hadn't answered that ad, I might have ended up at B.C. Hydro like some of my fellow students."

Now a multi-million dollar enterprise, CIA still uses range cameras for its coking drum inspection service. It serves forty-four customers at seventy-five sites in twenty-three countries around the world.

Irina Borisova's book of English stories, *Problems with Electricity*, based on some of her matchmaking experiences, which Curt edited and named, was published in 1999. Between 2004 and 2006, Irina wrote a column for the *St. Petersburg Rush Hour*. She also wrote a book in Russian *Lonely Place America*, which included some of the stories from her first book. It was published in 2005. After Curt died, Irina and Curt's friend, Tod Greenaway, became email buddies and she translated his book *Loitering* into Russian. Irina is no longer a matchmaker. She continues to write and is a real estate agent.

Ruth Lang drives a bus for Translink in Vancouver. Hope Pedrini died in 2006 as did Curt's friend David Marshall. Don MacLeod died in 2008. The bookstore bearing his name, MacLeod's books, is going strong under the aegis of Don Stewart. In March 2011, *Macleans* wrote a story about it, calling it the last great bookstore.

When I started speaking to Fred about Curt, he was sick, but he got better and taught for a few more years before retiring. Then he began work on his masterwork: a book about Vancouver, a magnificent layering of photography, painting and text, in some ways reminiscent of an illuminated medieval manuscript. It was named *Flutter* and *Farrago* at different times and Fred explained that it was like a magazine in concept with radically different subjects butting up against each other—a movie playing on Granville Street, a grisly murder in False Creek. It was going to be a compendium of all.

In February 2005, Greg told us that Fred's cancer had returned and he was in the palliative ward at Lion's Gate Hospital. We visited him twice. The first time, he was very much himself. He was still writing, an essay about the ephemerality of things, "I just wish I had more time to work on it," he said without a trace of irony. He railed about phony hipsters who think that if they've got the clothes and the talk they're it. He spoke about the history of the beats and the hippies and how they were different. We asked about his book. He said it was on sale at the Access Gallery. "You better buy a copy before all the assholes get them," he growled. But when we talked to his wife, Ev, she said the book was not finished and not for sale at any gallery. This was just Fred's fantasy. Recently, when I went to visit Fred's daughter, Lisa, I asked her whether anyone was doing something with the book. She said that it was last seen in the trunk of Ev's car, but that it had disappeared. Fred's Great Book of Vancouver is now a legendary lost text, like Homer's *Margites*, a comic epic about a fool, or Byron's memoirs.

And finally, because Curt should have the last word:

TIME THROWS FURNITURE

Time hits me with furniture.
I have been hit with a bed, a kitchen chair, a wardrobe,
A roll of rugs and several book cases.

Time doesn't bother to lie in wait;
He just throws furniture whenever the mood takes him
And never misses.

Time is very strong and can throw a chair very hard.
Chairs may not seem dangerous
But when thrown they hurt a lot.

I never expected this kind of behavior from Time
   And I am never ready when it happens.

       —CURT LANG, 1994

PORTFOLIO

Curt Lang's Vancouver Photographs, 1972

Light and Blinds, Angus Lodge

Bond's Books, 523 Dunsmuir Street

Street scene with woman and dog

View onto downtown from Ash Street near 8th Avenue

Quebec Manor, 101 East 7th Avenue

Marie Gomez tiled doorway, 578 Alexander Street

Pacific Central Station, 1150 Station Street (in 1972 the Canadian National Railway Station)

Waterfront Station, 601 West Cordova Street (in 1972 the Canadian Pacific Railway Station)

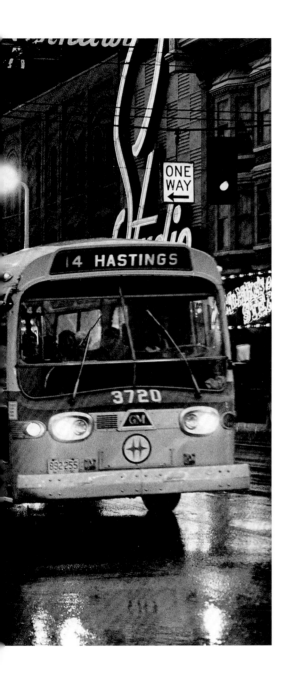

Looking south on Granville Street from Smithe
(formerly Smythe) Street

Woman and child in front of Harry's Market, 3313 Kingsway

Wild Rose cake and pastry sign on Gore Avenue

Security Market, 2996 East 22nd Avenue

Coke and bus reflection in store window, vicinity East Hastings Street near Princess Street

The Manhattan Building, 784 Thurlow Street

View of Golden A Mart

Service station on Pender Street

Hastings Street near Gore Avenue

Rear view of Singer Sewing Machine store

The Bluebird Beauty Salon, 1503 Commercial Drive

Vancouver downtown alleyway

Merit Café

Merit Café, Hastings Street

Canadian and Czechoslovakian restaurant

Superior Fruit & Produce with Orange Crush sign

Café men

Evelyn Wilson's Hat Shop

Leatherwear Dyers and Hatters, vicinity East Hastings Street and Princess Street

Pagoda Rice, Cordova Street store

Kitchen view from the vicarage of St. James Anglican Church, 303 East Cordova Street

People walking along Pender Street in Chinatown

Chinese import store, 550 Main Street

View of city toward the Woodword's building from CNR *Pier*

View looking toward the North Shore mountains from the CNR *Pier*

Corner of Gore Avenue and Pender Street

Signs around 24 East Hastings Street

Store interior

Earles Corner Grocery, 4895 Earles Street

Earles 29th Grocery, 4502 Earles Street

Marble Rooms, 107 Cordova Street

Curt Lang, self portrait

Endnotes

Will the real Curt Lang please stand up?

The quotations from people who knew Curt are drawn from my conversations with them as well as from formal interviews. Those interviews were with Don MacLeod (May 1999), Denise Goodkey (March 1999) Bob Sutherland (April 2011), Gill Collins (March 2011), Nina Raginsky (2002), Fred Douglas (April 2002), Jim Polson (April 1999), Tod Greenaway (May 1999) and Michael de Courcy (February 2011). For Michael de Courcy's website, see http://www.vancouverartinthesixties.com/archive/612 (accessed April 14, 2011).

For this quotation from Homer's *Odyssey* (and the other that appears subsequently) I used the Robert Fitzgerald translation of Homer's *Odyssey*, New York: Alfred A. Knopf, 1992.

1. Wild and memorable poets

This chapter is informed by my interviews with Jim Polson (April 1999), Doug Kaye (February 2011) and Jamie Reid (May 2001).

Curt's descriptions of visiting Pier B.C. and of twanging the lamp posts are undated. They are unpublished and like his published (and unpublished) writings in subsequent chapters appear with permission from Greg Lang. More information about the science fiction club Curt joined, as well as local sci-fi fandom and fanzines can be found at this website, The Canadian Fancyclopedia http://efanzines.com/CanFan/CanFan-V.pdf (accessed June 18, 2011).

I made use of published reminiscences, Al Purdy's *Reaching for the Beaufort Sea*, Madeira Park: Harbour Publishing, 1993; "Lowry: A Memoir" *Books in Canada*, vol. 3, no. 1 (January / February 1974), pp. 3–4; "A Memoir of Malcolm Lowry," *Canada Month*, September 1962, which appear here with permission from Eurithe Purdy, as does Purdy's other published work. I also used Sheryl Salloum's *Malcolm Lowry: Vancouver Days*, Madeira Park: Harbour Publishing, 1987.

Curt's poem "On the Death of Dylan Thomas," was published in *Canadian Poetry Magazine*, Winter, 1953–1954. Al Purdy's poem "For Curt Lang" appeared in Al Purdy and Sam Solecki, eds., *Beyond Remembering: The Collected Poems of Al Purdy*, Madeira Park: Harbour Publishing, 2000. (In the poem, Al Purdy was mistaken in saying that Curt was seventeen years old in 1952. He was fifteen.)

Malcolm Lowry's letter about Curt is from Sherrill E. Grace, ed., *Sursum Corda! The Collected Letters of Malcolm Lowry, Volume Two: 1946–57*, ed. Toronto: University of Toronto Press, 1997; Ralph Gustafson's response is in Harvey Breit and Margerie Bonner Lowry, eds., *Selected Letters of Malcolm Lowry*, ed., Philadelphia: J.B. Lippincott, 1965.

2. That beautifully unworldly, reasonless rampaging of my old self

Again, I made use of my interviews with Jim Polson and Doug Kaye and Al Purdy's published memoir, *Reaching for the Beaufort.*

Curt's poem "Paris 55" was unpublished. I used Curt's letters to Jim Polson and Al Purdy. Eurithe Purdy kindly gave me permission to quote from Al Purdy's unpublished letters to Curt here, and in subsequent chapters.

3. If one casts completely free

Sources for this chapter are Curt's diary as well as the unpublished correspondence between Curt and Al Purdy. Curt's letters to Al Purdy are held in the Special Collections Department of the University of Saskatchewan Libraries. I also used my interview with Jamie Reid.

Readers who wish to learn more about Curt's friend, David Marshall, can find it in Monika Ullmann's *The Life and Art of David Marshall,* part of the Unheralded Artists of BC series. Salt Spring Island: Mother Tongue Publishing, 2008. The film in which Curt acted was Donald Wilder's *The Legendary Judge,* National Film Board, 1958.

The picture of Curt and William Kurelek can be found in Patricia Morley's *Kurelek: A Biography,* Toronto: Macmillan of Canada, 1986.

Al Purdy's letter about Curt is from Sam Solecki, ed. *Yours Al,* Madeira Park: Harbour Publishing, 2004.

4. Naked in the VAG

I found Paul Wolf's recollection of Curt and Fred in "The Answer's Straightforward," *quint,* University College of the North, June 2009. It can be found here: https://www.ucn.ca/ics/icsfs/quint_june_09_1rev_edit_adobe.pdf?target=38b9137d-84cf-4d3b-b60f-494cf64ba0 (accessed April 16, 2011). I also interviewed Paul in February 2011.

I made use of interviews with bill bissett and Lisa de Bourcier, both in January 2011. I interviewed the inimitable Fred Douglas several times (February and April 2000, May 2001, January 2002 and October 2003). I spoke to David Marshall in February 1999, Jock Hearn in May 1999, and to Bob Sutherland in April 2011. The article about Bob Sutherland can be found here: "A Painter's Painter," *Vancouver Sun,* Andrew Scott, January 31, 1978.

The quote from William Dale comes from Chuck Davis's website "The History of Metropolitan Vancouver, http://www.vancouverhistory.ca accessed May 4, 2011).

I used my interview with Greg Lang at his home in Victoria (April 2000) as well as an email (April 2011). The Alcazar was a very popular hang-out for artists and writers at 337 Dunsmuir Street. Peter Trower wrote a reminiscence about the pub, which was demolished in 1981: "Countdown for the Alcazar," *Vancouver,* April 1982.

Jamie Reid's recollections come to me via my interview with him as well as his "Curt Lang" in Bill Jeffries, Glen Lowry, Jerry Zaslove, eds. *Unfinished Business: Photographing Vancouver's Streets, 1955 to 1985,* Presentation House and *west coast line,* 2005.

The program about the Exhibition of Geometric Abstract Painting and Sculpture was in the Vancouver Art Gallery library and information about the analogous show in the New Design

Gallery was in a program amongst Fred Douglas's private papers. Robert Clothier, whose sculptures appeared in the show, is the same man who acted in *The Legendary Judge*—acting was his day job. The review of the exhibition appeared in the *Vancouver Province*, March 10, 1960, page 17.

5. Smoking Gideon

I interviewed Clara Hague in July 1999 at her home in Surrey. I spoke to John Newlove, the mainstay of this chapter, in October 2000, and Peter Auxier in May 2001. I made use of interviews with Jim Polson and Paul Wolf, previously referenced. George Bowering sent me a couple of emails in January 2011. I dated the confrontation between Curt and the TISH poets with the help of "Brock becomes fairground," *Ubyssey*, November, 28, 1963.

For more on TISH, see Frank Davey, *When TISH happens*, Toronto: ECW Press, 2011.

6. Just arson around

I used my interview with Hope Pedrini (June 1999) as well as my interviews with Denise Goodkey and Clara Hague.

Biographical information about Stephen Dillingham came from The Biggar Encyclopaedia, http://biggarencyclopædia.wetpaint.com/page/Dillingham,+Stephen (accessed May 4, 2011). Stuart McGowan provided *The Trial of Stephen Dillingham: The Newspaper Wars, 1911*, the script of the mock trial, restaged by the Fort Saskatchewan Sheeptown players in 2009. Historical background about Fort Macleod came from Wikipedia, http://en.wikipedia.org/wiki/Fort_Macleod,_Alberta (accessed May 4, 2011).

More information about how the vets took over the Vancouver Hotel can be found in my article, "The Night War Vets Seized the Vancouver Hotel," published online on November 13, 2006, by *The Tyee*.

7. A wolf in the West End

I talked to Fred Douglas, Lisa de Bourcier, Jock Hearn, Paul Wolf and bill bissett, in interviews already referenced, I used Norman Hacking's, "He's stoked on ship and combed Africa," *Province*, September 7, 1959. I interviewed Keith Ralston by phone (March 2001). I spoke to Abby Benjamin in her home in Half Moon Bay, B.C., in March 2011 and to Al Neil in his, on July 2001. I also made use of emails from Abby, Lisa and Jamie Reid.

More information about Evelyn and George Fertig can be found in Mona Fertig's book, *The Life and Art of George Fertig*, in the Unheralded Artists of BC series. Salt Spring Island: Mother Tongue Publishing, 2010.

I tried to locate a photo of Curt's sculpture that became a well-known landmark in front of Mr. Mikes, but to no avail.

8. The vault

Curt's poem first appeared in the April 1964 issue of *blewointment*. "Kurt" is not a misprint. For several years, during the sixties, Curt spelt his name with a "K," but later reverted back to the original spelling.

For more information about Stephen McIntyre, see, George Fetherling, "The Man of a Hundred Thousand Books," *Geist*, Issue 80. I relied on my interviews with Don MacLeod, in Robert's Creek, in 1999 and with Gill Collins in 2011. I used my interviews with Peter Auxier and Fred Douglas previously referenced. I found Chuck Davis's column about the book trade in Vancouver in "The Magazine," *Vancouver Province*, on October 9, 1983.

9. I could not send it out

I used my interviews with Fred Douglas, Denise Goodkey (March 1999) and Ruth Lang (April 1999). Curt's poem and letter is unpublished. Abby's note to Curt is also unpublished and quoted by permission from her.

10. It was a blast

I was helped by my interviews with Don MacLeod, Jamie Reid, Fred Douglas and Peter Auxier, previously referenced. I talked to John Austin on the phone (May 2001). I used "Blasts at UBC legal," *Province*, June 8, 1965. The information about the play *In the Rough* letting out came from A Brief History of Theatre at UBC, available at http://www.library.ubc.ca/archives.pdfs/theatre/fw6506.pdf (accessed May 4, 2011).

11. Dreaming in black and white

My interview with Rod Gillingham was at his house in Saanich (November 2001). All the quotes from Rod in this chapter and the next are drawn from this interview. The information about the LIP grant was among Fred Douglas's papers. There are several editions of the *Dictionary of the Chinook Jargon*. The one Curt reprinted in 1972 was originally published in Victoria by T.N. Hibben & Co. in 1899. It was a knock-off of the first, written by George Gibbs and published in New York by Cramoisy Press in 1863. I used Aileen Campbell's articles "Grant puts city on camera," May 1, 1972, and "Taking snapshots of how we live," July 23, 1976, both in the *Province*. I used an email from Howard White in October 2010, and the introduction from *Unfinished Business: Photographing Vancouver's Streets, 1955 to 1985*, Presentation House and *west coast line*, 2005. I also interviewed Bill Jeffries (February 2011). The talk Fred Douglas gave at Presentation House was in January 2003.

12. Stubborn as the buffeted birds

For this chapter, I used my interviews with Peter Trower at his place in North Vancouver (May 2001) and my interview with Greg Lang previously referenced. Greg sent me some clarifying emails in January and February 2002 and Peter Trower gave me permission to quote his poem "The Poem Rower," which appears in *Chainsaws in the Cathedral*, Victoria: Ekstasis Editions, 1999. Curt surfaced in Peter's writing once more, in his novel *The Judas Hills*, Madeira Park: Harbour Publishing, 2000. Called Bert Prang, he appears along with a Purdy-like character named Hal Gurdy.

13. Always winging it

For this I referred to an email from Greg in March 2002 as well as to an interview already referenced. The boat drawings were in Curt's private papers. The Shipping Registry is available at http://www.apps.tc.gc.ca/Saf-Sec-Sur/4/vrgs-srib/d.aspx?lang=e&shipid=370645 (accessed April 28, 2011). In April 2002, I interviewed Joe Ginger on the phone and Ray Breckner at his house in Surrey. For the details about the storm, I used "Rescuers check on oil slick in search for 11 fishermen," *Vancouver Sun*, March 17, 1978; "Six fishermen feared dead in storm," *Province*, March 18, 1978; and "Hope fades for fishermen," *Province*, March 18, 1978.

Information about the speed and size of the old *Walter M.* was on the Canadian Shipping Registry when I accessed it in June 2003, but is no longer to be found there. The telegrams from Romeo LeBlanc and Curt's fishing notebook were among Curt's private papers.

14. Take the money and run

I quoted both from Gordon's diary and his essay, "Curt Lang as Technologist," in *Unfinished Business: Photographing Vancouver Streets, 1955 to 1985*, referenced earlier. When the quote is from Gordon's diary, I say so in the text. All other quotes from his writing are from the published essay. Gordon's misgivings about Krieger Data were justified. After he left, the promoters fired Ralf, he lost his shares *and* his house. When he appealed to the superintendent of B.C. brokers, for redress, he got none. What the promoters did was perfectly legal.

I used my phone interview with Mike Shields (February 2011). I spoke to Mike Collins at his house (March 2011), and with Jeff Chow at my place (September 22, 2000). I also used my interview with Greg, already referenced.

Tod Greenaway's piece on Curt is unpublished and was written shortly after Curt died in December 1998.

Everett Rodgers coined the phrase "early adopter" in the first edition of his book *Diffusion of Innovations*, New York: Free Press, 1962.

I got the quote about Lynn Richards from "vgh patient lost patience with 'chaos,'" Daphne Bramham *Vancouver Sun*, January 24, 2002. She also described Lynn's battle with cancer.

The information about Mattrick's game, *Evolution*, came from Peter Nowak, "The evolution of video games in Canada," cbc News, September 10, 2010. Mattrick went on to found Distinctive

Software which Electronic Arts California bought for $11 million in 1991. He is now a senior vice-president at Microsoft.

I learned that Sydney was desperately seeking a way to restructure its $3.5 million debt from Karen Howlett, "Troubled Sydney Development seeks aid from B.C. Government," *Globe and Mail*, September 27, 1984.

Gil Johnson's announcement is from *PR Newswire*, February 21, 1984. After Curt left, a member of the board, Larry Kostiuk, an ex-Mountie, but a shady character nonetheless, replaced Gil as president. In 1993, he fraudulently billed Evergreen International Technology for $390,000 and in 1995, the RCMP charged him with securities fraud and other violations. He pled guilty, received a six months conditional sentence and a fine of $50,000. See Ann Gibbon. "Stock promoter pleads guilty: Former head of Evergreen fined $50,000 for securities violations," *Globe and Mail*, October 24, 1996. Evergreen changed its name a couple of times after that and eventually merged with an American company, KnowledgeMax, which sank under *its* debt load in 2003.

The information about Maxwell and Columbia Computing came from several sources: "U.K. publisher moving into educational market" *Canadian Press, Toronto Star*, October 8, 1987; "*Pergamon* seeks all of Columbia," *Vancouver Sun*, December 23, 1989; "Investment News, Columbia Computing," *Globe and Mail*, April 7, 1989. This latter story reported that Columbia and Maxwell's company, Pergamon, "amalgamated." (This was a little like saying that when the elephant swallowed the fly, the two merged.) I also used Curt's business journals and Greg's email (March 2011).

15. The high-tech heartache blues

Gordon let me use his diary and his essay already referenced. I used the minutes from the RVI Board Meetings as well as Curt's journals. I spoke to Rick Clark on the phone in May 2011 and referred to his emails. I interviewed Norm Hooper via Skype (March 2011) and talked to Mike Ryan (May 2003)

Mike Ryan was vice-president of research at Pemberton Houston Willoughby Bell Gouinlock, when it helped take Joseph's Segal's company public. Mike described Joseph as a superb bottom-line operator. Maybe because of the connection between Joseph and Ron, he thought that Ron would share some of Joseph's fairy dust. See John Schreiner, "Mr. Jax's eye fixed on bottom line," *Financial Post*, August 31, 1987. I used interviews with David Marshall and Ruth Lang previously referenced.

The book I was writing was, *Letter from Vienna: A Daughter Uncovers Her Family's Jewish Past*, Vancouver: Douglas & McIntyre, 1995.

16. I am I

Curt and Jeff's book is *Data Base Publishing on the Web and Intranets*, Scottsdale, Arizona: Coriolis Group, 1996. I used diaries, both mine and Gordon's as well as Curt's business journal.

17. Dead man's chest

I used Curt's diary as well as mine and Gordon's, and Curt's unpublished poem.

This is not the end

Curt's poem at the beginning of this section is unpublished as is the one that ends the book. I drew on my own recollections and conversations with Gordon. I interviewed Georg Hoevel on June 10, 2011, and referred to a clarifying email. I used my interview with Rick Clark, already referenced. Irina Borisova brought me up to date via emails.

My information about famous lost books came from Stuart Kelly, *The Book of Lost Books*, New York: Random House, 2006.

Curt's 1972 camera, a Japanese Mamiyaflex
PHOTOGRAPHER: GREG LANG

Comments on the Mamiyaflex camera

The camera allowed for interchangeable lenses. The lens is a medium wide angle, good for working close to people or in cramped quarters. Diane Arbus used a similar camera and lens combination with a strobe unit. This kind of camera could be used on a tripod and also worked very nicely hand held. It used either 120 or 220 roll film which means it could expose 12 or 24 frames respectively of 2.25 inch square images per roll. In the hand-held mode it hung at the waist from a neck strap and the photographer would look down through the reflex finder to see the image on a ground glass where it could be composed and focused. The image would be right side up but reversed left to right. These cameras were sturdy and reliable and had a world wide reputation for excellent lenses and durable bodies while being substantially cheaper than Hasselblads. The Japanese Mamiyaflex and follow up cousin the Mamiya c330 were intended to offer more options than the German Rolleiflex by way of interchangeable rather than fixed body lenses.

Henri Robideau, an "Ironic Tragedy of Human Existence" photographer
and Canada's paramount Gianthropologist, Vancouver.

Image Notes

We gratefully acknowledge and thank the lenders of these photographs:

Irina Borisova–p. 178
Lisa de Bourcier–p. 42, 78, 83, 101, 102, 183
Canadian Museum of Contemporary Photography, Ottawa–p. xvi
Claudia Cornwall–p. 97, 175
Gordon Cornwall–p. 138, 161, 186
Rod Gillingham–p. 118
Norm Hooper & Railway Track & Structures–p. 173
Greg Lang and the Estate of Curt Lang–p. viii, 15, 34, 71, 84, 86, 90, 100, 105, 113, 117, 126,
    134, 168, 259
Ruth Lang–Front Endpage, p. 38, 57, 73, 136, 154
Vancouver Public Library, Special Collections:
    p. vii, 7th Avenue and Heather Street, vpl 86646
    p. 99, North Arm, Fraser River, Checkmate yarding, vpl 85862n
    p. 124, Log Salvaging, vpl 85860gg
    p. 128, Lane near Lonsdale in North Vancouver, vpl 85875g
Eurithe Purdy & Harbour Publishing–p. 4

Foncie Pulice Photos–*Front endpage*

Don Slade–*Back endpage*
Christopher Varley–p. 116 (Exhibited: Pender Street Gallery, 1976,
    Surrey Art Gallery, 1976)

PORTFOLIO PHOTOS:

Greg Lang and the Estate of Curt Lang for:
    Light and Blinds, Angus Lodge
    Bond's Books, 523 Dunsmuir Street
    View onto downtown from Ash Street near 8th Avenue
    Quebec Manor, 101 East 7th Avenue
    Waterfront Station, 601 West Cordova Street (in 1972 the Canadian
    Pacific Railway Station)
    Looking south on Granville Street from Smithe (formerly Smythe) Street
    Woman and child in front of Harry's Market, 3313 Kingsway
    Security Market, 2996 East 22nd Avenue

Coke and bus reflection in store window in vicinity of East Hastings Street near
    Princess Street
The Manhattan Building, 784 Thurlow Street
View of Golden A Mart
Rear view of Singer Sewing Machine store
The Bluebird Beauty Salon, 1503 Commercial Drive
Vancouver alleyway
Merit Cafe
Canadian and Czechoslovakian restaurant
Superior Fruit & Produce with Orange Crush sign
Café men
Evelyn Wilson's Hat Shop
Leatherwear Dyer's and Hatters, vicinity East Hastings Street and Princess Street
Pagoda Rice, Cordova Street store
Kitchen view from the vicarage of St. James Anglican Church, 303 East Cordova Street
Corner of Gore Avenue and Pender Street
Signs around 24 East Hastings Street
Store interior
Earles Corner Grocery, 4895 Earles Street
Earles 29th Grocery, 4502 Earles Street
Marble Rooms, 107 Cordova Street
Curt Lang, self portrait

Vancouver Public Library, Special Collections:
Street scene with woman and dog, VPL 86651
Marie Gomez tiled doorway, 578 Alexander Street, VPL 85872Z
Service station on Pender Street, VPL 85874KK
Hastings Street near Gore Avenue, VPL 85874L
Pacific Central Station, 1150 Station Street (in 1972 the Canadian National Railway
    Station), VPL 85872B
Merit Café, Hastings Street, VPL 85873G
People walking along Pender Street in Chinatown, VPL 85874U
Wild Rose cake and pastry sign on Gore Avenue, VPL 85874R
Chinese import store, 550 Main Street, VPL 85874E
View of city towards the Woodwards building from CNR Pier, VPL 85872S
View towards the North Shore mountains from the CNR Pier, VPL 85872T

Index

Italic page numbers refer to images

Acknowledgements

I am indebted to many people for their help and support. My husband, Gordon Cornwall, shared his memories, thoughts, his writing—and gave me valuable feedback on several drafts of the manuscript. Greg Lang was generous with his recollections, lent me Curt's diaries, papers, drawings, photographs, letters and journals—and wrote the introduction. Fred Douglas regaled me with stories. Lisa de Bourcier gave me photographs. Abby Benjamin described aspects of Curt's life in the early sixties, and Ruth Lang told me about Curt in the eighties and nineties. Denise Goodkey, Clara Hague, Sandra Foss and Hope Pedrini offered important insights into Curt's family. Many of Curt's friends were very happy to tell me how they remembered him: Jim Polson, Jamie Reid, Bob Sutherland, Evelyn Douglas, Peter Auxier, Don MacLeod, George Bowering, John Newlove, Gill Collins, Mike Collins, Douglas Kaye, David Marshall, Jock Hearn, Paul Wolf, Tod Greenaway, Gregg Simpson, Al Neil and bill bissett. Peter Trower shared his memories *and* his poem. Nina Raginsky gave me her insights and allowed me to use her photograph of Curt. I'd also like to thank Curt's colleagues and co-workers from various fields of endeavour: Rod Gillingham, Joe Ginger, Ray Breckner, Norm Hooper, Rick Clark, George Hoevel, Jerry Pedersen, Peter O'Brien, Jeff Chow and Mike Ryan. Eurithe Purdy let me use Al Purdy's unpublished letters as well as his published memoirs. Howard White generously allowed me to use material published by Harbour Publishing. Sheryl Salloum recalled her interview with Curt many years ago, and Bill Jeffries provided ideas about Curt-as-photographer. Thanks to Henri Robideau for his comments on Curt's camera. Stuart McGowan of the Sheeptown Players gave me permission to use the script of the Stephen Dillingham trial. I'd like to thank Jan Westendorp for her design and her infinite patience. I'm grateful to David Beers for writing the foreword and for publishing in *The Tyee*, the earlier versions of a couple of stories that found their way into the book. As well, I'd like to acknowledge the Vancouver Public Library for its help in accessing Curt's collection of photographs and the Canada Council for supporting my initial research for the book. I am indebted to George Fetherling whose mention of Curt in a book review of *The Life and Art of George Fertig* renewed Mona's interest in my friend. Finally, my heartfelt gratitude to Mona Fertig and Peter Haase, without whom none of this would have been possible.

A Note on the Type

Albertan Roman, used for the text, was designed and cut in metal at the 16 point size by Jim Rimmer in 1982 as a proprietary type for use in his private press and foundry, Pie Tree Press & Type Foundry. Only the Roman was cut for casting at the foundry. It was to be used for the hand-setting and printing of limited edition books, but was eventually rendered in digital form. Albertan Italic was drawn in 1985 to accompany the Roman. It has been designed to a narrow set width and has a very slight incline. The capitals have been taken from the Roman face, and have been condensed about 10 percent to blend with the lower case forms. The face has a full set of ligatures, and in addition, a font of Italic Small Capitals has been designed. It was named after Jim's wife Alberta.

Alexander Quill, used for the chapter titles, was designed by Jim in the 1980s with the intention to cut the type in 14 point for casting into foundry type for the setting and printing of limited edition books at Pie Tree Press & Type Foundry.

Jim Rimmer (1934 – 2010) was a beloved Canadian designer, letterpress printer, and proprietor of Pie Tree Press in New Westminster, BC, and is especially known as a designer of type faces. Over 200 digital faces, distributed among 18 families, have been made from Rimmer's designs. In 2007, Jim received the honour of becoming a fellow of the Society of Graphic Designers of Canada. Jim also generously shared his skills and knowledge through his teaching and mentor support of many type designers and printers. Included among them is Peter Haase of Mother Tongue Publishing whom Jim trained in letterpress printing.